SOFR Futures and Options

Founded in 1807, John Wiley & Sons is the oldest independent publishing company in the United States. With offices in North America, Europe, Australia, and Asia, Wiley is globally committed to developing and marketing print and electronic products and services for our customers' professional and personal knowledge and understanding.

The Wiley Finance series contains books written specifically for finance and investment professionals as well as sophisticated individual investors and their financial advisors. Book topics range from portfolio management to e-commerce, risk management, financial engineering, valuation, and financial instrument analysis, as well as much more.

For a list of available titles, visit our Web site at www.WileyFinance.com.

SOFR Futures and Options

Options

A Practitioner's Guide

DOUG HUGGINS
CHRISTIAN SCHALLER

WILEY

Published by John Wiley & Sons, Inc., Hoboken, New Jersey.
Published simultaneously in Canada.

Neither the authors nor the publisher are affiliated with the New York Fed. The New York Fed does not sanction, endorse, or recommend any products or services offered by the authors or the publisher.

For general information on our other products and services or for technical support, please contact our Customer Care Department within the United States at (800) 762-2974, outside the United States at (317) 572-3993 or fax (317) 572-4002.

Wiley also publishes its books in a variety of electronic formats. Some content that appears in print may not be available in electronic formats. For more information about Wiley products, visit our website at www.wiley.com.

Library of Congress Cataloging-in-Publication Data is Available:
ISBN 9781119888949 (Hardback)
ISBN 9781119888963 (ePDF)
ISBN 9781119888956 (epub)

Cover Design: Wiley
Cover Image: Graph by Doug Huggins and Christian Schaller from data Courtesy of CME, (background) © Digital_Art/Shutterstock

SKY10035479_072522

Contents

Foreword

by Galen Burghardt
February 2022

Writing this foreword is a little like writing an obituary for a dear friend. LIBOR, and the Eurodollar futures and options contracts that have been tied to it for nearly 40 years, will be put to bed soon. And so ends a remarkable era of financial innovation that transformed the world of interest rate risk management and academic research.

Still, if you're reading this Foreword, chances are that SOFR, and its related futures and options contracts, have made the competitive cut and are serving as replacements for my old friends. So let's spend the next few paragraphs reflecting on what we've learned.

I think I can be most helpful by recounting some of the reasons the Eurodollar futures contract helped to revolutionize the world of banking and finance. And by finance, I mean both applied and academic.

A LITTLE BIT OF HISTORY

First, it's worth remembering that at the time Eurodollar futures were first listed in the 1980s, there had never been a futures contract that cash settled to an abstract concept. In talking with Rick Kilcollin, who was largely responsible for the contract's design, I learned that the LIBOR market in the early 1980s was thin, and that the development of an index that could capture a relevant financing rate and resist attempts at manipulation was still unfinished. With that in mind, what the Chicago Mercantile Exchange (CME) devised was an ingenious survey in which banks of whatever credit rating were not asked what rate they were paying for interbank funds in London. Instead, they were asked to provide the rate at which they perceived funds were offered to prime quality banks. This, combined with the practice of throwing out the high and low responses, produced a survey outcome with an astonishing degree of agreement.

Second, it's worth remembering that when the contracts were first listed, they were the runty cousins of the certificate of deposit contract. A special, and less expensive, membership was created by the CME for trading the contract, which took place in a small corner of the CD pit. I may have made up this story, but I recall someone saying that Fred Arditti, who was the CME's head of research at the time, would visit the pit each day and come back saying, "I die a little each day when I see how little is going on there."

Then all hell broke loose. Continental Illinois, whose CDs were deliverable into the CD futures contract (and whose motto was "We will find a way") suffered some substantial loan losses and took a hit to its credit rating. It didn't take long for the market to start worrying about credit risk in the deliverable instrument and to look elsewhere.

At the same time, the interest rate swaps market was beginning to take hold and grow, and the Eurodollar futures market was poised perfectly to go along for the ride.

A REVOLUTION IN FINANCE

Eurodollar futures proved to be a financial engineer's dream tool. In the 1980s, the idea of zero-coupon bonds was largely found in textbooks. As was the idea that one could break up the yield curve into three-month (3M) segments and use those segments to study yield curve behavior and the sensitivity of one's financial position to each of those segments.

Now these ideas seem commonplace, but at the time, the world of bonds was almost unbelievably primitive – at least in the world of actual bonds. And the market for forward rates was nearly nonexistent. Try to imagine, for example, what it was like to extract a continuously compounded forward rate curve from the traded bond market. Even if one used data from the Treasury market – possibly the deepest and most liquid bond market in the world – the results could be almost hilariously erratic. In contrast, with Eurodollar futures, one had the next best thing – a quarterly compounded forward rate curve – served on a platter.

Well, almost. It's one thing to know that convexity matters, and another to know just how much. In the late 1980s, Terry Belton and I published a piece for our clients at Discount Corporation of New York Futures called *The Financing Bias in Eurodollar Futures*. The idea was a simple one based on the daily settlement of gains and losses on futures. That is, if one were short Eurodollar futures, one would be able to invest cash coming in at higher rates (i.e., when rates were going up and you were making money on your short position) and borrow the cash you paid out at lower rates when rates were falling. This was an obvious advantage to the shorts, and if you could do it long enough and over big enough swings, the advantage could add up to real money. At the time we published the note, though, the Eurodollar futures curve only went out a year or two, and the advantage proved not to be worth much for such short-dated contracts. So that research note sank without a trace.

In time, though, the CME extended the Eurodollar futures curve out to 5 years and then to 10 years. And when it did, the interest rate swaps market used these newly available futures rates to price their swaps. The problem, though, as Bill Hoskins and I discovered when we published *The Convexity Bias in Eurodollar Futures* – perhaps one of the most important research notes of our working lives – was that the market had failed to take the value of convexity into account. Swaps were priced as if futures rates were forward rates so that it was possible to receive fixed on a swap and hedge the position by shorting Eurodollar futures and make completely riskless money as rates rose and fell. Not long after we published that note, the market became aware of the mispricing and completely readjusted.

Another lesson that Bill Hoskins taught me, although it took him a while, was that forward rates (or prices) are breakeven values. That is, if you finance a position to any given forward date, you know just how much the price of what you have can rise or fall before you make or lose money as of that forward date. This is a hugely valuable tool.

One example of just how valuable a tool it is came when Gavin Gilbert, a wonderfully voluble friend of mine, rang me one day to announce, more or less at the top of his lungs, "Galen! You won't believe it! I just bought the forward 2-year TED for zero!" For this to make sense, you need to know that we had just published a good piece of work called *Measuring and Trading Term TED Spreads*. This was the basis for much of what you could find on Bloomberg if you visited that particular page. We had not, however, considered the buying and selling of term TEDs forward. But Gavin had. He found that if he bought a two-year note two months forward and sold the appropriate strip of Eurodollar futures, he basically owned the spread at 0. Since the two-year TED spread at the time was trading at roughly 20 basis points, he expected to make 20 basis points on the trade. And he also knew that the spread would have to go negative for him to lose money.

I, of course, checked into it and found that by the time I got there, the spread could be bought forward for 10 basis points. So we published a note (as Gavin knew we would) telling our clients about the trade. What made the trade remarkable, though, was that even with highly sophisticated and integrated markets, the term repo market was not yet in sync with the term LIBOR market. Hence the glaring mispricing.

One of the things you learn in any class on derivatives is that the gains and losses on the derivative look just like the gains and losses you would experience on a trade that you could construct in the cash market. So, for example, a long Eurodollar futures position has the same payoff as a cash position in which you borrow money for a term equal to the contract's expiration date and lend for a term that is three months longer. As a result, a long Eurodollar futures position is the equivalent of a simple borrow short/lend long yield curve trade.

Once, during one of our classes on Eurodollar futures, a young man from Panagora asked me what the Sharpe ratio of a Eurodollar contract would look like. It was the first time I'd ever heard the question, so I had to beg off. But when we got back to the office, we tackled the question and found that we could analyze the gains and losses combined with their standard deviations and calculate very straightforward Sharpe ratios. When we did this, we learned that the most profitable part of the yield curve carry trade was in the first two or three years of the yield curve. If you're interested, you can find these early results on page 64 of *The Eurodollar Futures and Options Handbook*, at least until it disappears from the face of the earth. Or you can look for one of our yield curve carry notes such as *Yield Curve Carry Rides Again.*

It was neat, too, that these results conformed to what Antti Ilmanen had written in one of his extraordinary monographs at Salomon Brothers. The note was called *Does Duration Extension Enhance Long-Term Expected Returns?* (Ilmanen 1995). He concluded that once you got past the two-year mark, you had more or less exhausted any useful excess returns and that no, you didn't get paid for taking extension risk.

I should add that one of the greatest contributions of Eurodollar futures in the banking industry can be attributed to one of its most prosaic features. That is, they were futures contracts, which meant that one could buy them in the morning and sell them in the afternoon and have the positions off-set. For asset/liability managers, this feature was a godsend. The chairman of JPMorgan's asset/liability committee once volunteered in casual conversation that they had revolutionized his life. He was no longer bound to deposit, swap, and forward rate agreement positions that would stay on the books for weeks, months, or years (and that carried with them all kinds of credit risk). Instead, if his bank's risk position changed during the course of a trading day, he could simply add to or offset open futures positions without having to worry about being stuck with them.

ALL THE BEST

To conclude, before I wear out my welcome here, I would like to thank Doug and Christian for inviting me to contribute this Foreword. It gave me a chance to think back over some of the great joys of being in these markets at a time when financial history was being made and to reconnect with some old friends. I would also like to thank my colleagues at the CME for all the support they have given me over the years. The time I spent there from 1983 to 1986 were great fun and set me up for a career that I could never have imagined. And, of course, the CME's financial support for *The Eurodollar Futures and Options Handbook* made it possible to produce a volume that has been paying dividends for nearly 20 years.

So, with that, thank you all. And let's hope that the next 40 years of trading and innovation are just as thrilling as the past 40 years have been. Or as my old boss and mentor, Morton Lane, liked to say, "May we all have prosperous futures with many options."

Galen Burghardt
Evanston, IL
February, 2022

Introduction

This book is about the SOFR futures and options complex at the Chicago Mercantile Exchange (CME). Before providing an overview of its topics, we take a look at the relevant history. To understand SOFR futures and options, we need to understand SOFR; to understand SOFR, we need to understand LIBOR; and to understand LIBOR, we need to understand Eurodollars.

EURODOLLARS

The most basic definition of a Eurodollar is a US dollar held in a bank outside of the United States. Given that dollars are fungible, it may not be obvious that a dollar held offshore should differ in any respect from a dollar held onshore. But depository institutions in jurisdictions other than the United States are subject to different regulations than those in the United States. For example, the US government is typically unable to confiscate assets held by banks domiciled outside of the United States. And this fact figures prominently in some of the origin stories of the Eurodollar market.

One such story is that the Chinese government, fearing confiscation of its dollar balances after the outbreak of the Korean War in 1950, transferred most of these balances to *Banque Commerciale pour l'Europe du Nord*, a Paris-based bank that had been started by Russian exiles in 1921 and acquired by Gosbank in 1925 (Dormael 1997, pp. 1–9). These offshore dollars, opened in the name of the Hungarian National Bank, became the first Eurodollars. They were later leant to various French banks and to the Paris branch of Bank of America. Over time, other communist countries channeled their dollars through Europe, with the business expanding to another Russian institution, the Moscow Narodny Bank, based in London. These offshore dollars were leant to various Western European governments, and by the late 1950s, American multinationals were using funds obtained in this market to finance their expansion throughout Europe.

Another feature of the Eurodollar market was that these offshore dollars were not subject to the typical exchange rate controls that governed onshore deposits. For example, in 1955, Midland Bank found it profitable to acquire 30-day offshore dollar deposits at a rate of 1.875% for the purpose of buying sterling in the spot market and selling it 30 days forward at a premium of 2.125%. In this FX swap, Midland paid an effective rate of 4% for pounds sterling at a time when the official rate at the Bank of England was 4.5%. The rate Midland paid for these offshore dollars was well above the maximum rate of 1% for 30-day deposits specified at the time by Regulation Q in the United States. But exchange controls prevented the arbitrage using onshore dollars. By tapping the Eurodollar market, Midland was able to pursue the arbitrage despite exchange rate controls – and despite the interest rate premium paid in the offshore market.

Eurodollars include other benefits as well. For example, they don't attract an FDIC insurance fee, estimated currently to be on the order of 8 to 9 basis points for large banks (Keating and Macchiavelli 2017). And they aren't subject to central bank reserve requirements. So while dollars are fungible in a broad sense, dollars can sometimes be put to a wider variety of uses when they're held overseas.

EURODOLLAR FUTURES

As the market matured, various futures exchanges considered the possibility of introducing futures contracts on Eurodollars. At one point, the Chicago Mercantile Exchange considered a futures contract that required the seller to open an offshore time deposit for the buyer. But this procedure was considered too cumbersome, so the CME designed the contract to be cash-settled. No other futures contract had settled with a simple cash payment at expiration, so the CME was taking a bit of a risk with this contract (Burghardt 2003).

In order for the contract to be settled in cash, the CME needed a way to construct an index to be used in calculating the final settlement price of the contract. To that end, the CME designed an interesting process. Each day, it would randomly select 20 banks from a pool of London banks active in the Eurodollar market and ask each bank for the rate at which it believed prime quality banks could borrow dollars for three months. The highest and lowest quartiles were discarded, and the two middle quartiles were averaged. Then, at some randomly chosen time during the subsequent 90 minutes, the process was repeated with a second set of randomly chosen banks. The CME then averaged the two results (Robb 2012).

It's important to note that the CME did not publish the identities of the banks that participated in either of the two surveys.

This system worked well for quite some time. But in 1996, the reference rate for Eurodollar contracts was no longer the dominant index for the massive market over-the-counter interest rate swaps, and CME applied for permission to switch from the reference rate it had been calculating since 1981 to LIBOR.

LIBOR

In the early 1980s, the market had a need for standardized reference rates that could be used to settle various forms of interest rate swaps, and members of the British Bankers Association (BBA) asked the BBA to arrange a standardized interest rate for this purpose. In 1984, the BBA introduced the BBAIRS code – the British Bankers Association Interest Rate Swap code. This code suggested terms and conditions to govern interbank transactions with maturities up to two years. And as part of this process, the BBA in 1984 introduced BBA interest settlement rates. The rate-setting process continued to evolve and was standardized by the BBA in 1986 as LIBOR – the *London Interbank Offered Rate.*

The LIBOR rate determination process was similar in spirit to the process the CME had used since 1981 for its Eurodollar futures contract. But there were a few differences. For example, the BBA polled the same 16 banks every day. And since the same banks were polled each day, there was no need to poll them a second time during the day. And, unlike the CME, the BBA publicly displayed the rate submitted by each bank in the panel.

The fact that the rate submitted by each bank was made public mattered even more when, in 1998, the question submitted to each bank was changed. The original question was, "At what rate do you think interbank term deposits will be offered by one prime bank to another prime bank for a reasonable market size today at 11 a.m.?" The new question was changed to read, "At what rate could *you* borrow funds, were *you* to do so by asking for and then accepting interbank offers in a reasonable market size just prior to 11 a.m.?" [Emphasis added.]

And it was *this* new question to which banks were responding when the Great Financial Crisis of 2008 hit.

THE GREAT FINANCIAL CRISIS

The subprime mortgage crisis, which started in 2007, eventually led to a number of bank failures in 2008. The most notorious examples were Bear Stearns in March of that year and Lehman Brothers in September, but the entire banking system was deeply affected, and the Federal Reserve orchestrated a large-scale infusion of capital into the banking system, largely via the purchase of preferred shares in 42 US banks. Similar assistance was provided in one form or another to banks in many other jurisdictions, including the UK and many other parts of Europe.

One of the consequences of the great financial crisis is that banks largely stopped lending to one another on an unsecured basis, as each bank was unsure about the creditworthiness of the others. Central banks quickly stepped into the breach, providing substantial funding via repo operations and collateralized currency swap lines with other central banks.

With unsecured interbank lending greatly reduced, the LIBOR polling process became somewhat academic. How would a bank know where it could borrow in the interbank market if it wasn't active in the interbank market? And if no banks were active in the interbank market, what was the LIBOR polling process measuring *precisely*?

Perhaps Citigroup's Willem Buiter put it best when he said, "LIBOR is the rate at which banks don't lend to one another." Questioned about this comment in a Parliamentary committee hearing, Bank of England Governor Mervyn King commented:

> The world has changed totally; people are very worried about lending, and indeed hardly anybody is willing to lend to any bank around the world for three months unsecured; they want to lend secured. . . . I think that in future we will see far less lending to banks on an unsecured basis and far more on a secured basis. The inter-bank market has very often been a market in which overnight or short-term cash holdings can be distributed around the banking system, and banks were willing to do it with each other unsecured at Libor. I just do not think it plays that role now, and I think we are going to see developing over the next few years a much more intensive method in which banks can redistribute cash surpluses and shortages among each other on a more secured basis. At present they are doing it directly with the central bank, and that is true around the world, not just in the UK.[1]

THE LIBOR RIGGING SCANDAL

If LIBOR's days were numbered as a result of the switch from unsecured to secured interbank lending, the nail in the coffin was evidence that the process had been manipulated by some of the traders at some of the banks in the LIBOR survey panel.

---

[1] Oral evidence taken before the Treasury Committee on Tuesday 25 November 2008.

As early as April 2008, the *Wall Street Journal* published an article suggesting some banks were submitting LIBOR rates that were unjustifiably low (Mollenkamp 2008). Two reasons were offered for this behavior. First, some of these banks – and their clients – stood to gain if the published LIBOR rates could be suppressed. Second, some of these traders hoped to give the appearance that all was well with their particular bank. For example, it came out in hearings that Paul Tucker, then executive director of markets at the Bank of England, had called Barclay's CEO, Bob Diamond, regarding Barclay's LIBOR submissions. Diamond's notes from that call are quite revealing:

> *Further to our last call, Mr Tucker reiterated that he had received calls from a number of senior figures within Whitehall to question why Barclays was always toward the top end of the Libor pricing. His response was, "You have to pay what you have to pay." I asked if he could relay the reality, that not all banks were providing quotes at the levels that represented real transactions; his response: "Oh, that would be worse."*
>
> *I explained again our market rate driven policy and that it had recently meant that we appeared in the top quartile and on occasion the top decile of the pricing. Equally I noted that we continued to see others in the market posting rates at levels that were not representative of where they would actually undertake business. This latter point has on occasion pushed us higher than would otherwise appear to be the case. In fact, we are not having to "pay up" for money at all.*
>
> *Mr. Tucker stated the level of calls he was receiving from Whitehall were "senior" and that while he was certain we did not need advice, that it did not always need to be the case that we appeared as high as we have recently.* (House of Commons 2012).[2]

In the end, a slew of bankers were convicted for their roles in the LIBOR rigging scandal, and fines totaling more than USD 9 billion were levied against large banks, including Barclays, Citigroup, Deutsche Bank, JP Morgan, Lloyds, RBS, Rabobank, and UBS.

Perhaps most significant for our purposes is that regulators in many jurisdictions concluded that LIBOR was not fit for purpose and that it needed to be retired. In different parts of the world, authorities have suggested

---

[2]It's worth noting that Bob Diamond, an American, was forced to resign from Barclays by the Bank of England and the UK Financial Services Authority, while Paul Tucker went on to become Deputy Governor of the Bank of England and was later knighted for his services to central banking.

different candidates for replacing LIBOR. But in the US, authorities have settled on SOFR – the *secured overnight financing rate*.

SOFR AND REPO MARKETS

To understand SOFR, one needs first to understand repo – short for repurchase agreement. As the name suggests, a repo transaction is one in which a security – typically a bond – is sold and *simultaneously repurchased* at an agreed price with settlement on an agreed date in the future. In other words, the bond is sold in the spot market and simultaneously bought back on a forward date for a different price. The repurchase price is typically greater than the sale price, and the difference between the two prices reflects the cost of borrowing between the sale date and the subsequent repurchase date, with the bond serving as collateral.

For example, imagine that I could sell USD 100 million par amount of bonds for an invoice price[3] of 101,000,000 in the spot market and that I simultaneously could arrange to repurchase those same bonds tomorrow for an invoice price of USD 101,000,280.56. The difference between the sale price and the purchase price – USD 280.56 in this case – is the interest I pay to borrow USD 101 million overnight. In this example, the overnight repo rate is $(280.56 / 101,000,000) \times (360/1) = 0.001$ – i.e., 0.1%.

The mechanics of this repo transaction involve me selling a bond today and simultaneously agreeing to repurchase the bond tomorrow at a price we agree on today. But the economic rationale for repo transactions is to borrow money using a bond as collateral for the loan – i.e., to arrange a secured financing – in this case, an overnight secured financing. Not surprisingly, the repo rate associated with this overnight secured financing is called the secured overnight financing rate (SOFR). We describe the mechanics of the repo market and the secured overnight financing rate in much greater detail in Chapter 1.

As it happens, the repo market is a very large, very active market. The Brookings Institution estimated the average daily turnover in the US repo market in 2021 at somewhere between USD 2 trillion and USD 4 trillion *per day*. Repo agreements can be arranged for various terms, but the most common term is one day – i.e., *overnight*. In fact, even when people intend to borrow funds for a longer period, they often simply arrange to leave the repo agreement "open," meaning the repo arrangement will keep rolling over for

---

[3]The invoice price of the bond is the total price one must pay for the bond, including accrued interest. Bond prices are typically quoted on a "clean" basis – i.e., without accrued interest. But the invoice for the bonds will add the accrued interest to this amount – hence the term *invoice price*. In practice, bond prices are expressed assuming a par amount of USD 100.

a term of one day until otherwise ended by one of the two parties to the transaction.

Many large institutions are required to report repo transactions, with the result that the Federal Reserve has a wealth of daily repo transactions that it can use to monitor the market for overnight secured financing.[4]

With LIBOR viewed as an unreliable benchmark, the Board of Governors of the Federal Reserve and the Federal Reserve Bank of New York in 2014 jointly convened the Alternative Reference Rate Committee (ARRC) for the purpose of identifying a risk-free replacement for USD LIBOR. Over time, the membership of ARRC was expanded to include quite a number of regulators, banks, GSEs, exchanges, and investment managers. By 2017, the ARRC had settled on SOFR – Secured Overnight Financing Rate – as the replacement for LIBOR and had proposed a transition plan for moving the market from LIBOR to SOFR, the key steps of which are summarized in Figure Intro.1.

Lesser-used USD LIBOR values ceased on 31-Dec-21.

Remaining USD LIBOR values will cease on 30-Jun-23.

Supervisory guidance instructed banks to stop using LIBOR for a reference rate on new products by 31-Dec-21. In fact, continued use of LIBOR as a reference rate for new products was to be considered a "safety and soundness risk."

For derivatives, LIBOR-SOFR fallback spreads (to be used in legacy products) were set by currency and by tenor on 5-Mar-21.

Legacy Eurodollar futures contracts will be converted to SOFR futures at a fixed spread of 26.161 bp.

For consumer cash products, the LIBOR-SOFR fallback spread for each tenor will be:

> Before 1-Jul-23: the median difference between USD LIBOR and SOFR compound in arrears during the previous 10 working days

> After 30-Jun-24: the median spread for that tenor during the five years prior to 5-Mar-21

> Between 1-Jul-23 and 30-Jun-24: the linearly interpolated value between the two rates above

For institutional cash products, such as corporate loans and floating rate notes, for each tenor the fallback spread is the median of the historical differences between USD LIBOR and the compounded in arrears SOFR value over a five-year period prior to 5 March 2021.

FIGURE Intro.1   Transition from LIBOR to SOFR
Source: Authors

---

[4]For example, US bank holding companies with total assets equal to or greater than USD 100 billion are required to report these transactions, as are foreign banking organizations with total assets of at least USD 50 billion.

SOFR FUTURES AND OPTIONS: TOPICS AND STRUCTURE OF THIS BOOK

While the International Swaps and Derivatives Association (ISDA) has been overseeing the practical implementation of the LIBOR-to-SOFR transition for over-the-counter derivatives, and while the ARRC has been overseeing the practical implementation of the transition for cash products, the CME has been working to facilitate the transition for listed derivatives, namely futures and options.

The last step of the historical evolution of money markets summarized thus far leads to the subject of our book, SOFR futures and options, and links it with the transition from an unsecured term-rate to a secured overnight rate, implying two fundamental changes:

1. Term-lending, which used to be based on the term-rate LIBOR, needs to be based on an overnight reference rate.
2. The transition from LIBOR to SOFR involves the basis between unsecured and secured rates.

The main goal of this book is to provide a conceptual framework for these changes in section 1 and practical help for dealing with them in section 2. Like the subject of this book, SOFR futures and options are historically and conceptually linked to these two fundamental changes. It is the structure of the first part: Chapters 1, 2, and 3 address the implications of switching from a term rate to an overnight rate, and Chapter 4 focuses on the basis.

Chapter 1 outlines the construction of SOFR from the repo market. Since liquidity in the repo market is sufficient only for the shortest tenor, the decision to base lending on a secured reference rate implied the decision to base lending on an overnight rate. This fact is the reason behind the need to migrate the cash loan and derivatives markets from a term rate (LIBOR) to an overnight rate (SOFR).

Chapter 2 describes this migration in the futures markets by comparing SOFR with ED (Eurodollar) contracts. It turns out that it can easily be implemented in the futures market; with the exception of the front month contract, the transition from LIBOR to SOFR as the underlying rate is, for practical purposes, little more than a renaming exercise of ED and FF (Fed Funds) futures. Chapter 2 also provides a fair value model for the spread between 1M and 3M SOFR futures:

  ▪ The three-month SOFR futures contract settles to a compounded average of SOFR values produced daily by the New York Federal Reserve. This compounded average is quite similar to a geometric average, and it means the SOFR futures *rate* (100 less the SOFR futures price) is equal to the forward rate between the first and last days of the three-month reference period for that contract.[5]

■ In contrast, the one-month SOFR futures contract settles to a *simple average* of SOFR values during the respective calendar month. As a result, the futures rate for a one-month SOFR futures contract is not identical to the forward rate between the first and last days of the relevant reference period. The nature of these differences is highlighted in Chapters 2 and 6.

Chapter 3 discusses the implications of this migration in the cash loan markets. Here, unlike for futures, the transition from the forward-looking term rate LIBOR to the backward-looking overnight rate SOFR met significant resistance. Chapter 3 explains how the tension between the goals of regulators and the needs of borrowers has resulted in the compromise of introducing a term rate for SOFR calculated via a model from the SOFR futures market. As a result of using a model, the cost of hedging the term rate with futures is high, and regulators keep it at a high level by prohibiting a secondary market for the SOFR term rate. This chapter finishes by analyzing two possible scenarios for the further evolution of the tension: It could be resolved either by the high hedging costs for the term rate driving cash loan markets to embrace in-arrears conventions, making the term rate superfluous, or by regulators allowing a secondary market for the term rate, which supports its permanence by reducing the hedging costs – maybe after the frictions caused by the prohibition will have become clear.

Chapter 4 then addresses the implications of switching from an unsecured to a secured reference rate. It provides an economic framework and a statistical model to understand the unsecured–secured basis and applies it to analyze the spread between ED and FF futures on one hand and SOFR futures on the other hand. As the model establishes a link between the unsecured–secured basis driving the ED–SOFR futures spread and the CCBS (cross currency basis swap), it allows replacing the CCBS, which is part of many relative value trades, but involves high capital and transaction costs, in some trades with the much cheaper spread future.

Chapter 5 describes the options on SOFR futures and finds that the transition from the term rate LIBOR to an averaged or compounded overnight rate has major implications for the future options:

---

[5]There are some circumstances in which the equivalence is approximate rather than exact.

- As soon as the reference period starts, the future option transmogrifies into a path-dependent exotic Asian option. Options on 1M SOFR contracts are then Asian options of the American type with arithmetic averaging, which are a mathematical challenge and for which no pricing formula exists. One consequence of the absence of a way to determine the Greeks – specifically, the delta required for delta hedging – is the relatively late migration of liquidity from ED to SOFR future options; another consequence is an increased difficulty of using SOFR rather than ED future options for hedging caps and floors.
- On the other hand, before the reference period starts, options on SOFR futures are standard options referring to a forward rate, which can be priced and analyzed by well-established methods – though the values are quite sensitive to the statistical process chosen. Here, the conclusion from Chapter 2, that for most practical purposes the conceptual difference between a term rate and an average or compound of overnight rates can be reduced to a renaming exercise of already known analytic concepts with some extra caution for the front-month contract, can be applied again – precisely by excluding the front month from the consideration. Chapter 5 summarizes the realized and implied volatility analysis for the secured yield curve, including the distribution of risk and return, which Galen has mentioned in his Foreword. Expanding the secured versus unsecured theme from Chapter 4, we also highlight the opportunities for trading options on SOFR futures versus options on ED contracts and hope that the attractiveness of these spread positions will support the transition of liquidity.

Chapter 6 considers some of the idiosyncrasies of SOFR futures contracts. We find that, while the Eurodollar futures suffered from a much-discussed convexity bias, the three-month SOFR futures contract suffers from no such bias, as the contract has no convexity. On the other hand, there is a slight bias in the one-month SOFR futures contract, owing to the fact that it settles to a simple, arithmetic average of SOFR rates during its reference period. We also consider the conditions under which market participants need to be concerned about any financing bias affecting the SOFR futures contracts. In Chapter 6, we also discuss the way in which SOFR futures prices, possibly with adjustment, can be used to create a term structure of overnight forward rates along the SOFR yield curve.

Section 2 has the objective to help the market practitioner applying the new products, SOFR futures and options, for concrete tasks, such as hedging. The conceptual discussion of section 1 gave a sense for those parts, where the approaches known from ED contracts can simply be transferred, and for those, where extra caution is required – specifically the term rate and options. Section 2 uses these results and outlines the necessary adjustments of analysis and hedging techniques in the SOFR universe.

Chapter 7 illustrates basic principles using the simplest possible examples – namely, of a corporate treasurer who wishes to convert a portion of his floating-rate balances to fixed rate using SOFR futures contracts. We pay particular attention in this chapter to the pernicious effects of date mismatches. When the reference period of your hedging instruments doesn't precisely coincide with the reference period of the underlying quantity you want to hedge, this date mismatch risk is inevitable. In Chapter 7, we offer a few suggestions for ways in which this date mismatch risk can at least be mitigated.

Chapter 8 considers hedging the Term SOFR rate. The CME adopted its Term SOFR valuation methodology for a number of good reasons, but the simplicity of the calculations wasn't one of them. Their computation methodology creates some unique issues for anyone using or hedging the Term SOFR rate. For example, the methodology allows the possibility that the prices of futures contracts with reference periods well beyond the end date of the Term SOFR reference period can influence the published Term SOFR rate. This is in contrast to methods traditionally used to calculate term rates and forward rates along LIBOR curves built with Eurodollar futures contracts, and market participants at least should be aware of this effect when using or hedging the CME's Term SOFR rate.

Chapter 9 builds on the discussion of the secured–unsecured basis in Chapter 4 and explains how the elimination of that basis in the asset swap spreads of government bonds results in the three key markets, futures, swaps, and bonds, all becoming conceptually similar. Welcome consequences of this convergence in the SOFR universe are a straightforward hedge of swaps and bonds, with futures and the exclusion of the basis risk in hedges of government bonds with futures.

Chapter 10 builds on the discussion of options in Chapter 5 and explains – in sharp contrast to Chapter 9 – how the migration to SOFR has necessarily resulted in major difficulties for hedging caps and floors with options on futures. On top of this, the recommendation of ARRC to apply the floor of some loans on a daily basis has added another layer of challenges.

IMPLICATIONS OF SOFR FOR MARKET ANALYSIS

In addition to the focus on the conceptual and practical aspects of the transition from LIBOR to SOFR, from time to time this book offers insights into the general implications of a secured reference rate for market analysis:

- All analysis tools developed for the unsecured yield curve can now be transferred to the secured yield curve. For example, like Eurodollar futures provide consecutive 3M forward segments of unsecured lending rates, so do SOFR futures for secured lending rates. Hence, the entire arsenal of risk/return, carry analysis, etc., which has been developed over decades for LIBOR, can be replicated for SOFR. This book does not intend to perform that Herculean task, but will give a few glances at the results, specifically in Chapter 2 for yield curve and in Chapter 5 for volatility curve analysis, while Chapter 6 highlights the different convexity.

■ From a general analytic viewpoint probably the most important consequence of the switch from LIBOR to SOFR is the elimination of the secured–unsecured basis in government bond swap spreads. While LIBOR-based swap spreads are conceptually a LIBOR-repo basis swap over the life of the bond (Huggins and Schaller 2013, p. 161), the switch to SOFR as reference rates eliminates this basis in swap spreads – and even makes the LIBOR-repo basis swap tradable via a strip of SOFR versus ED futures.[6] Chapter 4 will briefly touch on this and also address the implications for the CCBS – and for the model using the CCBS – of exchanging secured rather than unsecured rates in different currencies in future. Chapter 9 will exploit the absence of basis risk for hedging a Treasury with SOFR futures.

■ While the unsecured reference rate LIBOR has provided lenders with an automatic exposure to the unsecured–secured basis, following the transition to the secured reference rate SOFR maintaining exposure to this basis will require additional transactions. A lender who wants to continue profiting from a banking crisis will need to look for products that continue to depend on unsecured lending. Due to the migration to SOFR these products will become rare and Chapter 4 concludes that SOFR versus FF spread contracts will probably offer the cheapest way to add exposure to the basis in a world of SOFR-based loans.

In general, every analysis that is possible with ED futures can be *repeated* with SOFR futures, and the spread between the two is the basis for *new* analysis and trading opportunities. Chapter 4 uses these new opportunities to link the CCBS to SOFR–ED future spreads. As long as the reference period is excluded, the same is true for options on SOFR futures, and Chapter 5 both repeats the analysis of implied and realized volatility for the secured yield curve and links it via SOFR–ED future option spreads to the implied and realized volatility of the unsecured yield curve. But Chapter 5 also shows that as soon as the options on (1M) SOFR futures enter the reference period, the picture changes fundamentally and requires a completely new pricing model for exotic options not known from the Eurodollar complex.

---

[6]More precisely, the LIBOR-GC basis swap.

Some key concepts are encoded in Excel sheets.

Usually, yellow cells indicate user input.

Main results are highlighted in red.

If random numbers are used in simulations, confirm the recalculation setting (F9).

All these sheets are provided to illustrate concepts and should not be used in a professional context, including for trading and investing. For professional use, much more robust implementations (and more simulations) are required.

FIGURE Intro.2   Explanations of Excel sheets accompanying this book
Source: Authors

For some key concepts, this book provides Excel sheets in addition to verbal explanations (Figure Intro.2). You may access the additional complementary resources by visiting: www.wiley.com/go/sofrfuturesandoptions. (Password: Huggins123)

REMAINING HURDLES IN THE TRANSITION FROM LIBOR TO SOFR

In the course of this book, we will identify the reasons of some remaining hurdles in the transition to SOFR and share suggestions for addressing them:

- While SOFR is based on actual market transactions, the rate is determined by the Fed *without* sharing the raw data. This counteracts the proclaimed goal of a fully transparent reference rate and limits the usability of SOFR published in this way. Moreover, it leads to SOFR-based lending markets being constructed on a reference rate, which can be considered as being no level playing field: Large banks with a repo desk can see the repo market real-time and therefore estimate SOFR well before it is released to the general public on the next business day. This could be one fundamental reason behind the general perception that SOFR is a project imposed by regulators for the benefit of large institutions, which explains the reluctance of the cash loan market to welcome this project.

  Suggested solution: Publish the raw data used for SOFR calculation on a timely basis.
- The calculation of the SOFR term rate via a model results in high hedging costs with futures. By prohibiting the alternative hedge through a secondary market, regulators violate free market principles in order to force their preferred solution on loan markets – which most likely will cause inefficient markets and arbitrage opportunities.

  Suggested solution: Allow a secondary market for the term rate.

- CME's term rate uses a pure jump process, contains no diffusion and is therefore unsuitable for pricing options. Hence, traders dealing in both CME's term rate and options on SOFR contracts need different models for both, which is likely to result in discrepancies. Moreover, not all details of CME's calculation process are known, which further complicates replication and hedging.

  Suggested solution: Publish all details and research alternative processes for CME's term rate.

- An unintended but necessary consequence of the transfer to SOFR is the more complex option pricing and hedging of caps and floors. This situation is aggravated by the specifications of options on SOFR futures: Those on 3M contracts end trading before the reference quarter begins and are therefore not available as hedging instruments anymore; those on 1M contracts have the set of specifications that make pricing most difficult.

  Suggested solution: Change the specifications of options on SOFR futures to make them (somewhat) more accessible to pricing and suitable for hedging.

THE TRANSITION CONTINUES

This book is being written at the turn of the years 2021–2022 and hence right in the middle of the transition from LIBOR to SOFR. While SOFR futures volumes are increasing, Eurodollar futures volumes are still relatively robust – perhaps because market participants are relying on the fact that legacy Eurodollar futures contracts will be converted to SOFR futures at a fixed spread (of 26.161 basis points). And very little of the liquidity in Eurodollar futures options has moved to SOFR futures options[7] – probably as they suffer from more complicated pricing and less suitability for hedging.

Regulators have placed a big bet on SOFR as a replacement to LIBOR, and it's still not entirely obvious that this bet is going to pay off the way regulators hope. But the point of *this* book is to contribute to a successful transition by describing the instruments in the CME's SOFR complex and by illustrating the way these instruments can be used to help manage short-term interest rate risk.

---

[7]During the editing process of this book in the first half of 2022, liquidity in options on SOFR futures has started to increase.

One

Concepts

1

SOFR

THE REPO MARKET

The Secured Overnight Financing Rate (SOFR) is based on data collected from the market for overnight repurchase agreements (i.e., the repo market). A repo transaction is a loan collateralized by a bond, usually of very high quality, such as a US Treasury note. Since a repo agreement is a secured loan, the interest rate associated with a repo transaction is usually lower than interest rates for otherwise similar unsecured loans, such as LIBOR.

This difference also leads to a lower Bank for International Settlements (BIS) risk weighting (e.g., 0% for US Treasuries) and thereby to lower capital costs (Huggins and Schaller 2013, p. 148). Hence, the motivation for the borrower in the repo market is the lower interest rate that can (usually) be obtained with a secured financing. The motivation for the lender in the repo market is the significant reduction of credit risk and a lower cost of capital.

In addition, lenders may be motivated to receive a specific bond as collateral in the repo transaction in order to cover a short position in this bond. The fact that the repo market can be used to cover short positions makes it a vital component of many relative value trades – and therefore the repo rate appears in many relative value relationships and arbitrage equations. For example, the "classical" relative value trade of buying a bond futures contract and selling a bond deliverable into that contract requires covering the short position in the bond until the delivery date of the futures contract. As a result, the repo rate is a direct determinant of the spread between the forward price of the bond and the price of the futures contract. Seen from another perspective, the price of each deliverable bond can be expressed in terms of its implied repo rate – i.e., the repo rate that would be earned by purchasing the bond in the spot market, selling the futures contract, and delivering the bond into the short futures position (Huggins and Schaller 2013, p. 121).

The vital function of the repo market for relative value trading also means that relative value relationships, at times, can exert a significant influence on the repo market. For example, if a futures contract were trading cheap to the cheapest-to-deliver bond, one could buy the futures contract and sell the bond, using the repo market to cover the short position in the bond. This situation often results in traders being willing to lend cash at lower rates in exchange for the cheapest-to-deliver bond as collateral. A borrower of cash in the repo market can then enjoy an especially low rate, provided he secures the loan with the cheapest-to-deliver bond rather than a generic US Treasury. Accordingly, a bond is said to be "special collateral" or "on special" when its repo rate is below the repo rate earned by general collateral. Apart from bonds that are cheapest-to-deliver in futures contracts, specialness tends to occur in bonds for which there are significant short positions, such as new issues and benchmarks (Huggins and Schaller 2013, p. 291).

If the lender of cash in a repo transaction is unable to return the collateral to the borrower at maturity, this is called a *failure,* which carries penalties. In order to avoid the risk of failures, tri-party repo can be used, where a custodial bank holds the collateral as a third party to the repo transaction. In tri-party repo, no specific bonds can be selected as collateral, so the tri-party repo rate can be considered as a general collateral rate, (almost) without the risk of failure. For this reason, on any given day, the probability distribution for tri-party repo rates tends to be narrower than the probability distribution for bilateral repo rates. On the left tail of the distribution, it excludes special repo rates and any premium charged for the possibility of the counterparty failing.

SOFR: DEFINITIONS AND FEATURES

One can formulate general goals for the task of condensing the overnight repo market into a single number, which is intended to serve as a reference rate for collateralized overnight private sector lending and to replace LIBOR:

- On one hand, the portion of the repo market considered needs to be large enough to be representative, not easily manipulable, and provide enough liquidity even in times of crisis.
- On the other hand, the intended use as a reference rate requires sufficient stability. Given the structure of the repo market, it has at least one inherent source of instability from special bonds, which needs to be excluded from the reference rate as much as possible.

■ Given the experience of LIBOR, which motivates the whole exercise, the new reference rate should be based on actual market transactions rather than on surveys of panel members.

The Secured Overnight Financing Rate is the solution suggested by the Alternative Reference Rates Committee (ARRC) and proposed to the Federal Reserve. Figures 1.1, 1.2, and 1.3 summarize the main characteristics of SOFR, which the New York Fed publishes on its website, https://www.newyorkfed.org/markets/reference-rates/sofr, with historical data being available from April 2, 2018.

These definitions and features reflect the status at the time of writing (December 2021). We encourage the reader to monitor the sources mentioned (specifically, Figure 1.2 source) for changes and updates.

Data input:	TGCR (Tri-Party General Collateral Rate)	Tri-party repo conducted with BNYM (Bank of New York Mellon) as clearing bank Excluding repo transactions, in which the Fed is a counterparty
	BGCR (Broad General Collateral Rate)	As for TGCR plus Tri-Party repo executed through GCF (General Collateral Financing) Repo of FICC (Fixed Income Clearing Corp)
	SOFR (Secured Overnight Financing Rate)	As for BGCR plus Bilateral repo cleared through FICC's DVP (delivery-versus-payment) service, filtered for special bonds (i.e., removing transactions below the volume-weighted 25th percentile)
	Minus trades between affiliates, as far as visible from the data (hence, not possible for anonymous repo transactions) Plus "open trades," as far as possible	
Contingency mechanisms:	In case of unavailable data for a segment: use adjusted data for prior day	
Data exclusion:	Manual exclusion of doubtful data by New York Fed	
SOFR calculation:	Volume-weighted median of data after contingency and exclusion (i.e., the repo rate associated with the 50th percentile of the transaction volume)	

FIGURE 1.1 SOFR: Calculation
Source: Authors, based on https://www.newyorkfed.org/markets/reference-rates/additional-information-about-reference-rates#information_about_treasury_repo_reference_rates and Federal Register Vol. 82, No. 167

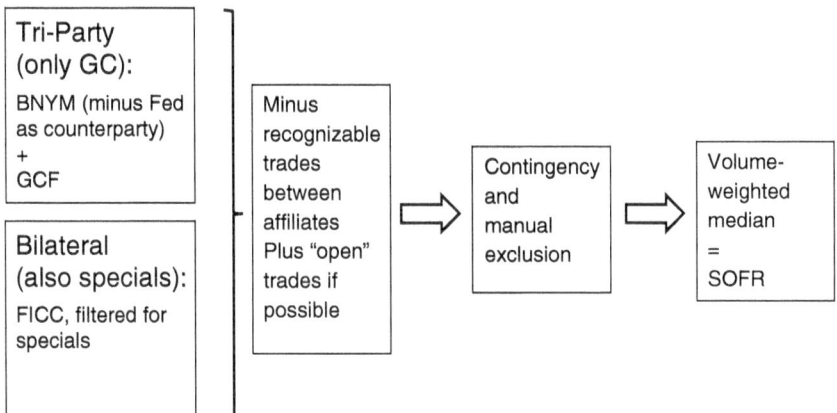

FIGURE 1.2 SOFR: Segments of the repo market used as data input for SOFR calculation
Source: Authors, based on https://www.newyorkfed.org/markets/reference-rates/ additional-information-about-reference-rates#information_about_treasury_repo_ reference_rates and Federal Register Vol. 82, No. 167

Page:	https://www.newyorkfed.org/markets/reference-rates/sofr
Time:	Approximately 8 a.m. ET for the previous business day
Revisions:	Approximately 2:30 p.m. ET for the previous business day
	Revisions are possible if additional data became available or an error has been detected and the revised rate differs from the initial one by at least 1 bp.
Scope:	1st, 25th, 50th, 75th and 99th volume-weighted percentiles (50th percentile = SOFR)
	Volume
	Note: The individual repo transactions are not published

FIGURE 1.3 SOFR: Publication
Source: Authors, based on https://www.newyorkfed.org/markets/reference-rates/ sofr

Since liquidity in the repo market is greatest for overnight transactions and decreases rather quickly as the term increases, only the overnight repo market provides the depth required for a reliable reference rate. Hence, the decision to switch from LIBOR to a repo-based reference rate necessitates switching to an overnight term rather than a one-month term or a three-month term, as was the case for LIBOR. This is a key challenge in the transition from LIBOR to SOFR, which will be discussed in Chapter 3.

CALCULATING A REFERENCE REPO RATE

The first task in constructing a reference rate from the repo market consists in collecting data:

- For the bilateral repo market, only data from trades cleared through the delivery-versus-payment (DVP) service of the Fixed Income Clearing Corporation (FICC) is practically accessible.
- For the tri-party repo market, data can be more easily and completely collected from third parties: the FICC offering General Collateral Financing (GCF) repo for its members; and Bank of New York Mellon, acting as clearinghouse. While the former anonymizes brokers, the latter collects data about the counterparties, which can be used to identify repo transactions between affiliates.

The Fed has agreements in place to collect these data from Bank of New York Mellon and from DTCC Solutions LLC, affiliated with FICC. At roughly 8 a.m. the next morning, the New York Fed publishes the volume-weighted median repo rate, rounded to the nearest basis point, as the daily secured overnight financing rate. *On publication day only*, the Fed will amend this reported SOFR value, in the event it subsequently receives amended data.

The NY Fed does not share the underlying data with the public, the consequences of which will be considered below.

ORIGIN OF REPO RATES USED FOR SOFR CALCULATION

The Fed publishes the volume figures for data used to calculate SOFR, as well as for the Tri-Party General Collateral Rate (TGCR), and the Broad General Collateral Rate (BGCR). As a result, it is possible to gain some insights into the relative volumes that the different sectors of the repo market contribute to the SOFR calculation. The TGCR volume directly represents the volume of tri-party repo rates provided by Bank of New York Mellon. The difference between BGCR and TGCR volumes represents the volume contributed by GCF Repo. And the difference between SOFR and BGCR volumes represents the volume originating from cleared bilateral repo (in each case after the adjustments described in Figure 1.1, such as filtering for specials).

Repo Market Contributions to the SOFR Calculation

Figure 1.4 shows that the volume contributed from GCF repo has been consistently low compared to the other two data sources. The volume provided by Bank of New York Mellon and from cleared bilateral repo has been

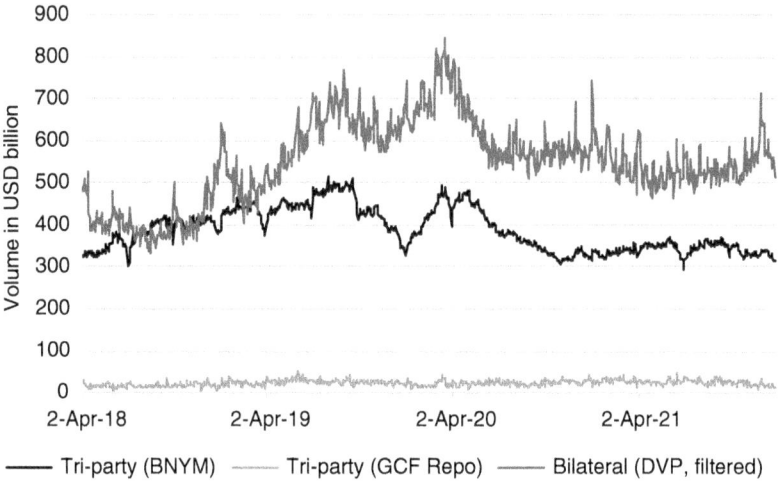

FIGURE 1.4   Volume in different sectors of the repo market
Source: Authors, from data provided by the Fed (https://www.newyorkfed.org/markets/reference-rates/sofr) Disclaimer: These reference rate data are subject to the Terms of Use posted at newyorkfed.org. The New York Fed is not responsible for publication of the reference rate data by the Authors and Wiley does not endorse any particular republication, and has no liability for your use.

roughly the same initially, while the latter has been higher since 2019. This graph also suggests that the bilateral repo market, which is only partly captured in the data in Figure 1.4 (only cleared trades, filtered for specials), remains the larger sector compared to tri-party repo.

Distribution of Repo Rates Used for SOFR Calculation

In addition to the reference rate, defined as the volume-weighted 50th percentile, the Fed also publishes the 1st, 25th, 75th, and 99th percentiles. Figures 1.5 and 1.6 show a history of the rate spreads associated with different percentiles, thereby giving an impression of the width and shape of the distribution. A few observations are worth noting:

- There are significant spikes in the width of the distribution. Most of them coincide with a spike in the level of repo rates (and of SOFR), but not all of them.
- Until the low-interest-rate period starting in April 2020, the distribution tended to be wider on the right-hand side. This may reflect the impact of filtering out most of the special bonds.
- After April 2020, the spikes subsided, and the distribution has exhibited a more symmetric and narrow shape.

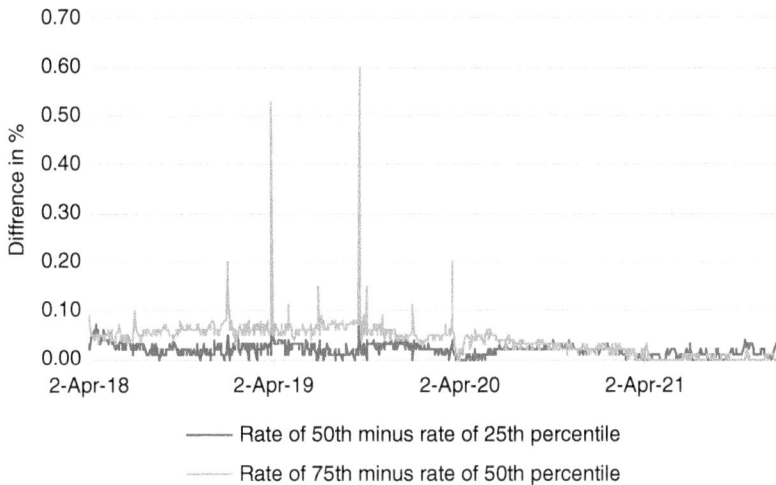

FIGURE 1.5 Difference of rates associated with percentiles
Source: Authors, from data provided by CME

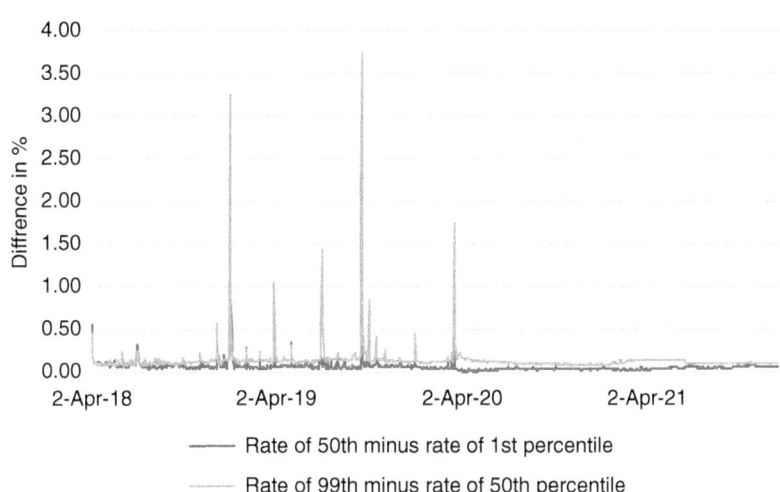

FIGURE 1.6 Difference of rates associated with percentiles
Source: Authors, from data provided by CME

The data filtering applied in SOFR therefore seems to exclude a significant part of the specialness, which results in a relatively narrow distribution on the left-hand side. On the other hand, there is no filtering applied on the right-hand side of the distribution, which means that excessively high repo rates also enter the SOFR data pool, even if they are caused by counterparty-specific factors, such as the difficulty of a bank in accessing funding. On one hand, if funding problems are sufficient to affect the volume-weighted median, they cause a spike in the width of the distribution *and* the SOFR rate. On the other hand, if funding problems are limited to a smaller subset of banks, they cause a spike *only* in the width of the distribution. This explains the first observation.

In summary, the data pool for SOFR excludes most *bond-specific* influences (e.g., specialness) but not the *counterparty-specific* influences. In other words, the construction of SOFR tends to successfully exclude from the reference rate any instability caused by specialness but not by funding problems. The result is a distribution tilted toward the right-hand side and reflecting general funding stress in a spike of the SOFR rate *and* of the distribution.

Based on the recent symmetric shape of the distribution, we have calibrated a normal distribution to the percentiles. Specifically, we have calculated the mean and standard deviation of the normal distribution, so that the sum of the absolute differences of its 1st, 25th, 50th, 75th, and 99th percentiles versus those of the SOFR rate becomes minimal. Repeating this calculation for every day, we have obtained the history shown in Figure 1.7.

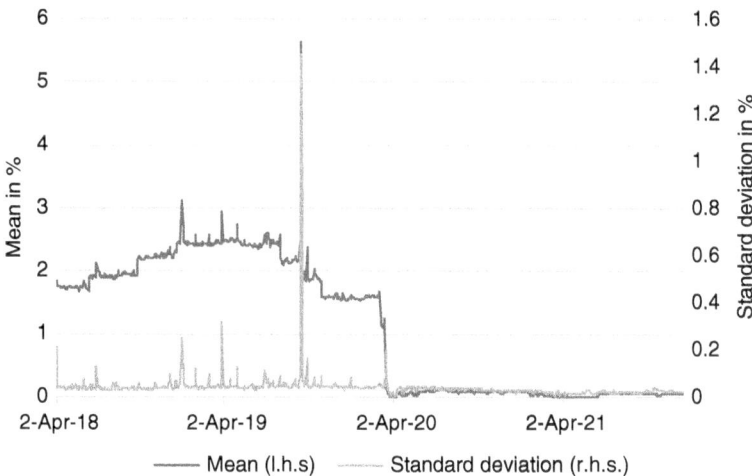

FIGURE 1.7 Mean and standard deviation of a normal distribution fitted to the percentiles of the SOFR data pool
Source: Authors, from data provided by CME

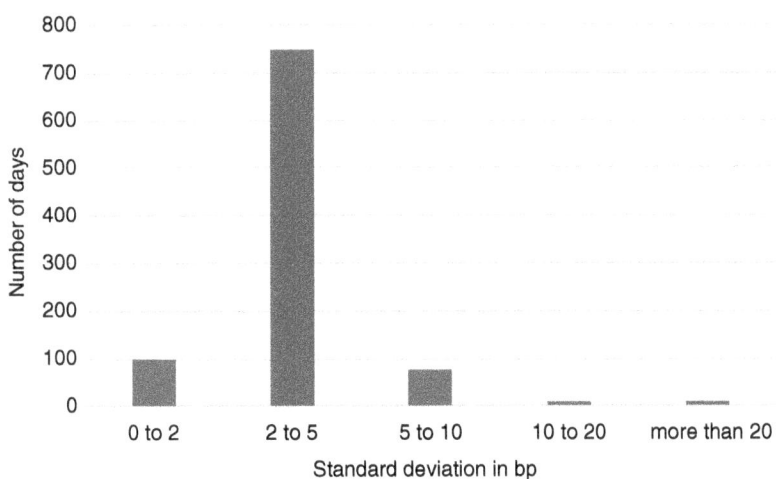

FIGURE 1.8 Histogram of observed standard deviations
Source: Authors, from data provided by CME

As the data of the repo transactions used for SOFR calculation are not published, the distribution obtained in such a manner from the published percentiles can serve as an (imperfect) substitute for further analysis of the repo market underlying SOFR. For example, one can create a histogram of the standard deviation as depicted in Figure 1.8.

On average, the individual repo transactions have exhibited a standard deviation of 4 bp; a standard deviation of more than 10 bp is exceptional.

Repo traders using SOFR (futures) as a hedge should keep in mind this non-negligible standard deviation as well as its sources. In the histogram shown in Figure 1.8, the lower standard deviations tended to occur more recently, so in the current market environment the mismatch between individual repo transactions and SOFR appears to be more benign.

SOFR VERSUS FED FUNDS

Figure 1.9 shows the history of SOFR, a secured overnight rate, along with the history of Fed Funds, an unsecured overnight rate. For scaling reasons, Figure 1.10 shows only the last part of this history, when both rates and their volatility were low. Two basic observations can be made:

- There are instances, even some prolonged periods of time, when SOFR is above the effective Fed Funds rate (EFFR).
- There are significant spikes in SOFR, which are less pronounced in EFFR.

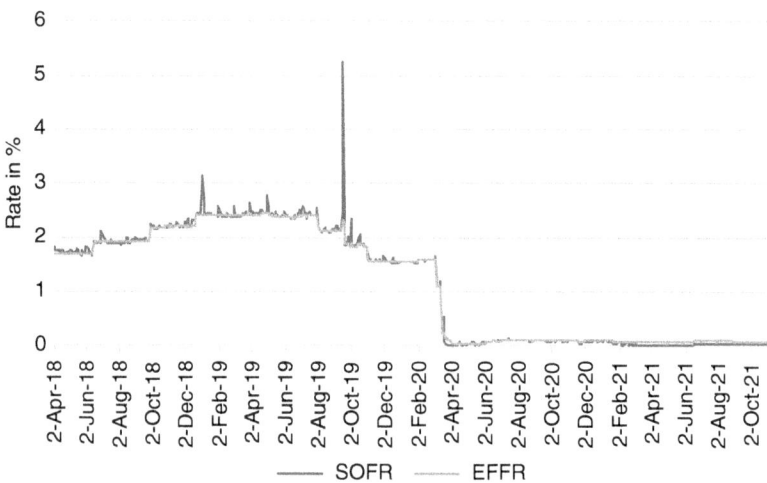

FIGURE 1.9 SOFR versus EFFR
Source: Authors, from data provided by CME

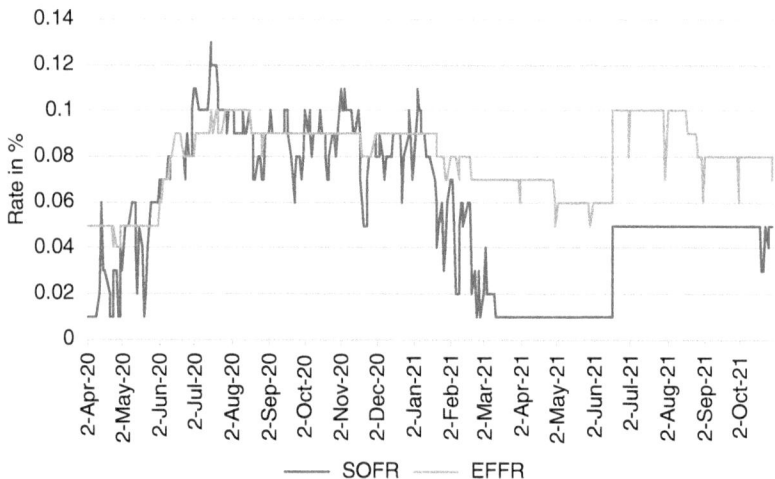

FIGURE 1.10 SOFR versus EFFR
Source: Authors, from data provided by CME

This can be puzzling: Why should a secured rate trade above an unsecured rate for the same tenor? Actually, taking June 29, 2018, as an example, with SOFR at 212 bp and EFFR at 191 bp, a trader could borrow unsecured in the Fed Fund market and lend secured in the repo market overnight, realizing both a profit of 21 bp *and* a lower risk from collateralization.[1] Hence, this transaction fulfills the definition of an arbitrage. Therefore, in efficient markets, SOFR should trade below EFFR. While this has been the case more recently (Figure 1.10), the history of Figure 1.9 tells us that there have been many instances of that arbitrage opportunity, which persisted at times for several weeks.

As a first step to explain the reasons behind this puzzle, we note that participants in secured and unsecured lending markets are partly different. For example, a hedge fund using the bilateral repo market to fund his long positions (and to cover his short positions) in bonds has no access to the Fed Funds market. If hedge funds experience funding problems, the repo rate can therefore rise above the level of Fed Funds (assuming banks using Fed Funds do not experience the same or bigger funding problems). This also explains the counterparty-specific influences on the distribution of repo rates – and why they are usually more pronounced in bilateral repo than in tri-party repo.

Since there exist market participants, such as banks with repo operations, that can participate in both markets and therefore execute the arbitrage, this first step does not solve the puzzle, but only translates it in to the question: Why don't these market participants exploit the arbitrage opportunities whenever they occur?

Following the financial crisis, banks have been subjected to increasing regulation in general and to balance sheet constraints in particular. As a consequence, they need to assess an arbitrage opportunity not only in isolation (as we did in the example of June 29, 2018, above), but also with regard to various balance sheet constraints, such as leverage. When constraints on bank balance sheets are non-binding, banks can execute this arbitrage at relatively low cost. This explains the periods of history when the arbitrage has "worked" as expected and kept SOFR below EFFR. (See Figure 1.10.) On the other hand, when many banks face binding constraints on their balance sheets, increasing the balance sheet via an additional arbitrage position would be costly (e.g., require issuing additional equity). These situations explain the periods of history that exhibited the puzzling observations. Of course, when the arbitrage profit exceeds the cost of executing it, banks are enticed to enter it even when balance sheets are constrained. This explains why the spread remains capped by arbitrage – though the level at which the arbitrage occurs depends on the specific balance sheet situation of banks and can be different from zero.

---

[1] This becomes particularly clear if one assumes that he can use the same counterparty for both loans.

In summary, therefore, the SOFR–EFFR spread is subject to the arbitrage relationship SOFR $\leq$ EFFR *under the condition* that balance sheet constraints allow the bank to execute the arbitrage without additional regulatory costs. The adjustment for regulatory costs will affect the discussion of the basis between secured and unsecured funding rates in Chapter 4.

SOFR SPIKES AND THE SRF

Applying this explanation to the observation of spikes in SOFR, one can see two driving forces:

- A high demand for funding (e.g., during a liquidity crisis) increases both secured and unsecured funding rates.
- A high cost for executing the arbitrage increases secured versus unsecured funding rates.

There is a correlation between both forces. In a general funding crisis, the leverage of banks is usually high, as is the cost of equity required to expand the balance sheet with an arbitrage position. This explains the observation that general spikes in funding rates tend to be more pronounced in SOFR than in EFFR. Imagine a situation of general stress in the financial system, causing hedge funds to push up repo rates versus Fed Funds. A bank may see an arbitrage opportunity but also that its execution would require a costly expansion of its balance sheet at the worst point in time. Hence, the bank will wait for the arbitrage to become large enough to cover the exceptionally high regulatory costs of executing it. A high cost of altering the balance sheet thereby translates directly into the high spikes of SOFR versus EFFR.

Realizing this problem, the Fed decided to assume that role. Specifically, as reaction to the spikes of SOFR, the Fed announced on July 28, 2021, the implementation of a standing repo facility (SRF), providing liquidity to the repo market independently of the balance sheet constraints of banks, with the minimum rate being usually set at the top of the current policy window. In other words, with capital costs becoming too high to make banks a reliable provider of liquidity in repo markets in times of stress, the Fed has introduced, via its repo facility, the SRF rate $(SRFR)$ as an additional constraint,[2] i.e.,

$$SOFR \leq SRFR$$

---

[2]Violations of this constraint are theoretically conceivable, for example, due to some participants in the repo market influencing SOFR not being eligible to participate in the SRF.

The relationship between SOFR and EFFR is therefore determined simultaneously by both of the two constraints, of which the capital cost is unobservable and *SRFR* is observable. Together this can explain both observations in Figure 1.9, specifically the disappearance of large SOFR spikes once the Fed had introduced the repo facility.

Hence, analysts should keep in mind the structural break in the SOFR time series, which contains both SOFR before and after the Fed repo facility existed (i.e., without and with the *SRFR* constraint). This situation can be compared to looking at a series of swap rates, to which a cap is added in the middle of the time series. However, due to low interest rates at the point of time the cap was added, this is not immediately visible from the data – but will be once interest rates rise.

While the Fed provides a proxy for SOFR going back far before its introduction (Federal Reserve Bank of New York 2018), it is of limited analytic use, as the SOFR data points were observed in the absence of the constraint. For this book, this leads to the practical problem that at the time of writing (December 2021), there were only a few months of SOFR history available after the introduction of the standing repo facility, which would not have allowed for any meaningful statistical analysis. We therefore needed to ignore the structural break in order to be able to present historical analysis. However, readers should consider this only as an example and repeat the methods presented here once a sufficient history is available with data from August 2021 onward only.

In particular, this has an implication for volatility considerations. (See Chapter 5.) The introduction of the second constraint on SOFR rates also results in a structural break between realized SOFR volatility before and after the point of time of introduction. Consequently, SOFR volatility calculated from time periods before the introduction should be treated with caution. Also, while one could expect some increase in realized SOFR volatility when rates rise, it seems unlikely that the frequency and extent of the spikes visible in Figure 1.9 at higher yield levels will occur again. In fact, from the historical perspective of Figure 1.9, it appears as if the reduction in rates close to zero put an end to SOFR spikes well before the SRF was introduced. However, the existence of the SRF should help mitigate SOFR spikes even in an environment of increasing yield levels. Using the cap analogy from above, the existence of the cap, which is not visible in a low-rate environment, is likely to appear in an environment of higher rates.

As an aside, an Austrian economist would consider the evolution described above as an example of an interventionist cycle (Mises 1924, p. 232). After the state had subjected banks to balance sheet constraints, they became unable to provide repo funding in times of a crisis. This "market failure" gave the state an excuse to "help out" with a repo facility – i.e., to acquire another function that the free market had provided reasonably well before the state intervened.

BENEFITS AND (POTENTIAL) PROBLEMS OF SOFR

Let's finish this chapter by assessing SOFR versus the goals for the new reference rate mentioned at the beginning of this chapter:

■ The volume of repo transactions in the data pool for SOFR calculation has been at a consistently high level, as Figure 1.11 demonstrates. While there has been no crisis of the dimension of 2009 since the introduction of SOFR, the pandemic-related crisis did not cause a discernible drop in repo volumes. And repo markets remained functional during 2009 as well. Moreover, the spikes in SOFR do not coincide with significant decreases in volume, meaning that the repo market seems to work well, even during times of general funding stress. These features make SOFR appear favorable in comparison with other reference rates, including LIBOR, which are based on a smaller and/or more unstable transaction volume.

■ We have concluded above that SOFR provides a partial solution to the stability goal. It isolates the reference rate from most bond-specific disruptions (e.g., specialness) but not from counterparty-specific disruptions

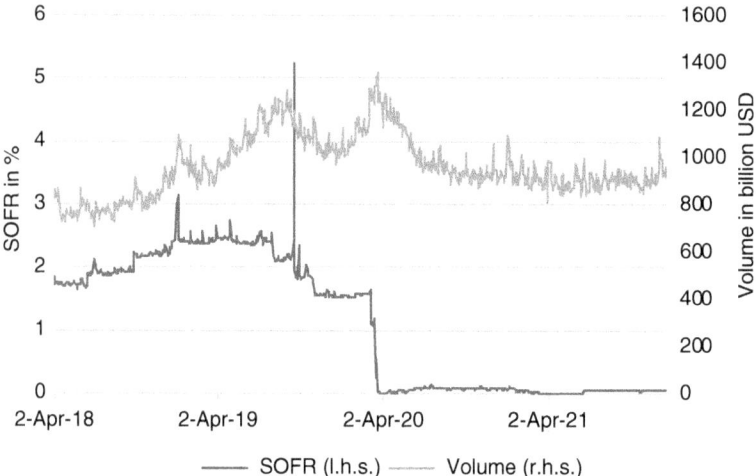

FIGURE 1.11 SOFR rate and volume of repo transactions used for SOFR calculation
Source: Authors, from data provided by CME

(e.g., funding problems). As a consequence, funding problems affecting a large portion of the financial system cause spikes in SOFR (as in Figure 1.9) *and* in the width of the distribution (as in Figures 1.5 and 1.6). Funding problems affecting only a small subset (and hence not the volume-weighted median) cause a spike *only* in the width of the distribution.

The introduction of the Fed's standing repo facility provides an additional part of the solution to the stability goal: It isolates the reference rate also from most counterparty-specific disruptions, such as funding problems.

Taken together, the calculation process excludes most disruptions from the left-hand side of the distribution (e.g., specialness) and from the right-hand side of the distribution (via the SRFR in the equation above).

■ So far, SOFR seems to have fulfilled the motivation for its introduction to exclude the possibility of manipulation from the reference rate. However, we see in the construction of SOFR outlined in Figure 1.1 the theoretical loophole of manipulating SOFR via internal repo transactions between affiliates. While these transactions are removed from the Bank of New York Mellon data, where counterparts are visible, this is not possible for the FICC data. On the other hand, given the size of the repo market, the definition of SOFR as the volume-weighted median, and the power of the Fed to exclude doubtful datapoints manually, it appears hard to exploit this theoretical loophole in practice.

It's also worth noting that, while LIBOR calculations are a cross-sectional average, SOFR (like Fed Funds) is a volume-weighted, time-series average. And without access to the volume data, it is impossible for market participants to replicate SOFR via market transactions.

This has two consequences for market participants. First, it's not possible to price SOFR futures purely through no-arbitrage considerations the way we price Treasury bond futures and Eurodollar futures. Anyone trying to trade an arbitrage involving SOFR futures necessarily runs the risk that the published SOFR values that determine the final settlement price of a contract will be different from the repo rate used in the arbitrage. Even for a trader who was active in the repo market throughout the day, it's not possible to replicate the SOFR value with certainty, as the volume information used in the published SOFR calculation is opaque.

The second consequence is that anyone using SOFR futures for general risk management faces this inherent risk every time the contract is used. In most of the examples appearing in this book, we maintain the simplifying assumption that the parties in the example can trade whenever they want at the prevailing SOFR rate. But of course this isn't the case in practice. In practice, market participants are quite likely to be able to trade within a few basis points of the published SOFR value, but there's no way to reduce the residual uncertainty beyond that few basis points. Over time, one would expect the law of large numbers to help, with roughly as many transactions above the reported SOFR value as below. But on any given day, including the day on which the final settlement price of the futures contract is determined, that residual risk remains.

For similar reasons, the decision of the Fed not to share the repo data used for SOFR calculation with the public results in several (potential) problems:

- While some analysis can be done using the percentiles (as above), some important questions remain unanswered. For example, it is impossible to analyze the daily distribution of repo rates and volumes. But this is vital information for a repo dealer quoting an overnight rate in the morning and using SOFR as a hedge. Consequently, obscuring the raw data may result in lesser suitability of SOFR for hedging.
- Likewise, while we have estimated a standard deviation of 4 bp between SOFR and individual repo trades, we needed to assume a normal distribution and calibrate it to the published percentiles. The possibility to conduct analysis on the raw data would lead to better analysis and therefore to better hedges of repo transactions with SOFR and hence to a greater demand for SOFR.
- Big banks with repo desks have access to a part of the raw data in real-time by participating in the repo market determining SOFR, while the general public, including "end users" of SOFR such as smaller banks and corporate borrowers, does not. Consequently, they are in a better position not only to perform some of the analyses mentioned above, but

SOFR, TGCR, BGCR, EFFR	https://www.newyorkfed.org/markets/reference-rates/sofr
SOFR averages and index	https://www.newyorkfed.org/markets/reference-rates/sofr
Long history of a proxy for SOFR	https://www.newyorkfed.org/markets/opolicy/operating_policy_180309
3M SOFR futures	https://www.cmegroup.com/markets/interest-rates/stirs/three-month-sofr.quotes.html
1M SOFR futures	https://www.cmegroup.com/markets/interest-rates/stirs/one-month-sofr.quotes.html
SOFR term rate	https://www.cmegroup.com/market-data/cme-group-benchmark-administration/term-sofr.html

FIGURE 1.12 Data resources
Source: Authors

also to estimate the SOFR during the day, *before* the Fed releases it to the general public on the next business day.

▪ Hence, the secrecy about the raw data may lead to concerns about SOFR being a level playing field. In fact, there seems to be a perception among end users that regulators and big banks have forced SOFR on them, to their potential disadvantage. This perception appears to be the result of several factors, including that the transition from LIBOR to SOFR makes lenders unable to profit from an increase in unsecured versus secured lending rates (see Chapter 4). But sharing the raw data in a timely fashion with the general public would be an essential step for addressing these concerns at their most basic level, by providing more equal knowledge about the reference rate itself. This would enable every participant in SOFR markets at least to see the determinants of its basic reference rate at about the same time and to roughly the same extent.

Overall, the decision not to share the raw data seems to be an "unforced error" in the construction of SOFR, limiting its usability and hence the demand for it, even in its most basic and direct application as a hedge for overnight repo transactions. Fortunately, it can be easily rectified by making its input data publicly available, as the raw data for most other financial transactions and reference rates, such as LIBOR. If the raw data are shared in a timely manner with the general public, the disadvantage of end users versus big banks with repo desks can be mitigated, supporting the acceptance of SOFR as new reference rate.

In case the concern of exposing repo counterparties to squeezes was the reason behind the decision to hide the raw data from the public, anonymizing the counterparties (and maybe also the bonds) could be a solution, which would avoid exploitation of the raw data for squeezes, while at the same time allowing the legitimate analysis described above. Swap Data Repositories might serve as models for publication of the repo data underlying SOFR. A revision of this decision would support the switch from LIBOR to SOFR by allowing smaller end users the same relative degree of transparency enjoyed by banks and other large participants in the repo market.

CHAPTER 2

SOFR Futures

While three-month Eurodollar futures\uline{a} settle to a three-month term rate at the end of the contract, SOFR futures settle to the average of an overnight rate during the last three months prior to the expiration of the contract – referred to as the *reference period* of the contract. Despite this difference, SOFR futures share several characteristics with Eurodollar futures, since prior to entering the reference period both contracts are functions of the forward rate associated with the reference period. As a result, Eurodollar futures and SOFR futures represent consecutive three-month forward segments of the yield curve – for unsecured borrowing in the case of Eurodollars and for secured borrowing in the case of SOFR. It follows that we can apply many of the same analytic techniques to SOFR futures that have been developed for Eurodollar futures.

Accordingly, this chapter starts by describing the specifications for 3M SOFR futures (SR3), before showing how analytic approaches common to the Eurodollar complex can be applied after the migration to SOFR. It then adds 1M SOFR futures (SR1) and analyzes the spread between 3M and 1M SOFR futures. Finally, it outlines more advanced modeling and hedging techniques via processes, again by building on the work done for LIBOR products.[1]

However, once the reference period of a SOFR futures contract begins, the aggregative function stops, and we must keep track of each of the overnight rates that span the reference period, as illustrated in Figure 2.1. Readers should keep this break in mind whenever considering SOFR futures and options. As soon as the reference period of a SOFR future starts, one does not deal with a LIBOR-like aggregation of daily rates into a

---

[1]The calculations of settlement prices and spreads for these contracts are illustrated in the Excel sheet "3M versus 1M" accompanying this chapter.

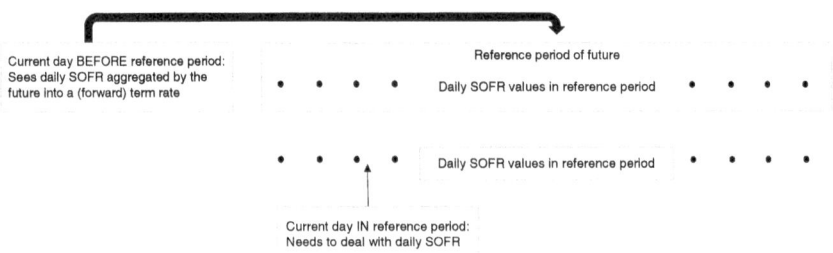

FIGURE 2.1 The aggregation of daily SOFR via the future before the reference period starts
Source: Authors

forward term rate anymore but rather, with a collection of already-known and still unknown daily SOFR values. This difference means that the front-month SOFR futures contract requires extra attention and new analytic approaches. Fortunately, in the case of futures, the necessary adjustments of terminology and analyses are rather simple, and this chapter offers some suggestions for strips and rolls. In the case of options on futures on the other hand, this conceptual difference will result in path-dependent Asian options and confront us with a much bigger challenge, as we'll see in Chapter 5.

3M SOFR FUTURES: CONVENTIONS

The key difference between a Eurodollar (ED) and a three-month SOFR (SR3) future is the fact that the underlying rate of the former is a traded, forward-looking, unsecured term rate, while the settlement rate of the latter needs to be calculated from overnight rates for secured borrowing and lending and is therefore by nature backward-looking. The basis between unsecured and secured borrowing will be analyzed in Chapter 4. Here we focus on the implications of the difference between forward-looking and backward-looking rates on the conventions of the futures. In order to account for this difference, as a first step, we need to adjust the terminology used to describe the contract month:

- The "Sep 2022 ED" future ends trading and settles in Sep 2022 on a 3M LIBOR rate, which begins in Sep 2022 and matures in Dec 2022.
- The "Sep 2022 SR3" future ends trading and settles in Dec 2022 to a (modified) geometric average of daily SOFR rates observed during a period, which begins in Sep 2022 and ends in Dec 2022.

Hence, while the *underlying rates* of a "Sep 2022" ED and SR3 future cover almost[2] the same period, *end of trading* and *settlement* occur in a SR3 future at the end rather than at the beginning of this period. This is a result of the different nature of the underlying rates: 3M LIBOR is a traded forward-looking term rate, while the 3M SOFR settlement rate needs to be constructed by looking back at the traded overnight SOFR during the past 3M. While even at the last day of trading of an ED contract, the underlying rate refers to a period completely in the future, at the last day of trading of an SR3 contract, the underlying rate refers to a period in the past, which is therefore completely known (except for the very last overnight rate, which is published on the business day after the last trading day). Consequently, during the last three months of the life of an SR3 contract, more and more of the rate determining its settlement price becomes known, typically resulting in reduced volatility – unlike in ED futures.

We will analyze these economic consequences below; for the moment, we focus on the consequences for terminology and conventions: The *contract month* (e.g., Sep 2022) of an SR3 future refers to the *reference quarter* (e.g., Sep 2022 to Dec 2022) of the *following* three months, whose SOFR will be used to calculate the settlement price at the *end* of the reference quarter, i.e., three months *after* the "contract month." While an ED contract ends trading when the underlying rate (the forward-looking 3M LIBOR) begins, the SR3 contract of the same "contract month" ends trading three months later, when all overnight SOFR values of the reference quarter (except the last one) and thus the term rate for settlement is (almost) known.

Using this adjustment in terminology, the conventions of ED contracts have been closely mirrored in those of SR3 contracts, as summarized in Figures 2.2 and 2.3. Crucially, the calculation of the settlement price uses ISDA compounding with Act/360 as the daycount convention.

The formula for the settlement price of an SR3 futures contract is defined as 100 less the settlement rate, R, given by the equation

$$R = \left[\prod_{i=1}^{n} \left(1 + \frac{\frac{SOFR_i}{100} \times d_i}{360} \right) - 1 \right] \times \frac{360}{D} \times 100$$

where

- n is the number of business days (for US government securities) during the reference quarter.
- $SOFR_i$ is the SOFR for day i
  (published on the next business day). In keeping with CME's conventions, the %-value of SOFR is entered (e.g., 1.5 for a SOFR of 1.5%), hence the factor 1/100.

---

[2]The differences will be discussed in Chapter 4.

Delivery months	Nearest 39 March Quarterly months (Mar, Jun, Sep, Dec)
Reference quarter	Begins on 3rd Wed (included) of 3rd month preceding the delivery month Ends on 3rd Wed (excluded) of the delivery month
Contract month	Month in which the reference quarter begins
Last trading day	Exchange business day preceding 3rd Wed of the delivery month
Delivery	Cash settlement First business day after last trading day, i.e., usually 3rd Wed of the delivery month (This is the day the Fed publishes SOFR for the last trading day)
Settlement rate	Compounded SOFR realized during reference quarter (see formula in text) Rounded to the nearest 0.01 bp
Settlement price	100 minus settlement rate
Online resource	https://www.cmegroup.com/markets/interest-rates/stirs/three-month-sofr.contractSpecs.html

FIGURE 2.2   SOFR futures: settlement calculations
Source: Authors, based on CME

Contract size	USD 25 per basis point per annum	
Minimum price increment	0.25 basis points per annum	for contracts with 4 months or less until last day of trading
	0.5 basis points per annum	for other contracts
Trading venues and hours	CME Globex and CME ClearPort: 5pm to 4pm, Sun-Fri	
Block trade minimum size	250 contracts	Asian Trading Hours (4pm–12am, Mon-Fri on regular business days and at all weekend times)
	500 contracts	European Trading Hours (12am– 7am, Mon-Fri on regular business days)
	1000 contracts	Regular Trading Hours (7am–4pm, Mon-Fri on regular business days)
Product codes	SR3 SFR Comdty	CME Bloomberg

FIGURE 2.3   3M SOFR futures: technical specifications
Source: Authors, based on CME

Delivery months	Nearest 13 calendar months
Last trading day	Last exchange business day of the delivery month
Delivery	Cash settlement First business day after last trading day (This is the day the Fed publishes SOFR for the last trading day)
Settlement rate	Arithmetic average of SOFR realized during delivery month (Average is taken over calendar days, not business days) (For non-busines days, the SOFR of the preceding business day is used) Rounded to the nearest 0.1 bp
Settlement price	100 minus settlement rate
Online resource	https://www.cmegroup.com/markets/interest-rates/stirs/one-month-sofr.contractSpecs.html

FIGURE 2.10 1M SOFR futures: settlement calculations
Source: Authors, based on CME

Contract size	USD 41.67 per basis point per annum	
Minimum price increment	0.25 basis points per annum 0.5 basis points per annum	during delivery month before delivery month
Trading venues and hours	CME Globex and CME ClearPort: 5pm to 4pm, Sun-Fri	
Block trade minimum size	125 contracts	Asian Trading Hours (4pm–12am, Mon-Fri on regular business days and at all weekend times)
	250 contracts	European Trading Hours (12am–7am, Mon-Fri on regular business days)
	500 contracts	Regular Trading Hours (7am–4pm, Mon-Fri on regular business days)
Product codes	SR1 SER Comdty	CME Bloomberg

FIGURE 2.11 1M SOFR futures: technical specifications
Source: Authors, based on CME

- d_i is the number of calendar days for which $SOFR_i$ is used.

  Until the next business day, the SOFR for the previous business day is used, e.g., on weekends and holidays. Thus, if Friday and Monday are business days, the SOFR for Friday (published on Monday) is used for Friday, Saturday, and Sunday, and the corresponding d_i is 3.
- D is the total number of calendar days during the reference quarter, i.e., $D = \sum_{i=1}^{n} d_i$.

The Excel sheet "3M versus 1M" accompanying this chapter implements these calculations for the Sep 2022 SR3 contract. The reader can define the SOFR either manually for each day during the reference quarter or set an SOFR level and slope for the whole reference quarter and observe the impact on the settlement price.

As outlined in Chapter 1, the Fed may revise SOFR published in the morning. If such a revision occurs for the SOFR of the last day of the reference quarter, it cannot be reflected in the settlement price of the future, which CME determines in the morning of the delivery day. By contrast, revisions for all other SOFR are taken into consideration for calculating the settlement rate (CME May 2018, p. 6).

Figure 2.4 illustrates the situation of SR3 contracts during the reference quarter: At the "current" day during the reference quarter, the SOFR values for the past period of the reference quarter are known, while the SOFR values for the future period of the reference quarter are not. Hence, as the "current" day progresses through the reference quarter, the share of known versus unknown values determining its settlement rate increases. This is similar to the situation in FF (Fed Funds) contracts, but different from the situation for ED contracts.

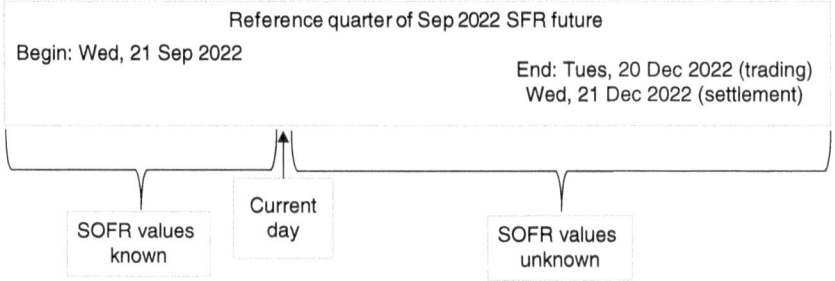

FIGURE 2.4   SOFR futures during reference quarter
Source: Authors

This is also the reason for the behavior seen in Figure 2.5, which shows the history of all SR3 future prices.[3] As SR3 contracts approach their end, an increasing portion of their settlement rate is known, and hence:

- Their volatility tends to decrease, as seen in the lines becoming flatter toward their end.[4]
- They respond less and less to changing market expectations about future interest rates. During the decreasing interest rate environment of 2019, expectations about Fed rate cuts affected all SOFR values in the reference quarters of back month contracts, but only some of the SOFR values in the reference quarter of the front month contract, which therefore tended to stick to a higher level.

Abstracting from this conceptually different behavior of front month SR3 futures, Figure 2.5 reflects the evolution of the market consensus of Fed policy over time. After a rather parallel curve shift down in 2019 and a flat curve around zero in 2020, the relatively steep curve of 2021 implies a long period of gradual rate hikes. This analysis is familiar from other future markets, since the Fed policy drives both secured (SOFR) and unsecured (ED) rates underlying future contracts.

One can therefore conclude that, with the exception of the front month contract, the transition from LIBOR to SOFR is little more than a renaming exercise for the futures market. This is a contrast to the problems this transition faces in cash loan markets, which will be described in the next chapter, and in option markets, which will be covered in Chapter 5. The similarity of conventions between 3M SOFR and ED contracts also facilitates the migration: Since LIBOR will end on June 30, 2023, ED futures expiring after this date will settle on a fallback clause, described in more detail in Figure Intro.1 and on https://www.cmegroup.com/education/files/webinar-fallbacks-for-eurodollars.pdf.

An important consequence of ED contracts after June 30, 2023, being spreads over a secured rate is that past this date only FF futures will trade on an unsecured rate. From mid-2023 onward, the unsecured–secured basis can therefore only be traded by SOFR–FF spread contracts, not by the currently more liquid SR3:ED spread futures anymore. The implications for analysis and positioning will be discussed in Chapter 4.

---

[3] A few data points have been excluded due to illiquidity.
[4] Chapter 5 will link this observation to Asian options.

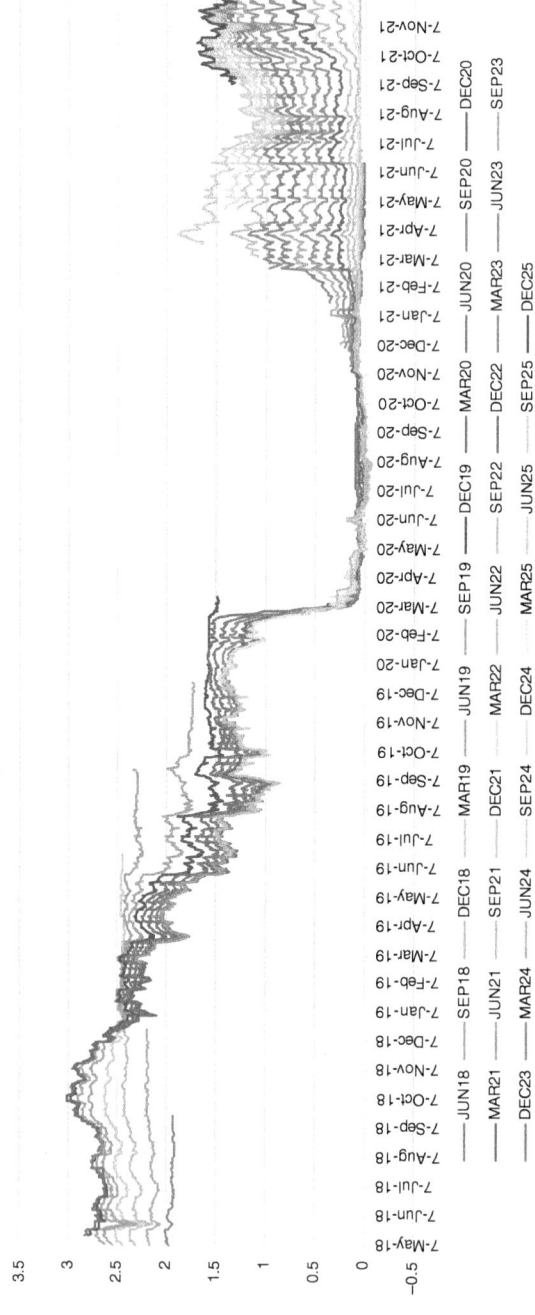

FIGURE 2.5 SOFR future price history

Source: Authors, from data provided by CME

3M SOFR FUTURES AS MARKET PRICES FOR CONSECUTIVE 3M FORWARD SOFR

The similarity of conventions between 3M SOFR and ED contracts, which facilitates the migration of *trading* after the end of LIBOR, also facilitates the migration of *analytic concepts* from the unsecured to the secured yield curve.

The importance of ED futures for yield curve analysis is based on the fact that they provide market prices for consecutive 3M forward periods of their underlying *unsecured* (LIBOR) rate – after adjusting for biases such as convexity. This is the foundation for many important analyses, such as:

- Using ED futures as building blocks for (forward) LIBOR rates via strips.
- The other way around, decomposing LIBOR rates into their individual 3M forward components and hedging them via futures (Burghardt et al. 1991).[5]
- Assessing the carry, rolldown, and risk/return of different parts of the yield curve and in different macroeconomic scenarios.[6]
- Extracting constant maturity zero or par rates, e.g., via spline models (Huggins and Schaller 2013, chapter 11), which are the basis for many further analyses.

The switch from LIBOR to SOFR as reference rate necessitates the transfer of this arsenal of analytic methods from the unsecured to the secured yield curve – and the proximity of ED and SOFR future conventions enables a straightforward transfer. While a complete treatment of secured yield curve analysis is outside the scope of this book, it offers a few examples of this transfer, specifically in this chapter for the secured yield curve and in Chapter 5 for the secured volatility curve, and focuses on its practical implications for hedging and trading in section 2. Chapter 6 discusses the different biases, such as convexity, in ED and SOFR contracts. As it turns out that there are no biases from nonlinearities in 3M SOFR futures, extracting secured forward rates from SOFR contracts is easier than extracting unsecured forward rates from ED contracts.

In fact, Figure 2.5 depicts the market prices for consecutive 3M forward periods of the *secured* yield curve. Slicing through the data in two dimensions, one can extract the historical evolution (one dimension) of

---

[5]Burghardt et al. (1991) can be considered as starting point for many for these analyses.
[6]Chapter 5 will provide more details on this.

the market expectations about the secured rate at different forward dates (second dimension). Figures 2.6 and 2.7 present the perspectives from these two dimensions.[7] The result confirms the similarity to pictures familiar from the unsecured yield curve: Expectations about Fed cuts led to an inversion of the curve from 2018 to 2019; the anticipation of low rates for a prolonged period of time is reflected in the compressed forward curve close to zero during 2020, while speculation about rate hikes led to more differentiation during 2021 again. One could now use these data as input into further analyses not performed here, for example, a macroeconomic analysis of the mismatches between the market consensus and actual Fed policy[8] or a relative value search for mispricings (e.g., opportunities for butterflies).

This analysis will be repeated in Chapter 5 to extract the evolution of the realized volatility in different parts of the forward curve for the secured rate. Both analyses can then be combined to assess the historical average and distribution of risk/return (e.g., Sharpe ratios, across the secured yield

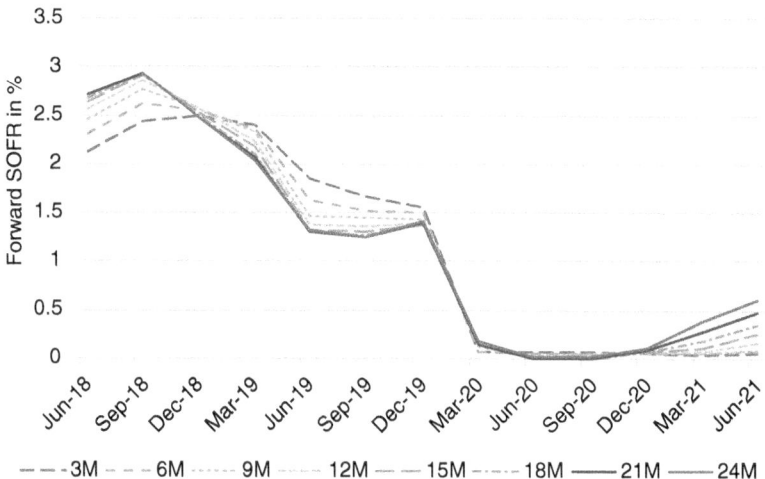

FIGURE 2.6 Consecutive 3M forward rates of the secured yield curve as implied by 3M SOFR futures
Source: Authors, from CME data

---

[7]The details of the data aggregation applied are explained in Chapter 5.
[8]An interesting question is whether market expectations for secured rates (as implied in SOFR futures) are a better predictor for actual Fed policy than those for unsecured rates (as implied in ED futures).

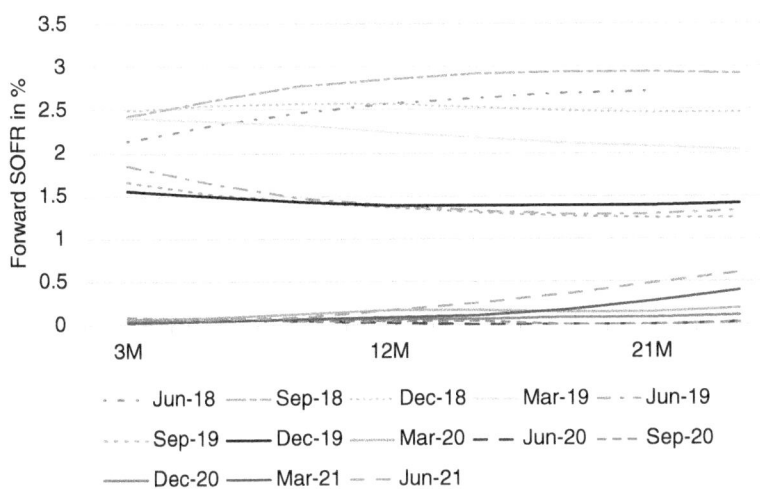

FIGURE 2.7 Consecutive 3M forward rates of the secured yield curve as implied by 3M SOFR futures
Source: Authors, from CME data

curve). This is an example of the transfer of established analysis techniques from the unsecured curve. In all these examples, readers should keep in mind the structural break due to the introduction of the Fed's standing repo facility (discussed in Chapter 1), which also affects statements based on the data from Figure 2.5. Readers also should repeat the analyses with post-SRF data exclusively once a sufficient amount of such data is available.

3M SOFR FUTURES: STRIPS

Since SR3 futures represent consecutive 3M forward interest periods (even without adjusting for nonlinearities as in case of ED futures), they can be easily combined into longer tenors. For example, buying the Sep 2022 and Dec 2022 SR3 futures on Sep 21, 2022, i.e., the beginning of the reference quarter of the Sep 2022 contract, gives exposure to the 6M interest period of all daily SOFR values during the reference quarters of both contracts.

This combination of successive ED futures is known as a *strip* and the corresponding interest rate as a *strip rate* (Burghardt et al. 1991, p. 86). It is a simple method to calculate term rates from the future markets; the example above corresponds to the 6M term rate implied by the futures market. However, when the term does not match the reference quarters, the results could be distorted. Imagine we want to calculate a 5M SOFR term rate from the

Sep 2022 and Dec 2022 SR3 futures contract on Sep 21, 2022, and that the market expects a Fed rate hike on Mar 1, 2023. This expectation would probably be reflected in the Dec 2022 SR3 price but should not affect the 5M term rate, which ends before Mar 1, 2023. Consequently, the simple method of calculating term rates from future markets via strips works well if the term matches the reference quarters (and in case of relatively constant forward SOFR during the reference quarter of the last future in the strip) but needs to be adjusted for the shape of the forward curve during the last reference quarter if it exceeds the term. We will address this issue later in this chapter.

When applying the concept of strip rates to the SOFR futures market to calculate term rates starting today, one needs to keep in mind the difference between front-month SOFR and front-month ED futures contracts, depicted in Figure 2.4:

- For ED strips, the first contract used in the strip covers an interest period entirely in the future. Hence, the time from today until the interest period covered by ED futures needs to be taken from the spot money market. For example, for a term rate starting on Sep 1, 2022, for the time until Sep 21, 2022, the 3W LIBOR is used.

- For SR3 strips, the first futures contract used in the strip covers with its reference quarter an interest period that is partly in the past and partly in the future. Hence, unlike for ED strips, it is not necessary to refer to the spot money market. In the example above, for a term rate starting on Sep 1, 2022, for the time until Sep 21, 2022, the price of the Jun 2022 SR3 contract can be used. However, it needs to be adjusted for the SOFR values already observed during the part of the reference quarter before Sep 1, 2022.

This difference is illustrated in Figure 2.8.

To calculate the yield for the period until the first full reference quarter from the front month SR3 contract, one needs to split its reference quarter into known and unknown SOFR values (Figure 2.4), i.e.,

$$
R = \left[\prod_{i=1}^{n_{known}} \left(1 + \frac{\frac{SOFR_i}{100} \times d_i}{360} \right) \times \prod_{i=1}^{n_{unknown}} \left(1 + \frac{\frac{SOFR_i}{100} \times d_i}{360} \right) - 1 \right] \times \frac{360}{D} \times 100
$$

One can then solve for the interest rate implied by the front month SR3 contract for the unknown period of its reference quarter. Conceptually, this can be considered as extracting the implied interest rate for the unknown

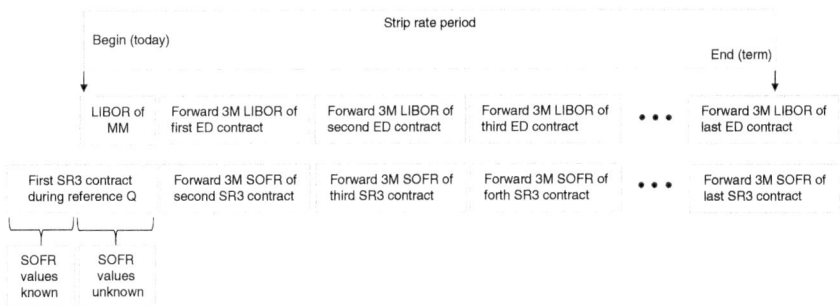

FIGURE 2.8 Calculating strip rates from ED and SR3 futures
Source: Authors

period from the future price (combining the known and unknown periods) and the SOFR values already known.

$$
R_{unknown} = \left(\frac{R \times \frac{D}{360} \times \frac{1}{100} + 1}{\prod_{i=1}^{n_{known}} \left(1 + \frac{\frac{SOFR_i}{100} \times d_i}{360} \right)} - 1 \right) \times \frac{360}{D_{unknown}} \times 100
$$

where (in addition to the variables from the formula above)

- R is the rate implied by the front month SR3 contract, i.e., 100 minus its price.
- D is the total number of calendar days during the reference quarter, i.e., $D = \sum_{i=1}^{n} d_i$.
- $D_{unknown}$ is the total number of calendar days during the unknown (future) part of the reference quarter, i.e., $D_{unknown} = \sum_{i=1}^{n_{unknown}} d_i$.

Using this rate calculated from the front month SR3 contract (rather than a LIBOR money market rate) for the first "short" interest period until the first "full" 3M reference quarter is the only conceptual adjustment required. Otherwise, strip rates can be calculated from SOFR futures in the same manner as from ED futures, i.e.:

$$
S = \left(1 + R_{unknown} \times \frac{D_{unknown}}{360} \right) \times \prod_{j=1}^{m} \left(1 + R_j \times \frac{D_j}{360} \right)
$$

where

- S is the strip rate.
- m is the number of SR3 contracts used after the front month contract (which is used for calculation of $R_{unknown}$).
    The last day of the term of the strip rate falls in the reference quarter of the mth future.
- R_j is the rate implied by the price of the jth SR3 contract, i.e., 100 minus its price.
- D_j is the total number of calendar days during the reference quarter of the jth SR3 contract for $j < m$ and the number of calendar days during the reference quarter until the term of the strip rate for $j = m$.

This calculation corresponds to compounding all daily SOFR values as implied by the SOFR future prices during the term of the strip. Using money market conventions, the strip rate S can then be annualized by solving the following equation for S_{ann}:

$$S = \left(1 + S_{ann} \times \frac{365}{360}\right)^N \times \left(1 + S_{ann} \times \frac{F}{360}\right)$$

where

- S_{ann} is the annualized strip rate using money market conventions.
- N is the number of whole years in the term of the strip.
- F is the number of days in the term of the strip minus N years.

The Excel sheet "strip" accompanying this chapter illustrates these calculations for the example of a 6M strip rate starting on Oct 3, 2022. Assuming hypothetical daily SOFR values of 95 bp for the known period of the reference quarter of the Sep 2022 contract and futures prices of 99, 98.5, and 98 for the three SR3 contracts in the strip (the user can change these numbers), in a first step the known SOFR values are compounded, just like when calculating the settlement rate (cell E13). Together with the price of the Sep 2022 contract, this allows determining the value $R_{unknown}$ (cell G7). Then, the D_j's are calculated, with the last one corresponding to the number of days from the start of the reference quarter of the Mar 2023 contract (Mar 15, 2023) to the end of the 6M term (Apr 3, 2023). Applying the formula above, the strip rate is determined (cell G9) and annualized (cell G10).[9] For the hypothetical values above, the annualized 6M strip rate is thus 1.34%.

---

[9]As in this example the term is less than one year, $N = 0$ and the annualization formula can be simplified.

3M SOFR FUTURES: ROLLS

We have already stated that the transition from ED to SOFR futures is basically a renaming exercise for back-month contracts, but not for front-month contracts during the reference quarter (see Figures 2.1 and 2.4). As a result, the transition has a significant effect on the roll from front-month into back-month contracts. Taking into account the increasing decoupling of front-month SOFR futures from the overall market during their reference quarter, which results in the reduced volatility and "stickiness" observed in Figure 2.5, it seems advisable to execute the roll *before* SOFR futures enter their reference quarter. Using the example of the Dec 19 SR3 future, which experienced a sharp drop of SOFR during its reference quarter, the roll into Mar 20 would have cost 138 bp if executed at the end of its reference quarter, but only 4 bp if executed at its beginning. Of course, this is a relatively extreme case, but Figure 2.9 suggests[10] that rolling at the beginning rather than at the end of the reference quarter has been better (i.e., closer to zero) in almost every circumstance.

This means that, for SOFR contracts, the roll should not be executed between front-month and back-month contracts, as usually done with ED futures, but between second and third listed contracts.

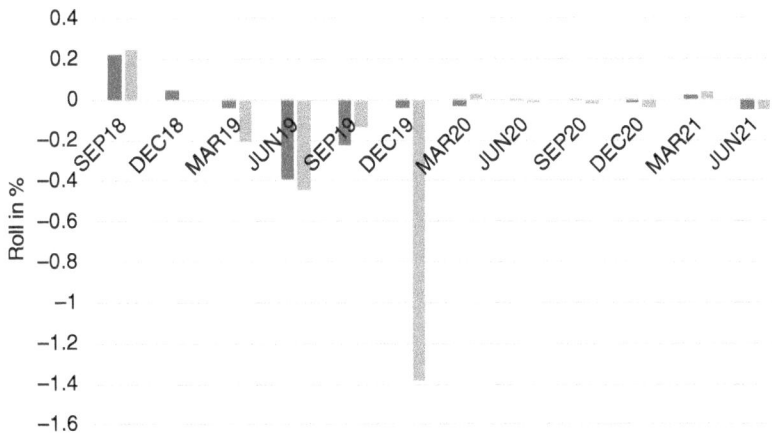

■ roll at begin of reference quarter   ▦ roll at end of reference quarter

FIGURE 2.9   Rolls for past 3M SOFR futures
Source: Authors, from CME data

---

[10]Also this figure and the numbers for the Dec 19 roll example apply the data aggregation outlined in Chapter 5.

1M SOFR FUTURES: CONVENTIONS

As the conventions of 3M SOFR futures (SR3) closely mirror those of
Eurodollar (ED) contracts,[11] the conventions of 1M SOFR futures (SR1)
have been modeled along the lines of Fed Funds (FF) contracts, as summarized in Figures 2.10 and 2.11. Crucially, the calculation of the settlement
price uses a simple arithmetic average over the *calendar* (not business)
days of the delivery month, which is also the stated contract month. As
with SR3 futures, the SOFR value for the previous business day is used
on each subsequent calendar day up until the next business day. In the
example of the Oct 2022 SR1 contract illustrated in the Excel sheet "3M
versus 1M," for the two first days of the contract month, Saturday, 1 Oct
2022, and Sunday, 2 Oct 2022, the SOFR value from Friday, 30 Sep 2022
(published on Monday, 3 Oct 2022), will be used. The settlement rate is
then calculated by dividing the sum of the SOFR values for each calendar
day by the number of calendar days in the contract month.

The similarity of conventions between SR1 and FF contracts has two
important implications:

- The simple, arithmetic average used in the SR1 contract does not reflect
  the conventions of most SOFR-related instruments. For example, if one
  repeatedly rolled a cash balance overnight earning the daily SOFR value,
  the balance on any given day would reflect daily compounding (i.e., the
  geometric average) rather than the simple, arithmetic average used in the
  1M SOFR contract. As a result, there is a risk that liquidity would be
  split between the two conventions, to the detriment of the SOFR complex generally. In addition, this also further complicates the pricing of
  options on 1M SOFR futures because there are formulae for geometric
  but not for arithmetic Asian options. (See Chapter 5.)
- An advantage is that the spread between SR1 and FF futures is not
  driven by different specifications, but (almost) only by the basis between
  secured and unsecured lending. This results in the spread contracts being
  a clean reflection of the market price for that basis. Hence, the fair value
  of the spread contracts can be determined via the basis. Likewise, the
  basis, which features in many relative value relationships, can be cheaply
  and easily traded via listed spread contracts. (See Chapter 4.)

---

[11] Again, a slightly different holiday schedule applies.

1M VERSUS 3M SOFR FUTURES

In contrast to trading SR1 versus FF futures, trading SR1 versus SR3 futures does not include exposure to a basis (as both have the same underlying secured rate) but exposure due to their different specifications. As such, spread trades between SR1 and SR3 do not depend on the secured–unsecured basis but mainly on two factors:

- As they cover different time periods, the spread depends on the *yield curve* and hence on its driving factors, such as Fed policy.
- As they use different specifications, the spread also depends on the *mathematical* formulas for determining final settlement prices, in particular, the difference between a simple average and daily compounding.

The effect of the first factor, different time periods, can be minimized by constructing spread trades with a good overlap. Specifically, one can trade a SR3 contract versus the two SR1 futures in the middle of its reference quarter. For example, the Sep 2022 SR3 future, with a reference quarter from Wed 21 Sep, 2022 to Wed 21 Dec, 2022, can be traded versus Oct 2022 and Nov 2022 SR1 futures. The relationship of the time periods covered is illustrated in Figure 2.12.

Since the overlap is good but not perfect, some exposure to the underlying yield curve remains:

- Parallel curve shifts only affect the SR1–SR3 spread via the mathematical issues described below, not via different time periods.
- The slope of the yield curve affects the SR1–SR3 spread also via the different time periods. While the construction shown in Figure 2.12 minimizes the impact, it should be noted that the time period covered by the two SR1 contracts is not precisely in the middle of the reference quarter. Actually, the precise position depends on the position of the third

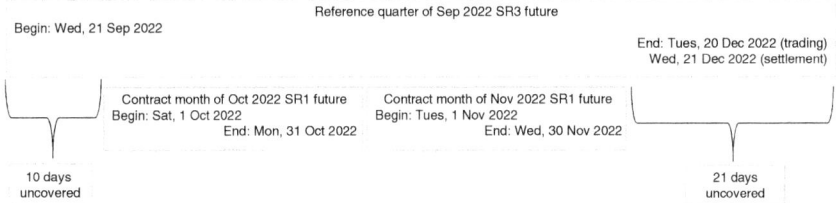

FIGURE 2.12 Time periods covered by 1M and 3M SOFR futures
Source: Authors

Wednesday in the contract month. In the example of Sep 2022 (which was chosen with the goal of illustrating this effect), the third Wednesday is late in the contract month (Sep 2022), and therefore a larger portion at the end than at the beginning of the reference quarter is not covered by the SR1 contracts. Thus, a steepening of the yield curve will affect the SR3 contract more, supporting a cheapening of SR3 versus SR1. This explains the impact of the curve slope on the theoretical spread shown in Table 2.1.

▪ Moreover, jumps in SOFR during the period of the reference quarter not covered by SR1 futures can have a strong effect on the spread. For example, a Fed rate hike on Dec 1, 2022, by 50 bp, driving the SOFR from 10 bp to 60 bp, results in a fair value for the SR1–SR3 spread of 12 bp.[12] By changing the values in the excel sheet "3M versus 1M," the reader can assess the impact of different scenarios of the SOFR evolution during the reference quarter on the fair value of the spread between the 1M and 3M SOFR contracts.

TABLE 2.1   Fair value of Sep 2022 SR1–SR3 spread

SOFR at begin of reference quarter (bp)	SOFR slope during reference quarter (bp)	Settl. Price Sep 2022 SR3	Settl. Price Oct 2022 SR1	Settl. Price Nov 2022 SR1	Fair Value of Spread Contract (bp) (CME convention)
0	0	100.00	100.00	100.00	0.00
0	25	99.88	99.93	99.85	1.33
0	50	99.75	99.86	99.69	2.67
100	−50	99.25	99.14	99.31	−2.59
100	−25	99.12	99.07	99.15	−1.24
100	0	99.00	99.00	99.00	0.12
100	25	98.87	98.93	98.85	1.49
100	50	98.75	98.86	98.69	2.85
500	−50	95.22	95.14	95.31	0.15
500	−25	95.09	95.07	95.15	1.62
500	0	94.97	95.00	95.00	3.11
500	25	94.84	94.93	94.85	4.59
500	50	94.72	94.86	94.69	6.09

Source: Authors

---

[12]This is a hypothetical assumption not in line with the FOMC meeting calendar in order to illustrate the point.

ICS (Inter-Commodity Spread)	Between SR3 and the two SR1 fully in its reference quarter (e.g., between Sep 2022 SR3 on one hand and Oct 2022 SR1 and Nov 2022 SR1 on the other hand)
Weighting	Three SR1 each versus ten SR3, resulting in almost equal BPV
Price display	Average of the two SR1 prices minus SR3 price (e.g., (Oct 2022 SR1 + Nov 2022 SR1) / 2 - Sep 2022 SR3)
Last trading day	Equal to the last trading day of the first of the two SR1 contracts contracts

For other specifications, refer to Table 04.01

FIGURE 2.13 1M–3M SOFR spread futures: specifications
Source: Authors, based on CME

The CME lists 1M–3M SOFR spread futures constructed according to the idea of overlapping time periods illustrated in Figure 2.12 and to achieve (almost) neutrality in basis point values (BPV).[13] Figure 2.13 summarizes their specifications. The key is the weighting, corresponding to three SR1 contracts each versus 10 SR3 contracts, almost netting out the BPV (6*41.67 = 250.02). The remaining BPV difference explains the difference between spreads calculated via the actual contracts and via the CME convention. However, this difference is less than 1 bp; accordingly, the Excel sheet and Table 2.1 show the spreads according to the CME convention only.[14]

Despite the (almost) BPV-equal weighting of 1M and 3M SOFR futures in the CME spread contract, there remains exposure to the slope of the yield curve due to time periods that do not perfectly overlap (as discussed above) and even to parallel curve shifts through different conventions. When SOFR is equal to zero, there is no difference between a simple, arithmetic average and daily compounding. But as SOFR rises, the difference becomes more important and reaches 3 bp for a constant SOFR at 5% during the reference quarter.

Table 2.1 shows the fair value of the 1M–3M SOFR spread (calculated from the Excel sheet) for different scenarios of SOFR during the reference quarter of the Sep 2022 SR3 future. Due to the reasons described above, at low interest rate levels and a flat curve, the fair value is small – which could explain the current illiquidity of the spread contracts. On the other hand, the spreads become more meaningful when rates rise (due to the different

---

[13] CME, April 2018.

[14] Still, especially in low interest rate environments, it may be useful to keep the slight deviation of the CME convention from the actual (3+3)-to-10 spread in mind.

conventions) and when the yield curve exhibits a shape (due to different time periods covered). In general, the higher the level and the steeper the slope of SOFR during the reference quarter, the higher the fair value of the spread. Hence, it is possible that liquidity in spread trading will increase with (speculation about) Fed rate hikes. Depending on the timing (see the hypothetical example of a Fed hike on Dec 1, 2022), the spread contracts could provide an attractive capital-efficient way to trade expectations about Fed policy.

1M AND 3M SOFR FUTURES: LIQUIDITY

Figures 2.14 and 2.15 show histories for volume and open interest for 1M and 3M SOFR contracts. Both on an absolute scale and relative to other newly introduced futures, SOFR contracts got off to an impressive start. Although there has been some concern about insufficient liquidity during the discussion about basing a term rate on SOFR futures,[15] the recent almost exponential rise in the liquidity for SR3 contracts is probably a good enough response to this concern.

Comparing both SOFR futures, while 1M contracts had a better start, only 3M contracts have benefited from the recent strong increase in liquidity. Actually, it appears as if liquidity might have started to concentrate in SR3 futures.

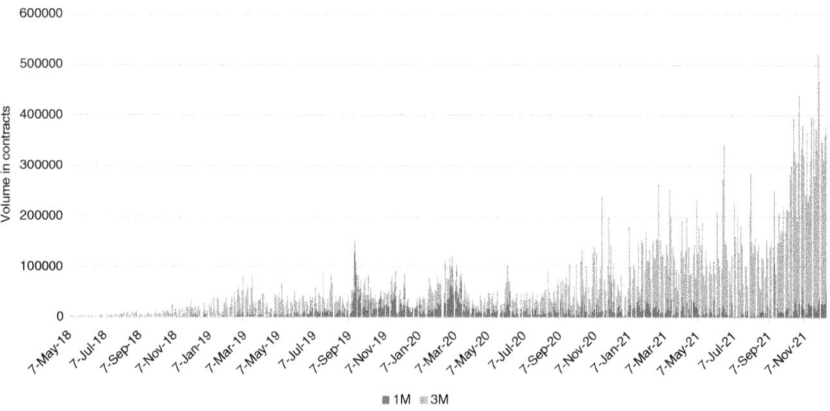

FIGURE 2.14 SOFR future daily volume
Source: Authors, from data provided by CME

---

[15] See Chapter 3.

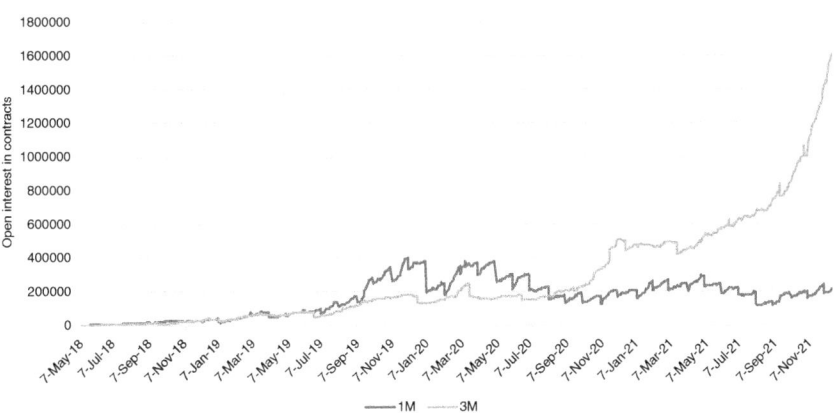

FIGURE 2.15 SOFR future open interest
Source: Authors, from data provided by CME

However, we think it is too early to "call the race" and will find in the following chapters some factors that are likely to impact the future liquidity situation of SOFR futures in general and the distribution between SR1 and SR3, including:

- The share of simple versus compound conventions of SOFR-based cash loans and securities will have an effect on the demand for hedging products with the same convention. Hence, the move toward using compounding for SOFR floating rate notes (FRNs) following ARRC's recommendation and model language could be one factor supporting the recent concentration of liquidity in 3M SOFR contracts. And the potential issuance of a Treasury SOFR FRN could further reinforce this trend. (See Chapter 3.)
- As SR3:ED spread futures give the biggest exposure to the secured–unsecured basis, demand and hence liquidity is highest for this spread (see Chapter 4). However, following the end of LIBOR in June 2023, the SR3:ED spread will disappear as a source for exposure to this basis. After this date, only the SR3:FF and SR1:FF spread futures cover the secured–unsecured basis. And among these two, SR1:FF provides the "cleaner" exposure to the basis, while SR3:FF is also subject to different time periods and conventions. Hence, one may expect the end of LIBOR to result in a boost in demand for 1M SOFR futures since SR1:FF could well become the best product to trade the secured–unsecured basis, as described at the end of Chapter 4.

▪ Liquidity in futures is influenced by liquidity in the options on futures (and vice versa). And the impressive liquidity in SR3 futures was achieved despite a lack of liquidity in its options. One can therefore expect another boost in liquidity for SR3 contracts when liquidity in options on 3M SOFR futures increases (despite the remaining challenges outlined in Chapter 5) – for example, due to migration from options on ED futures, hedging floored or capped SOFR loans, or the opportunities to trade options on SR3 and ED futures versus each other.

1M AND 3M SOFR FUTURES: ASSESSING THE EFFECT OF FOMC MEETINGS

Given the importance of Fed policy for the short end of the curve, analyzing and immunizing SOFR future positions against the exposure to policy rate changes is a key consideration:

▪ For 1M futures, the impact is easy to calculate: A rate hike by 1 bp should affect the SR1 contract in whose reference month the FOMC meeting takes place by the quotient of the number of days in the reference month after the FOMC meeting divided by the total number of days in the reference month. For example, a hike announced on May 4, 2022, by 25 bp is expected to affect the 1M May 2022 SOFR future by 25 bp * (27/31) = 21.8 bp.[16]
▪ For 3M futures, a method like the one encoded in the Excel sheet "3M versus 1M with FOMC hedge" needs to be applied due to the effect of daily compounding. For example, one can shift the SOFR values post the FOMC meeting by 25 bp, recalculate the fair future price, and obtain the sensitivity to a 25 bp rate hike by subtracting the two prices. The 3M Mar 2022 contract is expected to react by 11.3 bp to a 25 bp rate hike on May 4, 2022. Due to the compounding, this value depends on the level of rates, but small deviations from the actual rate level are usually negligible.

---

[16]One could argue that it is not certain that a change of 25 bp in the Fed Funds rate corresponds to a change of 25 bp in SOFR. However, as long as we are only dealing with SOFR futures, any difference is likely to net out: since 1M and 3M SOFR futures would need to be adjusted with the same factor for the move in SOFR/move in FF, it would cancel out in the hedge ratio. But when looking at spreads between SOFR and FF futures, this secured–unsecured basis will become important and will be discussed in detail in Chapter 4.

Alternatively, for 3M contracts, the following formula can be used:

$$100 - F_k = \left[\prod_{i=1}^{n_{pre}} \left(1 + \frac{\frac{SOFR}{100} \times d_i}{360} \right) \times \prod_{i=1}^{n_{post}} \left(1 + \frac{\frac{(SOFR + j_k)}{100} \times d_i}{360} \right) - 1 \right]$$
$$\times \frac{360}{D} \times 100$$

where

- n_{pre} and n_{post} are the number of business days before and after k in the reference period of F_k.
- SOFR is the rate at the beginning of the reference period (assumed to be constant except on day k) and j_k is the jump of SOFR following the FOMC policy announcement on day k.

Moreover, one can assess the impact of Fed policy on the spread between 1M and 3M contracts and adjust the hedge ratio between the two. To illustrate the problem, Figure 2.16 depicts two different positions of a FOMC meeting date in the 1M versus 3M SOFR future spread:

- If the meeting is right in the middle of the reference quarter of the 3M future and between the reference months of the 1M futures, distributing the hedge equally across the 1M futures – as in the standard 10 versus 3/3 hedge ratio – works well. The FOMC meeting schedule often comes relatively close to this ideal scenario, with the meetings in March, June, September, and December tending to be held at the 3rd Wednesday, i.e., at the start and end date of the reference quarters, while the meetings in the other months are often held around the turn of the month, i.e., near the start and end dates of the reference month.
- If, on the other hand, the meeting takes place at a distance from the middle, it affects the three contracts involved unevenly. The further the meeting date shifts to the right, the less it affects the 1M contracts relative to the 3M contract. Imagine the extreme scenario of the meeting taking place on May 30 rather than May 4. In this case, only one day of the reference month of the 1M futures would be affected, while there are still 15 affected days of the reference quarter of the 3M contract. Hence, in order to maintain the hedge against Fed policy shifts, the further the meeting date is to the right in Figure 2.16, the more of the later 1M future needs to be used relative to the 3M future, resulting in a deviation from the standard 10 versus 3/3 hedge ratio.[17]

---

[17]If the meeting takes place after the reference month, this hedge is not possible at all any longer; this corresponds to the example of a 50 bp hike on Dec 1 from above.

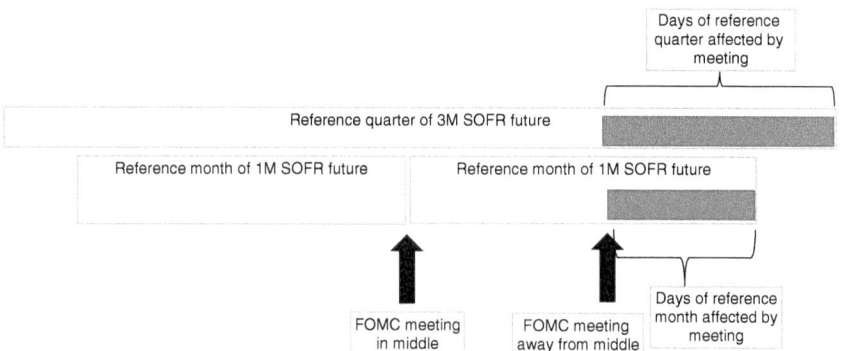

FIGURE 2.16 FOMC meeting dates relative to the reference periods of 1M and 3M SOFR futures
Source: Authors

A shift of the FOMC meeting date away from the middle to the right therefore results in a relative decrease of the sensitivity of 1M futures versus the sensitivity of 3M futures to the Fed policy and hence to a major source of yield volatility at the short end.

The sheet "3M versus 1M with FOMC hedge" illustrates how thc hcdge ratio for 3M versus 1M contracts could be adjusted to maintain neutrality versus the overall level of rates while also gaining neutrality versus Fed policy changes. Hence, in case the SOFR is only affected by Fed policy, i.e., follows a jump process,[18] the 3M–1M future spread should be completely hedgeable via such a method.

This sheet calculates the hedge of the 3M Mar 2022 futures contract versus the two 1M contracts Apr 2022 and May 2022. The start and the end dates of the reference quarter coincide with the FOMC meeting dates (March 16 and June 15). During the reference quarter, one FOMC meeting takes place on May 4, 2022. As this is slightly away from the middle, one may ask how to adjust the standard hedge ratio (ten 3M versus three 1M futures each) to account for the (slightly) different exposure to a rate hike on that date.

First, the sensitivity of the 3M contract to changes of the level of SOFR (at the start of the reference quarter) and to the Fed rate hike on May 4 needs to be calculated. This can be done by assuming reasonable starting values in cells C2 and G2 and assessing the impact of a 1 bp bump in each (separately)

---

[18]This is the assumption behind CME's Term rate discussed in Chapter 3.

(cell H8). The result is a sensitivity of −25.02 USD to +1 bp of the SOFR level and of −11.27 USD to +1 bp of the rate hike (cells H10 and H11).

Then, the sensitivity of the 1M contract affected by the Fed hike (May 2022) is calculated by dividing the days post-meeting by the total number of days in the reference month May. The result is a sensitivity of −36.29 USD to +1 bp of the rate hike (cell L2). In a first step, the 3M–1M future spread can be immunized against the Fed rate hike by taking the quotient of the two sensitivities, i.e., by selling 0.31 1M May 2022 contracts for every 3M Mar 2022 futures contract bought (cell K6). This approach works since the other 1M contract (April 2022) is not affected by the rate hike.

Hence, in a second step, the 1M Apr 2022 future can be used in order to obtain immunity against the rate level without influencing the hedge against the Fed rate hike already obtained in the first step. Selling 0.29 1M Apr 2022 contracts (cell K12) gives this immunity. Thus, the hedge consists in selling 3.1 1M May 2022 and 2.9 1M Apr 2022 contracts for every ten 3M Mar 2022 futures bought. The slight deviation of the meeting date from the middle therefore results in a slight deviation from the standard hedge ratio. The calculation of the hedge in two steps can be expressed in two simple formulae:

$$n_{May} = \frac{s_j}{\frac{d_{post}}{d_{total}} \times 41,67}$$

$$n_{April} = \frac{s_l}{41,67} - n_{May}$$

where

- n_{April} and n_{May} is the (short) position in 1M April and May SOFR futures for each one (long) 3M Mar 2022 future.
- d_{post} is the number of calendar days in the reference month of the 1M May future after the FOMC announcement.
- d_{total} is the total number of calendar days in the reference month of the 1M May future (31).
- s_j is the price sensitivity of the 3M Mar 2022 future to a 1 bp increase in the jump of SOFR following the FOMC announcement.
- s_l is the price sensitivity of the 3M Mar 2022 future to a 1 bp increase of the SOFR at the beginning of the reference quarter.

When the FOMC meeting date is further off the middle (Figure 2.16), the adjustment relative to the standard hedge ratio becomes larger. For the example of the 3M Sep 2018 contract, when the meeting took place on Nov 8, 2018,[19] the hedge ratio was 2.24 1M Oct 2018 and 3.79 1M Nov 2018 futures per ten 3M Sep 2018 contracts.

This mechanism implies that depending on the FOMC meeting schedule and policy expectations, 3M SOFR futures can be more affected by changing expectations about the Fed policy than the standard combination of 1M SOFR futures. That is another way of expressing the result from above, that a higher number than six for the sum of the 1M contracts is required in order to adjust for the lower sensitivity. For example, for ten 3M Sep 2018 contracts, a total of 6.03 1M contracts were needed to obtain immunity. This also explains the observation, that sometimes – i.e., depending on the FOMC meeting situation – 1M SOFR contracts appear to move less than 3M futures or the term rate.[20] The relatively small moves of 1M futures may seem puzzling if one only considers parallel shifts of the SOFR curve; they become clearer when one also considers their sometimes-lower exposure to Fed policy, a major source of rate volatility at the short end. Analysts are well advised to keep this in mind, in particular when using 1M futures to hedge or replicate other instruments, such as 3M contracts or the term rate.

PRICING AND HEDGING WITH SOFR FUTURES: GENERAL CONSIDERATIONS

Using the adjustments just outlined, one can easily transfer the pricing and hedging techniques from ED to SOFR contracts. For example, one could use a strip of SOFR futures to replicate and hedge a term SOFR. However, this method does not work well when the term and the end date of the futures strip are different – when an FOMC meeting falls between the two. In this case, an allowance for the curve between the two dates (e.g., the jump at the FOMC meeting date) is desirable.

Therefore, traders nowadays usually construct curves from futures markets and apply these to solve pricing and hedging questions. For example, focusing on the effect of Fed policy on the yield curve only, one could calibrate a jump process to the prices observed in the futures market and obtain the rates at any forward date from this process. Of course, after taking into account the required adjustments for the front month contract, SOFR futures also can be used as input into these common curve construction techniques.

---

[19]There was also a meeting on Sep 26, which needed to be included in the calculation.
[20]Due to illiquidity, it is not yet possible to compare the relative pricing of options on 3M and 1M SOFR futures in that light.

The first key decision is the choice of the functional form for the curve:

- The future strip used for the simple term rate hedge just mentioned corresponds to the assumption of the SOFR curve following a jump process, with the jumps occurring at the contract dates of the SOFR futures (in case of 1M SOFR contracts, the turns of the months). Between the contract dates, the same single forward SOFR value implied by the future price is used. Hence, if the forward point in time required (e.g., for hedging a term rate of a swap) does not fall on a contract date, the assumption of a constant curve between the two can lead to mismatches. There are a number of ways to react to this problem:
  1. The first possible approach is to use some sort of interpolation between the contract dates. Starting with linear interpolation, more sophistication can be reached by using exponential or cubic splines. This tends to produce good results from the middle part of the yield curve onward, where the impact of specific Fed policy decisions on the curve becomes less decisive and the FOMC meeting dates are unknown.
  2. The second possible approach is to stick with the jump process, but to use the FOMC meeting dates rather than the contract dates as the points in time when the jumps occur. Furthermore, specific points in time, such as the year-end, when spikes in SOFR are expected can be added as jump dates. This is useful for the short end of the curve, on which the Fed policy has an overwhelming effect and the FOMC meeting dates are known. Figure 2.17 illustrates the possibilities mentioned so far, for reasons of visibility for 1M SOFR futures only.
- In case the same jump process is used as the CME applies in its Term rate calculation (see Chapter 3), the construction of the SOFR curve simultaneously allows calculation of the Term rate; likewise, the same method used for hedging swaps with SOFR futures can be applied to hedge the CME Term rate with SOFR futures. The advantage of this approach is that it kills two birds with one stone. The disadvantage is that it subjects the SOFR curve and swap hedge to the same problems and criticisms of the Term rate mentioned in Chapter 3 and cannot be used for option pricing.
- Combining both approaches, one can add jumps to a cubic spline, for example. In the framework described in Chapter 11 of Huggins and Schaller 2013, the contract dates of the 3M futures could be used as anchor points for the cubic spline and the FOMC meeting dates as external variables. This combination has the advantage of producing a single yield curve from the short to the long end, which takes the effect of Fed policy on the short end into account but also minimizes frictions.

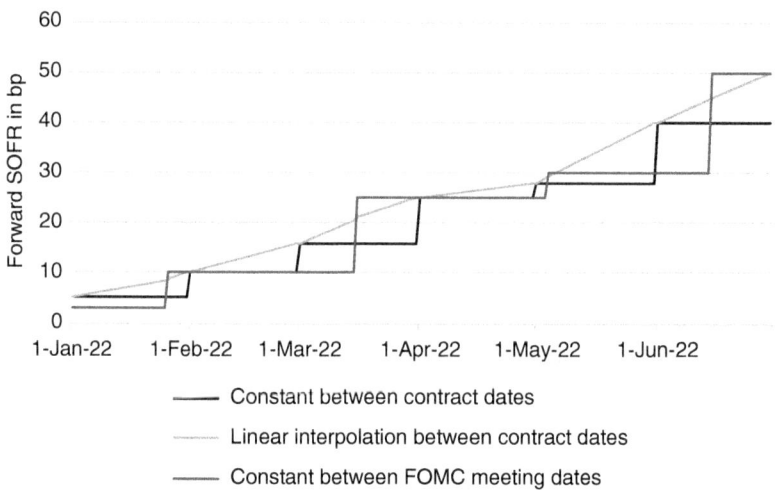

FIGURE 2.17   Different functional forms for the forward SOFR curve
Source: Authors

- Alternatively, one could combine the jump process with a stochastic process in order to account for the yield volatility not coming from Fed policy. A good candidate for a mixed jump-diffusion process could be a one-factor Hull-White model with jumps at the FOMC meeting dates. That is, when a jump occurs, both SOFR and the mean around which it reverts jump by similar amounts. Due to the diffusion, this process produces usually more reasonable option prices and can therefore be used to model both futures and the options on them, avoiding discrepancies.

Once the fundamental questions about the process are decided, the set of futures used for calibrating the process must be determined. Also this step offers several possibilities and requires therefore discretion and experience:

- When the number of futures contracts is less than the number of parameters used to describe the short rate process, the problem is said to be underdetermined. When the number of futures contracts is greater than the number of parameters, we say the problem is overdetermined. Calibrating a jump process with the FOMC meeting dates as unknown variables to all 1M and 3M SOFR futures as known variables, for example, is usually significantly overdetermined.
- One can either construct the SOFR curve from SOFR futures, and then separately the LIBOR curve (from ED contracts) and then separately the FF curve (from FF contracts), or all simultaneously. In the first case,

the basis between the curves is given by the *external* spread between the separately constructed curves; in the latter case, it is an *internal* parameter of the curves constructed from all futures simultaneously. The simultaneous construction can be thought of as decomposing the information contained in the whole STIR (short-term interest rate) future universe into information about market expectation about Fed policy (influencing all STIR contracts) and information about the secured–unsecured basis. When considering only SOFR-related instruments (e.g., a SOFR term rate hedge with SOFR futures), the separate construction offers the advantage of excluding influences from unsecured rates. The combined approach is useful whenever the basis between secured and unsecured rates is involved in the pricing (e.g., when the switch of an asset swap of a government bond from LIBOR to SOFR as floating leg should be hedged with SR1:FF spread contracts). (See Chapter 4.)

Pricing and hedging is not a mechanical procedure but requires the careful assessment of the different possibilities to achieve the specific hedging goals, which can be different from hedger to hedger. The selection of the process and its implementation introduces a significant degree of discretion: There is not *the* hedge, but several different possible hedges, which work better or worse for a given task. This also introduces the opportunity for analysts and traders to outperform competitors by improved hedging.

Given the number of possibilities already for selecting the functional form of the curve and the number of different hedging goals, a complete discussion is outside the scope of this book. But it does provide a few examples, which the reader may find useful as a starting point for constructing his own pricing and hedging tools.

EFFECT OF PROCESS SELECTION ON THE PRICING OF SOFR FUTURES

To assess the effect of the choice of the functional form and the parameters of the process used for pricing SOFR futures, one can start with a jump-diffusion process as a general framework, which covers both a pure jump process (by setting the volatility parameter to 0) and a pure diffusion process (by setting the probability for a jump to 0) as special cases. Moreover, one can add drift terms – for example, for mean reversion and momentum. The links between all these elements need to be considered (e.g., the impact of jumps on the drift and diffusion parameters). In the Hull-White model just mentioned, the mean could be shifted by the amount of the jump, for instance. Alternatively, one could consider jumps as being part of the mean reversion or diffusion.

Given our goal of demonstrating the effect of process selection on the pricing, and given the limitations of Excel spreadsheets, we use a simple Vasicek process – that is, one drift term for the mean reversion and one diffusion term – and add jumps at specific dates. We do not consider the links between these elements (e.g., the impact of jumps on the mean reversion parameters). Hence, this example should be considered a "heuristic framework." In the absence of an analytic solution for the combination of all the elements, numerical simulation needs to be applied. An example for such a simulation is encoded in the Excel sheet "SOFR future price simulation" accompanying this chapter. Please note that, like all sheets presented here, its goal is to illustrate concepts for educational purposes, and they are not fit for application in a professional context. Specifically, again due to the limitations of Excel sheets, we use only 200 simulations (in the columns), which is significantly too few; when applied with money at stake, many more simulations are required. (One million simulations would be more typical.)

Let us assume that on Jan 1, 2022, one wants to price the Mar 2022 SR3 contract (with a reference quarter from Mar 16 to Jun 15). To simplify the situation by reducing the parameters, we also assume that there is zero probability for a change in Fed policy at the FOMC meeting on Jan 26 and for any unscheduled FOMC meetings. This leaves two FOMC meetings to consider, on Mar 16 (i.e., right at the start of the reference quarter) and on May 4, for which we assume that the policy rate either increases by 25 bp or remains the same, with the probability for a 25 bp hike being set in cells E6 and E10. Cells E1 to E4 define the parameters for a Vasicek process, assuming that the start value for SOFR on Jan 1, 2022, is 5 bp. Based on this input, beginning in row 15, the SOFR evolution is modeled, assuming the standard deviation is the same for each calendar day.[21] For each of the simulated paths, the compounded SOFR during the reference quarter is calculated (row 135) and the average over all simulations is shown in cell H1.

Let us further assume that one decides to price the future according to the average of the simulated settlement prices (cell H2). This assumption ignores other influences on the future price. However, given the results of Chapter 6 and the short horizon of the simulation, this simplification could be acceptable for our current goal to obtain a first impression of the impact of different processes and their parameters on the future pricing.

---

[21]The user can change the assumption to business days by replacing the input from column C into the simulation with the annualized standard deviation (cell E2) divided by the square root of the number of business days in the year 2022.

Table 2.2 depicts the simulated future price, divided into the three main cases of a pure jump process,[22] a pure diffusion (and drift) process and a combined jump-diffusion (and drift) process, each with subcases for different parameters:

- As expected, the simulated settlement price depends heavily on the assumed probabilities for Fed rate hikes. This is in line with the common-sense perception that Fed policy has a major impact on the short end of the curve and hence the pricing of STIR contracts.
- Since the Vasicek process used assumes a symmetric distribution of the diffusion, the standard variation parameter has little impact on the simulated settlement prices; higher variance of the diffusion process – reflecting the volatility of SOFR not coming from Fed policy – does lead to some smoothing-out; however, the impact of jumps on future prices is more visible in an environment of lower diffusion.
- Also in line with the expectation, both the mean and speed of mean reversion parameter have a significant impact on the simulation result. One should note the correlation of these parameters with the jump probabilities: When rates are low as at the beginning of 2022, there is both a higher probability for Fed hikes than for cuts and a pull toward the mean from the drift coefficient in the Vasicek process. When building a jump-diffusion model, this link – which is not treated in the Excel sheet – should be taken into consideration.

The impact of the drift term is shown in Table 2.3 via a few combinations of the values for the mean and for the speed of mean reversion, represented in a two-dimensional matrix, and assuming 0.05% as start value and 2% as annualized standard deviation.[23] It can be seen that, even for the short horizon considered in this simulation, these two parameters have a major effect on the simulation results.

Therefore, even this simple simulation reveals the high dependency of the pricing on the choice of the process and its parameters. Extensive research into this topic is therefore a good investment. Under the impression of Table 2.3, in case of a drift term being part of the process, investigating the mean reversion of SOFR can be considered as a vital part of this exercise.

---

[22]Due to the simulation, the standard deviation (cell E2) cannot be set to 0; using a very small value like 0.00001 works.
[23]Due to the low number of simulations, we have taken the averages of several simulations. For a speed of mean reversion of 0, we have used the theoretical value.

TABLE 2.2 Simulated average settlement price of the Mar 2022 SR3 future

MAIN CASE 1: ONLY JUMP(S): Probability of +25 bp jump at		Settlement price
Meeting Mar 16	Meeting May 4	
0%	0%	99.9500
0%	50%	99.9010
0%	100%	99.8373
50%	0%	99.8251
50%	50%	99.7747
50%	100%	99.7198
100%	0%	99.7026
100%	50%	99.6468
100%	100%	99.5899

MAIN CASE 2: ONLY DIFFUSION AND DRIFT

Standard Deviation (ann)	Mean	Speed of mean reversion	
1%	1.50%	0	99.9212
2%	1.50%	0	99.8912
5%	1.50%	0	99.9099
2%	1.50%	0.002	99.7686
5%	1.50%	0.002	99.7130
2%	3.00%	0.002	99.5139
5%	3.00%	0.002	99.4326

MAIN CASE 3: JUMP-DIFFUSION (AND DRIFT)

Standard Deviation (ann)	Mean	Speed of mean reversion	Meeting Mar 16	Meeting May 4	
2%	1.50%	0	50%	50%	99.7469
2%	1.50%	0	100%	100%	99.5650
2%	1.50%	0.002	50%	50%	99.5466
2%	1.50%	0.002	100%	100%	99.3825
5%	1.50%	0.002	50%	50%	99.4828
5%	1.50%	0.002	100%	100%	99.4211
2%	3.00%	0.002	50%	50%	99.3066
2%	3.00%	0.002	100%	100%	99.1670

Source: Authors

TABLE 2.3 Simulated average settlement price of the Mar 2022 SR3 future using a pure Vasicek process

		Mean			
		0%	1,5%	3%	5%
Speed of mean reversion	0.000	99.9500	99.9500	99.9500	99.9500
	0.001	99.9563	99.8603	99.7101	99.5842
	0.002	99.9699	99.7686	99.5139	99.1756
	0.005	99.9840	99.4316	98.9558	98.2250
	0.010	99.9869	99.1365	98.2527	97.1213

Source: Authors

Since the history of SOFR is limited, one can use other short-term rates as proxies in order to assess the mean reversion characteristics over several rate cycles. When using a Vasicek model, it makes sense to estimate the parameters from historical time series by calibrating an Ornstein-Uhlenbeck process. Expanding the SOFR series with the overnight GC primary dealer survey rate back to 1998, we obtain an estimated mean of 1.18% and an estimated speed of mean reversion of 0.006. Figure 2.18 depicts the input and output of this mean reversion process. As the time series contains sharp spikes,[24] the question is whether to include these spikes when calculating the parameters given the recent establishment of the Fed's standing repo facility. (See Chapter 1.) If the spikes are excluded, the speed of mean reversion parameter decreases. This is one example for the discretion involved in every detail of the modeling process. When including the spikes and sticking to these parameters for a pure diffusion process, the average simulated settlement price of the Mar 2022 SR3 contract would be 99.4392.

The reasoning above is an illustration for the first step toward a pricing model for SOFR futures, with the remaining steps depending on the individual market assessment, specifically the weight given to Fed policy, and goals of the reader. But even at the end of the long journey to a pricing model, it is useful to remember alternative process and parameter choices. Coming back to the detail just mentioned, one could calculate the parameters of the mean reversion process without spikes in the input time series, obtain a speed of mean reversion of 0.002 and with this as input parameter into the simulation an average settlement price of 99.7615. Hence, even

---

[24] Even though we use weekly intervals in order to exclude daily fluctuations.

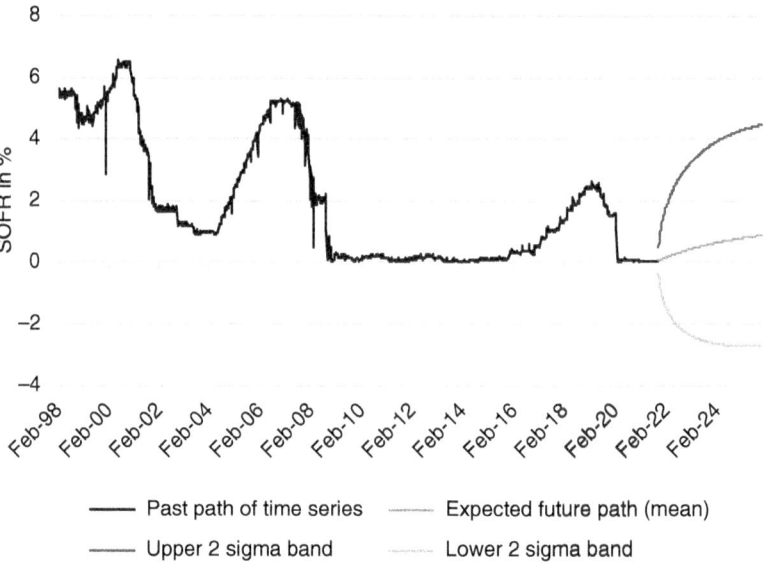

FIGURE 2.18 SOFR (proxy) as modeled by an Ornstein-Uhlenbeck process
Source: Authors, based on data from CME

the question of whether to include a few spikes or not in the historical time series, which might seem trivial at first glance, can have a material impact on the model prices. Obviously, this is even more the case for the fundamental decision about the relative weight given to jumps versus drift and diffusion, which is related to the fundamental worldview about the relative importance of Fed policy for STIR contract pricing. Even if a trader takes the extreme view that only Fed policy matters and hence uses a pure jump process, he is well advised to also look at a combined jump-diffusion process in order to stress-test his SOFR future pricing under the scenario of SOFR being influenced by factors not related to Fed policy as well.

Chapter 5 will expand this simulation and the Excel workbook to assess the impact of process and parameter selection on the pricing of options on SOFR futures. In line with the anticipation, we will find that the standard deviation parameter matters more for pricing options on futures than for pricing futures themselves. Hence, even if a trader decides to use a pure jump model for pricing futures, maybe arguing that the drift from mean reversion is sufficiently incorporated in the jumps, the trader will face the issue of the neglected diffusion term when turning to pricing options on futures. To use one model for consistent pricing of both SOFR futures and the options on them, therefore, the trader might want to consider including a diffusion term right from the beginning.

EXAMPLE FOR HEDGING A SOFR TERM RATE WITH SOFR FUTURES VIA A JUMP PROCESS

After the functional form of the curve and the set of futures used for calibration have been determined, the process can then be used to calculate the hedge ratios that immunize a portfolio. Using the example of the jump process, one can calculate the effect of a change in its parameters – i.e., the rate at the beginning and each jump, on every SOFR future on one hand and on a term rate on the other hand – and then construct a set of SOFR futures with the same exposure to all changes in the parameters as the term rate. This general approach, illustrated in Figure 2.19, can be modified to hedge a term rate (Chapter 3) and (asset and basis) swaps (Chapter 4) with SOFR futures.

Imagine the task is to hedge a 6M term rate starting on Jan 1, 2022, with a portfolio of SOFR futures, for example, because a dealer knows on Oct 1, 2021, that he is going to have exposure to a 6M SOFR term rate in 3M time. As mentioned above, the first key decision to take concerns the process used; for this example, we apply a simple jump process, assuming that FOMC meetings are the only source of interest rate volatility. Our reason for this choice is not that we consider this to be the only or the best alternative; actually, we will criticise this process in Chapter 3. We have selected it nevertheless because it fits both to the hedge against FOMC meetings described above and to CME's Term rate calculation described in Chapter 3. Note,

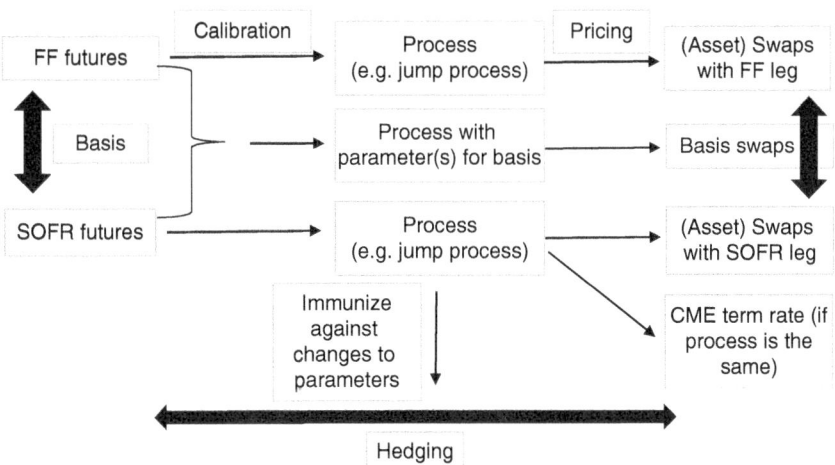

FIGURE 2.19 Futures as a hedge via calibrating a process
Source: Authors

however, that it is not identical to CME's Term rate; for instance, the jump process applied here cuts off after 6M, so that its 6M term rate does not depend on events beyond the 6M horizon, as does CME's Term rate. Hence, this example should be considered as illustration of one relatively easy (not necessarily the best) way to hedge a (not CME's) SOFR term rate; it shows *a* hedge of *a* term rate, not *the* hedge of *the* term rate. A precise hedge of CME's Term rate is significantly more complex and will be treated in Chapter 8.

For the sake of this example, we select the jump process

$$SOFR_t = SOFR_{t_0} + \sum_{k \in M} j_k$$

where

- t_0 is the start of the term.
- M is the set of all FOMC policy announcement dates between t_0 and t.
- j_k is the jump of SOFR following the FOMC policy announcement on day k.

In a first step, we calculate the sensitivities of both the 6M term rate and the SOFR futures to changes of the parameters of this jump process, i.e., the level ($SOFR_{t_0}$) and the jumps (j_k). This can be considered as an expansion of the method described as hedge against the impact of FOMC meetings above. It is encoded in the Excel sheet "Term rate hedge example" accompanying this chapter.

For this particular example, there are four FOMC meetings during the 6M term. The sensitivity table (cells G15 to N19) can be filled out as described above:

- Bumping the start value and the jumps (separately) gives the sensitivity of the term rate (cell G7) and the 3M Mar 2022 SOFR future (cell G10). The reference quarter of the latter is highlighted in bold in the compounding column D. Alternatively, the formula above could be applied.
- The sensitivity of the 1M contracts to FOMC meetings in their reference month is given by the formula above and encoded in cells L2 to L5. To the other FOMC meetings, the sensitivity is simply 0 or 1, depending on whether it is after or before the reference month.

At this stage, we face the overdetermination problem mentioned: Even though we use only futures whose reference period is fully inside the 6M term (not including the Dec 2021 and Jun 2022 SR3 contracts), there are seven of those, i.e., seven potential hedging instruments, for only five parameters to be hedged. Like for the selection of the process, discretion and experience is required to select the best set of hedging instruments. It seems that including the 3M future (Mar 2022) and excluding the 1M futures fully in its reference quarter (Apr and May 2022) is both reasonable and produces reasonable numbers. Of course, one can and should try different combinations and compare the results; if the results are too different, one could even think of going a step back and consider another process. While our experience is limited, we found that this method can sometimes lead to unrealistic results – in particular, when only 1M futures are used.[25]

Another point to consider when determining the futures used for the hedge is the number of days post the FOMC meeting (n_{post}). When it is small relative to the total number of days in a reference period, the number of futures required to immunize against this jump becomes large – and hence this "overhedge" needs to be corrected by a large number of offsetting positions in other contracts. This is one reason behind sometimes unrealistic outcomes. If such a situation occurs, it is advisable to exclude these contracts, perhaps by replacing them with 3M futures.[26]

With this in mind, we may decide to hedge the 6M term rate with Jan, Feb, Mar, and Jun SR1 contracts and the Mar SR3 future. This is now a well-defined hedging problem (five instruments for five parameters), which can be solved by usual matrix algebra, as encoded in the sheet below the sensitivity table. The resulting hedge portfolio of SOFR contracts shown in cells M31 to M35 consists of 0.17 Jan SR1, 0.14 Feb SR1, 0.19 Mar SR1, 0.17 Jun SR1, and 0.33 Mar SR3 futures. Note that these numbers are in bp terms, i.e., represent the hedge against a 1 bp move in the 6M term rate. To obtain the number of futures, they would need to be divided by the basis point values of the futures contracts (41.67 for 1M, 25 for 3M) and multiplied by the basis point value of the exposure to the 6M term rate.

---

[25] In the examples we have considered, including the 3M contract has solved these problematic instances. But we cannot rule out that there are cases in which this method does not work.

[26] If the first 1M contract (Jan 2022) was problematical, the replacement could be the Dec 2021 SR3 future, which would need to be adjusted for the days in its reference quarter before the term rate by the method described above.

3

SOFR Lending Markets and the Term Rate

As we saw in Chapter 2, the switch from the forward-looking LIBOR term rate to the backward-looking overnight SOFR is relatively easy to implement in the futures market. Both the Eurodollar (ED) futures contract and the SOFR futures contract refer to the same segment of the forward yield curve: ED futures via a forward-looking term rate, and SOFR futures via a backward-looking overnight rate. While the difference between the two has implications for the front-month contract, for back-month contracts the transition from LIBOR to SOFR is almost limited to an exercise in renaming the contract months.

In contrast to the easy implementation in the futures market, the transition to SOFR encounters more resistance in the cash loan market, which would require calculating the interest in arrears if implemented in the same manner as in the futures market. To understand the difficulties involved, consider the example of a borrower, such as a corporate treasurer, used to borrowing at LIBOR term rates. In theory, exactly the same method applied for futures also can be applied to cash loans. Rather than basing lending on forward-looking term rates such as LIBOR, it can be based on backward-looking overnight rates such as SOFR. But for the borrower in our example, this would mean that the rate is determined at the *end* of the reference period by the SOFR values observed during that period, rather than at the beginning of the loan by a forward-looking LIBOR term rate.

An advantage of applying the transition to backward-looking SOFR reference quarters in both futures and cash loans at the same time and with the same specifications is the ability to use SOFR futures directly as an effective and cost-efficient hedge for cash loans.

In practice, however, mirroring the transition from ED to SOFR futures in the cash loan market has run into several mental, organizational, and technical hurdles:

- Borrowers are used to knowing the interest they need to pay in advance of each period. The corporate treasurer in the example above can report the 3M LIBOR as interest costs to the CEO at the beginning of every lending period; he could therefore be hesitant to embrace the idea of reporting interest costs in arrears based on a reference period of SOFR observations.
- Implementing the same specifications as futures, where cash settlement occurs on the same day that the SOFR value for the last day of the reference quarter is published, would mean that the borrower only learns the size of his next interest payment on the same day he needs to make the payment. This is considered too tight a schedule by many borrowers.
- In addition, relics like simple averaging rather than compounding seem to stick around in some minds and systems, and more so in cash than in derivative markets.

This chapter first outlines these hurdles and possible solutions in greater detail before describing features introduced by the Fed, the ARRC, and the CME with the intention of supporting the cash market transition to SOFR. This concept of "supporting features" comprises

- Model documents and fallback language by the ARRC.
- The publication of simple averages and an index using daily compounding for SOFR by the Fed.
- Using simple averaging for the 1M SOFR contracts at the CME.
- The calculation of a SOFR term rate by the CME.

Overall, it appears that the resolve of regulators to rid the market of the real or perceived market failure inherent in LIBOR met with some resistance in the cash loan market, which led to the provision of several supporting features and compromises.

The biggest compromise from the viewpoint of regulators is the SOFR Term Rate, managed by CME Group Benchmark Administration, which replicates the forward-looking aspects of LIBOR without replicating the LIBOR panel survey process. However, the replacement of the panel survey with a model algorithm results in a different set of issues, as discussed below.

After describing how the tension between the resolve of regulators to switch from LIBOR to SOFR as reference rate on one side and the reluctance of loan market participants on the other side led to the compromise of a

SOFR Term Rate, the chapter ends by analyzing two possible scenarios for the further evolution of this construct:

- In the first scenario, the loan market eventually moves closer to the ideal loan mentioned above – a simple SOFR in arrears loan. We characterize this scenario as being "ideal" because the cost of hedging a SOFR loan would be lower in this case and because the structure is preferred by regulators. We expect that the lower costs of hedging this structure will provide an incentive for the loan market eventually to embrace the concept of a backward-looking reference period, in which case a forward-looking term rate may become superfluous.
- In the second scenario, we assume that the reliance on an SOFR term rate will become a permanent feature of SOFR-based lending. In this case, the problem of high hedging costs could be resolved via a secondary market for derivatives based on SOFR term rates – currently discouraged by regulators. Our analysis suggests that the absence of an active derivatives market involving SOFR term rates will likely lead to market imbalances (e.g., involving arbitrage opportunities between term rates and SOFR futures). In the event such imbalances become too disruptive, regulators may be forced to allow interdealer trading of SOFR term rate derivatives. In this scenario, the tension between market desire for a term rate and the regulator's caution may be resolved by regulators giving up on an "ideal" implementation of the transition and accepting the term rate as a permanent feature supported by a secondary market.

This chapter is also the basis for later use cases that analyze the application of SOFR futures and options to hedging cash loans. The further the loan market deviates from the conventions of SOFR futures, the more complex and costlier the hedge.

CONVENTIONS OF SOFR-BASED LENDING MARKETS

The most straightforward loan to hedge with 3M SOFR futures contract is one in which the interest is calculated with daily compounding and paid in arrears – i.e., at the end of the interest reference period. In fact, if the interest reference periods of the loan match the reference periods of the 3M SOFR futures contracts, a near-perfect hedge can be constructed cheaply and easily.[1] Similarly, the most straightforward loan to hedge with 1M SOFR

---

[1]We characterize the hedge as near-perfect rather than perfect due to the possible effects of any interest paid or received on variation margin.

futures contracts is one in which the interest is calculated as a simple arithmetic average and paid in arrears.

While these basic loans are straightforward to hedge, they may present problems for other reasons. For example, some borrowers appreciate knowing the size of their next interest payment well in advance of the day they need to make this next interest payment, which isn't the case in these simple loan structures. Given this situation, one can think of solutions, which can be classified by the issue they address:

- The solutions in the first class maintain averaging (arithmetic or geometric) to calculate the size of the next interest payment, but they adjust the date on which the interest payment needs to be made.
- The solutions in the second class allow determination of the interest at the beginning of the interest reference period rather than having to wait until the end of the interest reference period.

While solutions in this first class are designed to help the loan market with the transition to an overnight reference rate, the solutions in the second class can be considered as conceptual capitulations to the concerns of loan market participants. Rather than officials forcing the cash market to switch to interest calculations in arrears, the persistent demand for a term rate forces officials to provide a term rate, which can be used to calculate interest payments in advance.

The first category contains different ways to achieve a longer notification period by introducing a *lookback, lockout,* or *payment delay.* We summarize these technical features in Table 3.1 and refer to the comprehensive discussion in The Alternative Reference Rate Committee (ARRC 2021),[2] which also contains model language for loan contracts. However, we note that each

TABLE 3.1 Conventions for loans in-arrears until (day) T

	Payment due on day	Use SOFR from day ... as SOFR for day d
Plain	$T+1$	d (for whole period)
Lookback (n days)	$T+1$	$d - n$ (for whole period)
Lockout (n days)	$T+1$	d until $T - n$, then $T - n$
Payment delay (n days)	$T+1+n$	d (for whole period)

Source: Authors

[2]See also https://www.newyorkfed.org/medialibrary/microsites/arrc/files/2019/Guide_to_SOFR.pdf.

of these solutions faces new problems. In particular, the longer the look-back or lockout periods, the greater the divergence between the loan and the SOFR futures contracts – and hence the higher the costs and mismatches in a hedge. Chapter 7 will provide use cases illustrating this point.

Given these difficulties, officials have permitted two solutions in which the interest rate is known in advance of the interest reference period:

- From *historical* SOFR data, i.e., from a period *before* the lending period. For example, the counterparties could agree to base the interest for a loan during the second quarter on the average of SOFR values observed during the first quarter. While this is technically easy (one simply needs to look up the history of SOFR values[3]), it introduces the economic mismatch between the two periods. For most participants in the lending markets, this mismatch is unacceptable. In the current situation of low rates, which are expected to increase in coming quarters, this would mean that the borrower is able to pay an outdatedly low interest rate, based on Fed policy of the previous quarter.
- From *forward* SOFR values, i.e., from market expectations about SOFR values *during* the lending period. This solves the economic mismatch and the resulting problems of the example above: The lending rate for the next quarter is based on market expectations about Fed policy during that same quarter. And fortunately, as market prices for consecutive 3M forward sectors of the SOFR curve, the SOFR futures provide a good source for these market expectations.[4]

This overview explains how the tension[5] between the regulatory goal of moving from LIBOR to SOFR as reference rate and the practical hurdles of implementing this transition in cash loan markets produced two outcomes:

1. Features supporting the technical transition, such as providing model language for lookbacks.
2. The introduction of a SOFR term rate, allowing the cash loan market to stick to the "in-advance" structure of LIBOR-based lending (without economic mismatch between periods).

---

[3]For standard loan periods, the Fed even publishes historical averages.
[4]The predictive quality of forward rates for actual rates (and policy) has been subjected to an extensive and controversial analysis, which we will not repeat here.
[5]The Alternative Reference Rate Committee (ARRC 2020) and https://www.newyork fed.org/medialibrary/microsites/arrc/files/2019/Guide_to_SOFR.pdf are good historical documents for this tension and the discussion among officials and market participants.

After an overview of the current status of SOFR-based lending markets, we'll discuss these supporting features and term rates in more detail.

STATUS OF SOFR-BASED LENDING MARKETS

As a consequence of the recentness of the switch to SOFR as reference rate, SOFR-based lending markets are still under construction, with a number of conventions being used in parallel. While it is likely that the loan market will eventually settle on a set of standard conventions, at the time of writing (December 2021) it is unclear what this set will be. At the end of this chapter, we will present two scenarios for the future evolution of loan market conventions.

In addition to both in-advance rates and in-arrears rates being used, simple averaging and daily compounding are also currently used in parallel. This introduces an additional dimension to the classification of the SOFR-based lending market. A loan can be in advance or in arrears, *and* it can use simple averaging or daily compounding. The first dimension classifies loans according to *when* the interest is determined, the second according to *how* it is determined. For example, the counterparties may decide to use in arrears with a two-day lookback, i.e., to calculate the interest at the end of the loan period, and then take another independent decision how to calculate the interest, by simple averaging or daily compounding the SOFR observed during the lending period. Based on the choice in that second dimension and the lending period, the ideal hedging instrument may be 1M SOFR futures using simple averaging, or 3M SOFR futures using daily compounding.

And for both choices in the second dimension, supporting features have been introduced:

- The Fed publishes simple averages for standard loan periods of 30, 90, and 180 days.[6]
- The Fed also publishes an SOFR index implementing compounding, as explained below in more detail.

Under this classification in two dimensions, one can attempt to assess the current status of SOFR lending markets. Both the numbers and statements from market participants underline the importance of the introduction of term rates for activity in SOFR-based lending. Before term rates were introduced, market participants were hesitant to engage in SOFR-based loans;

---

[6]Also on the website https://www.newyorkfed.org/markets/reference-rates/sofr.

with the advent of SOFR term rates, the transition gained pace. Actually, for most market participants the transition appears to have started with SOFR term rates. This has resulted in in-advance loans using the SOFR term rate currently dominating the market for loans.

Regarding securities based on SOFR such as FRNs, the CME publishes the overall volume of SOFR issuance by tenor and date of issuance[7] (Figure 3.1). One can observe a trend toward increasingly issuing longer tenors as well.

Following the recommended model language provided by the Alternative Reference Rate Committee (ARRC 2019), FRNs tend not to use the term rate but an in-arrears interest calculation method. The differentiation between in-advance and in-arrears in the first dimension therefore also captures the overall current status between loans and securities using SOFR.

Regarding the second dimension of this classification, the first securities based on SOFR typically used simple averaging – for example, the first SOFR FRNs issued by agencies. Following the introduction of the SOFR

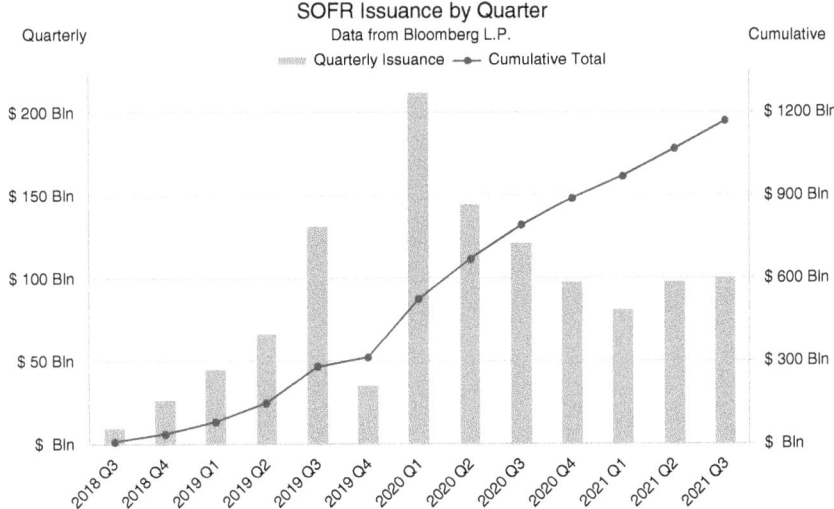

FIGURE 3.1   SOFR issuance by quarter
Source: CME

---

[7]See the CME Group website at https://www.cmegroup.com/trading/interest-rates/secured-overnight-financing-rate-futures.html?utm_source=cmegroup&utm_medium=friendly&utm_campaign=sofr&utm_content=sofr&redirect=/sofr#sofrissuance.

index, however, there seems to be a tendency to use it, and hence the daily compounding embedded in it, for more recent SOFR FRNs.

There is a discussion about the US Treasury issuing a SOFR FRN. This would support the transition by giving the market a benchmark and increasing liquidity. It would also set the standard for conventions; as it appears likely that it will also use the SOFR index, there is a good chance that it will collapse the second dimension for SOFR FRNs to daily compounding only.

SIMPLE AVERAGING VERSUS DAILY COMPOUNDING

Faced with the task of calculating a term rate from a series of known overnight rates, the economically correct approach is to use compounding. With Act/360 as daycount convention, the (ISDA) formula for the term rate R is

$$R = \left[\prod_{i=1}^{n} \left(1 + \left(\frac{SOFR_i}{100}\right)\left(\frac{d_i}{360}\right)\right) - 1 \right] \times \frac{360}{D} \times 100$$

where

- n is the number of business days during the term.
- $SOFR_i$ is the SOFR for day i.
- d_i is the number of calendar days, for which $SOFR_i$ is used.
  Until the next business day, the SOFR for the previous business day is used, e.g., on weekends and holidays. Thus, if Friday and Monday are business days, the SOFR for Friday is used for Friday, Saturday, and Sunday and the corresponding d_i is 3.
- D is the total number of calendar days during the term, i.e., $D = \sum_{i=1}^{n} d_i$.

This formula is used both for calculation of the 3M SOFR future settlement price[8] (where the term is the reference quarter), in the sample documents provided by ARRC (2019), in the SOFR index (Federal Reserve Bank of New York 2022), and for CME's SOFR term rate, described below (CME October 2021).

In the Excel sheet accompanying this chapter, this formula is applied for calculating the term rate for a one-year loan (from 3 Jan 2022 to 3 Jan 2023).

[8]SOFR Futures, "SOFR Futures Settlement Calculation," 2019, https://www.cmegroup.com/education/files/sofr-futures-settlement-calculation-methodologies.pdf.

The user can change the level of SOFR for all days or for individual days only and observe the effect. Table 3.2 summarizes the term rate for this loan for different levels of SOFR, assumed to remain constant throughout the year. Of course, rising rates result in a higher spread between the compound term rate and the simple average, which in this case is equal to the constant SOFR listed in the left column.

Simple averaging is still widely used, presumably due to its easier implementation in systems – though the formula above contains no mathematical challenge and can be easily encoded, as the Excel sheet demonstrates. While in the current yield environment the difference between simple averaging and daily compounding may be negligible, it becomes substantial for higher rates, as shown in Table 3.2. This will be an incentive to invest into upgrading the systems to daily compounding. We therefore anticipate increasing yields to be accompanied by an increasing share of daily compounding in the SOFR loan market.

However, as of now, simple averaging seems to be a relic sticking in many minds and systems. Accordingly, the first FRNs based on SOFR issued by agencies used this method. Also, while the 3M SOFR future uses the compounding formula from above, the 1M SOFR future is settled to a simple average. Given that the SOFR futures are leading the development of the SOFR lending market in many ways (as witnessed by the alignment of the conventions recommended by ARRC (2021) with the futures conventions), it appears that a chance has been missed to decide the question in favor of daily compounding for good. Rather than leading the market to use daily compounding by also applying this method to 1M contracts, the 1M and 3M SOFR futures conversely reflect the hesitance of the SOFR market to finally switch to daily compounding only. As a result, the spread shown in Table 3.2 is one influencing factor of the 1M–3M SOFR future spread, as discussed in Table 2.1 of Chapter 2.

TABLE 3.2 Compound term rate for a loan from 3 Jan 2022 to 3 Jan 2023

Constant SOFR (bp)	Compound term rate (bp)
0	0
100	101
200	202
300	305
400	408
500	513

Source: Authors

THE SOFR INDEX

In order to facilitate compounding calculations, the Fed has introduced a SOFR index with a base value of 1 for 2 April 2018 (when SOFR started) and updated every business day shortly after the SOFR rate, i.e., after 8 a.m. EST, on its website: https://www.newyorkfed.org/markets/reference-rates/ sofr-averages-and-index.

This index implements the formula from above and therefore corresponds to the amount that one would have if one had invested one dollar on 2-Apr-18, earning interest each day at the published SOFR value (i.e., with daily compounding). More specifically, the SOFR index is calculated as

$$SOFR\ index = \prod_{i=1}^{N} \left(1 + SOFR_i \left(\frac{d_i}{360} \right) \right)$$

where

- i is the counting number corresponding to a particular business day following 2-Apr-18.
- N is the number of business days since 2-Apr-18.
- $SOFR_i$ is the value of the secured overnight financing rate on the ith business day. Unlike CME, the Fed convention is to enter the SOFR value (e.g., 0.015 for a SOFR of 1.5%), hence there is no factor 1/100 in the formula.
- d_i is the number of calendar days for which $SOFR_i$ applies.

The daily SOFR index is rounded to eight decimal places and is subject to revision *on publication day only* in the same circumstances as those governing revision of the daily SOFR values.

The index is intended to make the use of SOFR products easier for market participants who would rather not have to perform so many calculations themselves. By using this index, the task of calculating the compounded SOFR term rate R simplifies to the equation[9]

$$R = \left(\frac{SOFRIndex_{enddate}}{SOFRIndex_{startdate}} - 1 \right) \times \frac{360}{D} \times 100$$

For example, if we wanted to calculate the interest paid on a SOFR-linked loan from 15-Sep-21 to 15-Dec-21, assuming a principal

---

[9]See the Federal Reserve Bank of New York, "Additional Information about Reference Rates Administered by the New York Fed," January 24, 2022, https://www .newyorkfed.org/markets/reference-rates/additional-information-about-reference-rates#sofr_ai_calculation_methodology.

amount of one million dollars, we would divide the SOFR index value for 15-Dec-21 by the SOFR index value for 15-Sep-21, subtract 1, and then multiply the result by one million. In this case the interest payment would be

$$USD\ 1,000,000\ \left(\frac{1.04235797}{1.04227169} - 1 \right) = USD\ 82.78$$

TERM RATE

We have attempted to explain above how the tension between the regulatory drive to switch from LIBOR to SOFR as reference rate on one side and the resistance of loan market participants on the other side has resulted in the compromise of introducing a term rate for SOFR, allowing the replication of LIBOR conventions. As with the forward-looking term rate LIBOR, a borrower can then use a forward-looking SOFR term rate and stick to the "in advance" specifications he is used to.

At this point of the evolving discussion, the question became how to determine the SOFR term rate. Reading through the following list of possibilities made the decision easy:

- The term rate could be set by administrative or expert judgment. However, this would introduce a potential friction between lending markets based on a term rate set this way and the actual SOFR markets.
- The term rate could be obtained via a survey of market participants about their perception of the current market for SOFR forward rates. For instance, one could call a number of contributor panel banks at 11 a.m. This option is obviously the nightmare of regulators as it would counteract the fundamental goal behind the whole SOFR project. Fortunately, as there exists an SOFR futures market, a survey is not needed to assess the market for forward SOFR. This decided in favor of the last option:
- A term rate could be calculated from the prices of SOFR futures contracts – being market prices for consecutive 1M and 3M parts of forward SOFR – via an automatic model without any expert judgment.

Hence, the existence of an active SOFR future market makes it possible to translate the market prices for forward SOFR into SOFR term rates without the interference of an administrator or a panel via the use of an automated model – which has its own set of potential problems, as discussed below. But given the alternatives, it seems to be the best way to translate an actual market for forward SOFR into an SOFR term rate. The SOFR term rate calculated this way allows loan market participants to calculate interest in advance while achieving the goal of regulators *not* to replicate LIBOR's method of determining term rates via a survey. This compromise was therefore the endpoint of the tension and discussion described above (ARRC 2021, p. 25).

To our knowledge, this is the first instance where term rates have entered a market via and after futures. The path of this construction is reflected in the sequence of chapters of this book: Overnight SOFR (Chapter 1) → SOFR futures (Chapter 2) → SOFR term rates (Chapter 3).

THE MODEL TRANSLATING SOFR FUTURE PRICES IN SOFR TERM RATES

The CME has implemented the model outlined by Heitfield and Park (2019) to extract 1M, 3M, 6M, and 12M Term Rates from SOFR futures. The details of this process have been published (CME October 2021). Summarizing the key aspects in Figures 3.2 and 3.3, in a first step, the data from future markets are aggregated by using sampling techniques and observation intervals in order to minimize effects from outliers and periods of illiquidity. While currently only data from the future markets are used, SOFR OIS (Overnight Index Swaps) may be considered as an addition in future.

At the core of the model is a jump process, which is then fitted to the aggregated data.[10] This process assumes that SOFR can change only after FOMC policy rate announcements and remains constant otherwise. That is a pretty strong assumption, which could affect the term rates calculated via this model, as discussed below. In more detail, an optimization algorithm fits the following process for SOFR to the observed data:

$$SOFR_t = SOFR_{t_0} + \sum_{k \in M} j_k$$

where

- t_0 is the start of the term.
- M is the set of all FOMC policy announcement dates between t_0 and t.
- j_k is the jump of SOFR following the FOMC policy announcement on day k.

CME term rates are then obtained by compounding the daily SOFR of this jump process using the ISDA formula from above.

---

[10]Chapter 8 describes the fitting in more detail.

CRITICISM OF THE CME TERM RATE

The CME Term Rate calculated via this approach can be criticized on two levels: in general, that a model is used at all for determining term rates; and specifically, which model is used. The published SOFR term rates reflect the future market *as seen through a specific model and its assumptions.* At the end of Chapter 2 (Table 2.2), we have demonstrated the significant effect of process and parameter selection on the pricing. And the assumptions of using a pure jump process are quite strong, e.g., they imply that neither mean reversion (other than captured in the jumps) nor momentum nor volatility unrelated to Fed policy has an effect on SOFR values, with a correspondingly high probability of distorting the information from future markets.

Given the list of alternatives above, it seems quite likely that determining term rates via a model (rather than by expert judgment or a market

Terms	1M, 3M, 6M, 12M
Publication	At 5 a.m. CT on every day SOFR is published
Start of term	Second business day (included) after publication day
Data input	Future market of the business day preceding publication day The first 13 1M SOFR contracts and the first 5 3M SOFR contracts are used (those during their reference quarter are adjusted for the known rates)
Observation Intervals	14 periods of 30 min from 7 a.m. to 2 p.m. CT
Sampling	VWAP (Volume Weighted Average Price) of executed transactions from DCM (1) and a snapshot of executable bids and offers at a random time during the interval (2)
Aggregation	An observation interval is eligible, if it contains an executed transaction in any SOFR future For futures with an execution, the VWAP (1) is used For futures with no execution, but with executable bids and offers, an optimized mid-price from (2) is used For futures with no execution and no executable bids and offers, the adjusted price of the previous interval is used
	Future price used as input in the model is calculated as VWAP over all eligible observation periods of the day
	(if there is no interval with an execution, the previous day's price will be used)

FIGURE 3.2 SOFR term rates: specifications
Source: Authors, based on CME

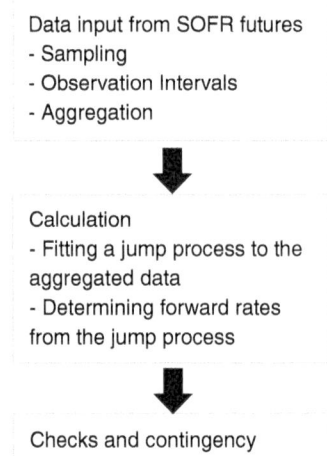

FIGURE 3.3 SOFR term rates: calculation process
Source: Authors, based on CME

survey) from the market prices for forward SOFR values observable in the future markets is the best among the available options. However, since using a model introduces its own specific problem of distorting the observed market by the model assumptions (rather than by expert judgment or a market survey), care should be taken when selecting the model in order to minimize the distortion. And from the documents available to the public, it does not seem that much discussion took place about the model selection. In fact, it appears that the approach of Heitfield and Park (2019) has been implemented without investigating less-restrictive alternatives:

- By construction, the jump process used allows changes of the interest rate only after FOMC policy announcements and hence ignores all other factors influencing SOFR values and all rate volatility between meetings. In light of the SOFR spikes (Figure 1.9) that appears to be a strong assumption imposed on the market, which puts the term rates calculated under this assumption at a significant risk of distorting the market information. While the introduction of the Fed's standing repo facility (SRF) may well bring the market somewhat closer to this assumption (see the additional constraint SOFR ≤ SRFR mentioned in Chapter 1), it is not sufficient to conclude that non-policy-related volatility will be absent from the repo market. This deficiency could be addressed by using a mixed jump-diffusion process.

▪ Moreover, the volatility not coming from Fed policy has a significant effect on the prices of options on SOFR futures. (See Chapter 5 and Table 5.2 in particular.) Hence, the pure jump process used to calculate the term rate cannot be used to obtain reasonable option prices. And using two different models opens the door for inconsistencies between both.

▪ There are alternative ways to achieve the extraction of constant-maturity term rates from curves, which have been proven to work well in other markets but which do not seem to have been considered for SOFR term rates. For instance, spline models – available in different forms[11] – tend to do a good job for obtaining constant maturity par (or zero) yields from bond markets. In the spline model we presented in Chapter 11 of Huggins and Schaller (2013), the Fed meetings could be easily incorporated as external variables. This would allow accounting for their effect as external shocks while preserving the internal dynamics and volatility of rates.

▪ Even if one accepts the process in general, one can still argue about its implementation. For instance, the optimization implemented by the CME results in the Term Rates being influenced by futures beyond the end date of the term. The 3M Term Rate could depend partly on futures whose reference periods start in 6M time, for example. By contrast, the term rate hedge described in Chapter 2 only uses futures, whose references periods coincide with the term. Market participants usually prefer this feature, since it is unintuitive that a term rate should depend on events such as FOMC meetings taking place after the horizon of the term.

Hence, while criticism on the general level about using a model at all can be countered by the lack of better alternatives, criticism on the specific level about the model selected for calculating the term rate appears to be valid. Researching other models with the goal of minimizing the impact of the model assumptions on the translation of future prices into term rates

---

[11]For the short end of the curve, cubic splines usually produce better results than exponential splines.

and depending on the results replacing the basic jump process in the CME's Term Rate model would be the best way to counter this specific criticism.

In addition, some participants have expressed concern about the limited liquidity of SOFR futures (i.e., of the data basis for the term rate calculation) (see, e.g., Bowman n.d.). In terms of Figure 3.3, this criticism focuses on the first step, the criticism of the model on the second. However, taking into account the sampling techniques and observation intervals mentioned above and the expected further increase of liquidity following the migration from ED contracts, the concern about liquidity seems to be both sufficiently addressed and of a temporary nature. A general adoption of compounding would also help by concentrating liquidity in 3M contracts.[12]

Chapter 8 will describe a precise hedge of the CME's Term Rate with CME SOFR futures and shed additional light on this discussion from the perspective of the practical hedger.

TWO SCENARIOS FOR THE FURTHER EVOLUTION OF THE TENSION AND HENCE THE TERM RATE

We have described the CME Term Rate as the product of a compromise between the goal of regulators to move the lending market away from LIBOR to SOFR and the demands of loan market participants and have seen that the introduction of this compromise product has been key to achieving acceptance of and activity in SOFR-based lending markets.

However, this compromise does not resolve the underlying tension but rather embodies it. It seems likely, therefore, that the tension will continue until it is resolved one way or another. In the following, we will present two scenarios for the further evolution of this tension and consider the effect on its current compromise product, the CME SOFR Term Rate.

Scenario 1: Shift Away from the Term Rate Due to High Hedging Costs

As we've seen, hedging a SOFR loan with the rate calculated and paid in arrears is a straightforward process, as SOFR futures can be used directly (1M futures when the loan rate is calculated via a simple average and 3M futures when the loan rate is calculated using daily compounding).

---

[12]On the other hand, this would introduce a specification difference between 1M SOFR and Fed Fund futures, losing this contract spread as a clean expression of the secured–unsecured basis for the next chapter.

By contrast, hedging CME's term rate requires replicating the rather complex data aggregation and calculation described in Chapter 8. In the end, the loan using a term rate is also hedged with SOFR futures – but via expensive replication (or by paying a premium to a dealer for taking the risk of imperfect replication). Currently, the cost of hedging the term rate is multiple basis points (E. Childs, personal communication), i.e., one order of magnitude greater than the cost of hedging directly with futures.

From an economic perspective, using term rates therefore seems to be a costly way to the same outcome – hedging with SOFR futures (ARRC 2021, p. 28).[13] Thus, the ability to achieve the same hedge in a much cheaper and more direct way should be a major incentive for borrowers to embrace loan structures that are very similar to the specifications of the CME SOFR futures contracts. While the costs of adjusting systems may vary between different companies, the more and the larger hedges are executed, the earlier this investment will pay off. The significant difference between direct and indirect hedging costs suggests that this breakeven could be reached rather soon except perhaps for the least active and smallest borrowers.

The more the lending market develops according to this forecast – that is, the closer it resembles the ideal situation described at the beginning – the less the supporting features will be required:

- The demand for the term rate, which allows for in-advance SOFR lending, depends on the resistance to move toward in-arrears, i.e., in the first dimension of the transition.
- The demand for simple averaging and related products (like 1M SOFR futures) depends on the resistance to move toward compounding (i.e., in the second dimension of the transition).

In other words, the more complete the transition of the lending market to SOFR will be, the more ephemeral the Term Rate and products using simple conventions are likely to be.

In this scenario, the "ideal" hedgeability of in-arrears loans supports via lower hedging costs the "ideal" envisioned by regulators. The current compromise product of a SOFR Term Rate could then be an ephemeral phenomenon only, which will disappear together with the reluctance of the cash loan market. The tension is solved by one part of it receding and its current product of a term rate will disappear with it.

---

[13]The Alternative Reference Rate Committee presents a similar argument for hedges with SOFR OIS swaps. We feel that the point becomes even clearer when considering hedges with SOFR futures.

At the core of this issue is the statement of the general model critique above: that Term Rates represent the future markets *as seen through the model and its assumptions*. This results in the hedging problem that (unlike loans using in-arrears) the term rate cannot be directly and cheaply hedged with futures, but only indirectly and expensively via an additional replication of the model and its assumptions. Chapter 8 will demonstrate how to do this and thereby give an impression of the complexity involved in hedging CME's Term Rate.

Scenario 2: Persistence of the Term Rate and Consequences

The hedging costs of term rates could be reduced via an active secondary market for term rates, allowing dealers to pass on term rate exposure rather than charging a high premium for either taking over that exposure or going through the complex exercise of replicating the model. However, regulators are prohibiting a secondary market: Banks are allowed to deal the term rate with "end users" only – for example, to hedge a loan based on the SOFR term rate, but not to deal the term rate between themselves.

We suppose that the reason for that prohibition of interdealer trading in the term rate is precisely the motivation to keep hedging costs for loans based on the term rate high and thereby maintain the incentive to move toward in-arrears described in scenario 1 above. While we have not found any official documents explaining the reasons behind the prohibition of a secondary market for the term rate, this appears to be the only possible explanation for US officials interfering in such a severe way with the development of free markets.

In terms of the tension between regulatory goals and market needs, which described the evolution toward the term rate, one can state that this tension is currently embodied in the hedging problem and the high hedging costs of term rates. Via prohibition of a secondary market for term rates, regulators keep this tension and the hedging costs high in order to nudge the loan market toward their preferred scenario 1, which resolves the tension in the hedge by the hedging product disappearing. An alternative solution to the tension currently embodied in high hedging costs for term rate loans would be the development of a secondary market, leading to efficient hedges of the term rate and hence supporting its permanence. Hence, by prohibiting this secondary market, regulators express their continuing disapproval of the term rate by depriving it of a cheap hedge.

Under the assumption of this scenario that the term rate remains as central to SOFR lending as it is now, we can analyze the likely consequences of the prohibition of a secondary market and thereby try to anticipate the possible future issues. Like the evolution of the tension has led to the current situation of lending markets using a term rate, the tension embodied in the term rate will determine their further evolution.

Taking the perspective of a dealer hedging loans based on the SOFR term rate, he cannot unload his risk by using a secondary market for the SOFR term rate, but needs to use other hedging products, specifically SOFR futures, e.g., by trying to replicate the calculation process of the term rate as closely as possible (see above). This introduces a bias into future markets, as all dealers hedging SOFR term rates are on the same side. Currently, the share of term rate hedging in overall SOFR future trading is still small, and such a bias is not visible to us – but this scenario assumes that lending based on the term rate will become the standard. The more loans using the term rate are hedged, the more visible the bias will be. Moreover, an increase of rates and volatility from the current historically low levels is likely to result in increased hedging activity, both of cash loan market participants hedging their SOFR term rate exposure with dealers and of these dealers hedging their SOFR term rate exposure with futures. In terms of our tension concept, this would mean that the tension currently embodied into the term rate (and the prohibition of a secondary market) evolves into a discrepancy between the markets for the SOFR term rate and for SOFR futures.

Thinking further through this scenario, this bias would be an attractive arbitrage opportunity for those who can make use of it, i.e., are not subject to the regulatory prohibition of interdealer trading in the SOFR term rate. For example, foreign banks might be able to execute this arbitrage – by using the CCBS (Cross Currency Basis Swap) to gain access to USD. In this case, their arbitrage may result in removing the bias from SOFR futures – but transform it into a bias in the CCBS market. Using the terms of our concept again, this would mean that the tension evolves into a mispricing in the CCBS market. This would be another arbitrage opportunity, which another group of market participants may be able to exploit, thereby continuing the evolution of the tension through different markets and countries.

Given that the consequences of this scenario, such as mispriced SOFR futures and arbitrage opportunities for foreign banks, are unattractive to regulators, it seems likely that they would reconsider the prohibition of a secondary market for the term rate. Hence, over time the persistence of SOFR term rates could lead to regulators accepting it as a permanent solution and allowing the interdealer trading necessary to support it. In contrast to the first scenario of the tension being finally resolved by the market converging to the "ideal" of regulators, in the second scenario the tension is resolved by regulators giving up their fight against the demand of loan markets for a term rate and accepting its permanence by giving up their fight against a secondary market. It seems unsustainable that banks will build large one-way exposures to SOFR term rates if they can't manage those exposures. It seems more likely that either banks will eventually pull back from offering loans linked to term SOFR rates or that regulators will relent and allow banks to manage these exposures in the OTC derivatives markets.

In a broader perspective, the possible evolution of this tension through the markets (maybe via futures to CCBS) is an example for arbitrage opportunities caused by regulatory intervention.[14] As long as demand for the term rate *and* the prohibition of a secondary market maintain the tension, it is likely to cause mispricings and hence profit for arbitrageurs.

In summary, the final resolution of the tension causing the current high hedging costs for loans using the term rate is achieved:

- In scenario 1 by regulators maintaining this high cost until the *hedged product* "term rate" disappears and the loan market has moved toward their ideal of in-arrears, which can be directly and cheaply hedged with futures.
- In scenario 2 by regulators finally allowing the secondary market as an alternative hedge for term rate loans, i.e., by the *hedging costs* for term rates becoming less prohibitive and the loan market achieving the permanence of its preferred alternative through a liquid interdealer market for the term rate.

---

[14]Chapter 18 of Huggins and Schaller (2013) outlines this process in general.

4

SOFR Spread Futures and the Basis

Broadly speaking, the switch from LIBOR to SOFR has two fundamental consequences:

- A switch from a term-rate to an overnight rate, from which term lending needs to be constructed as discussed in Chapter 3.
- A switch from an unsecured to a secured rate, which will be analyzed in this chapter.

This chapter begins with a classification of the STIR contracts and the forces driving the spreads between them. Together with the differences between 1M and 3M contracts discussed in Chapter 2, the basis is key to understanding and modeling spreads between STIR futures.

In a second part, this chapter describes the factors influencing the basis and presents a model linking the basis between secured and unsecured lending to other bases, such as the CCBS (cross-currency basis swap).

This model and its link are then applied in three ways:

- It derives a fair value[1] for the spread contracts affected by the secured–unsecured basis from other market parameters.
- Vice versa, since the SOFR versus ED/FF spread contracts depend almost exclusively on the secured–unsecured basis, the model shows how they can be used as a cheap replacement of the expensive CCBS in many relative value (RV) trades.
- Finally, it establishes a new RV relationship between some STIR future spreads and the CCBS.

---

[1]Based on statistical rather than no-arbitrage arguments.

From a general perspective, the analysis and trades possible for the unsecured curve and ED contracts can be transferred to and repeated with SOFR futures for the secured curve. Chapters 2 and 5 provide a few examples of this. But in addition, the spread between the two provides the basis for *new* analyses and trades, including a new source for alpha. This chapter presents the first steps in this direction.

In a third and final part, this chapter provides an overview of the implications of the switch from LIBOR to SOFR as floating legs in asset swaps. Using the terms of the two fundamental consequences again, these implications can be classified into

- Technical adjustments required to deal with the floating payment being determined in arrears.
- The elimination of the unsecured–secured basis in asset swaps of government bonds and the introduction of this basis in asset swaps of corporate (bank) bonds.

SOFR FUTURES IN THE STIR UNIVERSE

Figure 4.1 illustrates the fundamental feature of the introduction of the basis between secured and unsecured lending rates via SOFR futures. Before SOFR futures existed, STIR contracts were based on unsecured lending rates, such as LIBOR and Fed Funds (FF). Hence their spreads were only a function of different time periods covered (and hence of the expectations of Fed policy for these time periods) and of different specifications, such as simple averaging and daily compounding. In other words, the situation between 1M and 3M SOFR futures described in Chapter 2 was enough to understand the spreads in the STIR universe, such as between FF and ED futures.

With SOFR futures based on secured lending, a new dimension has been added to the STIR universe, reflected in the two dimensions of Figure 4.1. In addition to the horizontal relationship between contracts on the same type of lending rate (secured or unsecured) covering different time periods and with

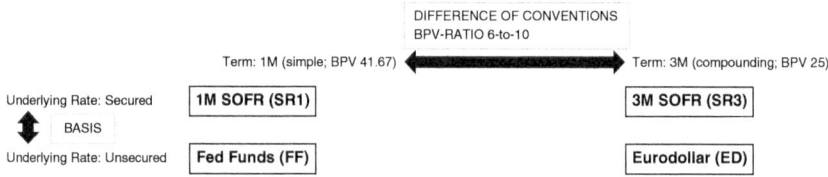

FIGURE 4.1 Relationship between CME's STIR futures
Source: Authors

different specifications, there is now also the vertical relationship between contracts covering (almost) the same time periods and with almost the same specifications for different types of lending rates.

DRIVING FORCES OF SPREADS IN THE STIR UNIVERSE

Hence, one can classify the driving forces of spreads between STIR futures by looking at Figure 4.1:

- The spread between futures in different columns is driven by the expectations about the interest rates (Fed policy) in different time periods, and the difference between simple averaging and daily compounding, which also depends on the general level of yields.

    This applies to the 1M–3M SOFR future spread discussed in Chapter 2 and to the FF–ED futures spread.
- The spread between futures in different rows is driven by expectations about the basis between secured and unsecured interest rates for the same time period.

    This applies to the SR1–FF and SR3–ED future spreads analyzed in this chapter.
- The spread between futures in different columns and rows is driven by both factors.

    This applies to the SR3–FF futures spread.

A few details need to be added to this broad conceptual perspective:

- While Fed Funds and LIBOR are different rates (unlike the same SOFR used for both SR1 and SR3 contracts), with very few exceptions they trade closely to each other. This is due to the fact that both represent unsecured lending rates – and validates our approach to classification based on secured vs unsecured lending.
- While SOFR futures have been constructed to mirror both the time period covered by FF and ED futures and their specifications, due to the different underlying rates and their conventions, there can occur slight differences from time to time. In particular, depending on the calendar situation, the underlying 3M LIBOR of an ED contract can deviate from the reference quarter of a 3M SOFR contract. And different holiday schedules apply.[2]

---

[2]https://www.cmegroup.com/education/files/sofr-futures-settlement-calculation-methodologies.pdf, page 3.

In most cases, however, these differences are negligible from a practical perspective.[3] Hence, the spreads between SOFR and FF/ED contracts can be considered to represent a "pure" market price for the secured–unsecured basis. This is the advantage of mirroring the specifications of FF and ED futures in 1M and 3M SOFR contracts. And this is also the foundation of using spread contracts as proxies for the secured–unsecured basis (and its links to other bases through the model) in RV trades. Specifically, it allows replacing CCBS in some RV relationships directly with SR3–ED spread contracts, without further adjustments.

CME'S SPREAD CONTRACTS

All "edges" of the square and the "diagonal" between SR3 and FF (not between SR1 and ED, though) shown in Figure 4.1 can be traded as inter-commodity spreads (ICS) on CME's Globex platform. Table 4.1 summarizes the specifications of these ICS. Given the margin offsets, this is a cheap and easy way to hedge against or gain exposure to the driving forces of these spreads, particularly to the secured–unsecured basis.

Figure 4.2 depicts the volume for the ICS involving SOFR contracts. We observe a clear correlation between the exposure of an ICS to the unsecured–secured basis and its liquidity: SR3:ED, which is exposed to a 3M basis, is most liquid, SR1:FF with exposure to a 1M basis less so. The SR1:SR3 spread, without any basis exposure, is currently without any liquidity. This suggests market demand for trading the basis via spread contracts.[4]

In fact, after switching from LIBOR to SOFR, banks cannot pass on their credit risk directly via LIBOR-based lending rates anymore.[5] In other words, banks engaging in SOFR-based lending face exposure to a secured–unsecured basis. And the need to hedge this basis explains the demand for ICS covering the basis.

As our model links the basis covered by ICS with other bases, like the CCBS, it could become the foundation for replacing the CCBS with ICS

---

[3]However, they should not be ignored. For example, a Fed rate hike on the last day of a 3M LIBOR period which is not in the reference quarter of the 3M SOFR future can have a material impact on the SR3–ED future spread.

[4]While it also indicates no current market demand for 1M–3M SOFR future spreads, this could be a consequence of the low interest rate environment and change in line with Fed policy, as discussed in Chapter 2.

[5]https://www.newyorkfed.org/newsevents/speeches/2020/wue200918.

TABLE 4.1 Spread contracts between CME's STIR futures

ICS	SR1:SR3	FF:ED	SR1:FF	SR3:ED	FF:SR3
Exposed to basis	No	No	Yes	Yes	Yes
Exposed to diff. conv. and BPV	Yes	Yes	No	No	Yes
Ratio	(3+3)-to-10	(3+3)-to-10	1-to-1	1-to-1	(3+3)-to-10
Price convention	Average of SR1 minus SR3	Average of FF minus ED	SR1 minus FF	SR3 minus ED	Average of FF minus SR3
Number of spreads listed	3	4	7	20	4
Minimum price increment	0.25 bp	0.25 bp	0.5 bp (0.25 bp for front month contract)	0.5 bp	0.25 bp
Last trading day	Last trading day of the contract in the ICS, whose last trading day is earliest				
Block trade size	ICS can be executed as block trades provided that each leg of the spread meets the smaller of the threshold requirements for the underlying products				
Holiday schedule	https://www.cmegroup.com/tools-information/holiday-calendar.html				
Margin offset	Possible				

Source: Authors, based on CME

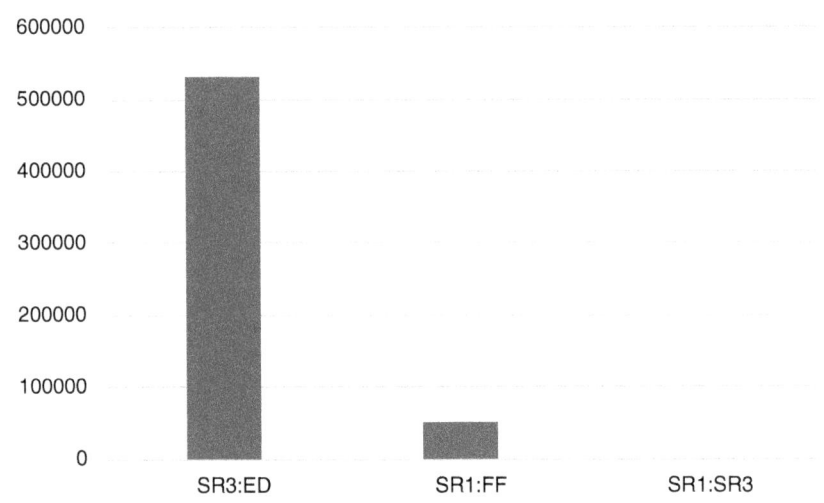

FIGURE 4.2 Volume of spread contracts during 2021
Source: Authors, from data provided by CME

in some RV trades, thereby further increasing demand and liquidity in the relevant ICS, especially the SR3:ED spread.

As mentioned in Chapter 2, ED futures settling after the end of LIBOR on June 30, 2023, trade on a fallback rate calculated as a spread over SOFR compounded in-arrears.[6] Hence ED futures expiring after this date are basically 3M SOFR contracts plus a fixed spread. This means that only SR3:ED spread contracts until June 2023 incorporate the secured–unsecured basis; afterward, only SR1:FF and SR3:FF spread contracts will be suitable to trade this basis and to analyze it through the model developed below. Due to the currently higher liquidity, we present the analysis for SR3:ED spread contracts and encourage the reader to repeat the same analysis for SR1:FF and SR3:FF spread contracts after liquidity will have shifted (and in case the legs of the CCBS change, as discussed at the end of this chapter).

DRIVING FACTORS OF THE SECURED–UNSECURED BASIS

As a start, we summarize a simple model for the spread between the secured repo rate R (for any term, not just overnight) and the unsecured LIBOR L

---

[6]Figure Intro.1.

presented in Huggins and Schaller (2013, p. 149):

$$L = \frac{R}{1 - p(1 - c)} + \frac{p(1 - c)}{1 - p(1 - c)} + \frac{qd(g - b)}{1 - p(1 - c)}$$

where

- p is the probability of default and c the recovery rate for the unsecured loan.
- q is the BIS risk weighting for the unsecured loan, d the BIS capital ratio, g the cost of equity, and b the marginal cost of funds (such as deposits).

Conceptually speaking, the higher cost of capital for unsecured loans should translate into a higher rate for unsecured loans. Assuming no default risk ($p = 0$) and $L = b$ (i.e., the bank using the LIBOR market rather than deposits as low-cost funds) and using the usual BIS risk weighting $q = 20\%$ and $d = 8\%$, the equation simplifies to:

$$L - R = 1.6\% \times (g - L)$$

This means that an increase in the cost of equity g by 5% versus LIBOR should result in a widening of the LIBOR-Repo spread by 8 bp, since unsecured loans become more costly to fund relative to secured ones. This relationship can explain the increase in (LIBOR-based) asset swap spreads of government bonds in times of stress in the banking sector and the fact that asset swap spreads tend to be higher in those markets when the cost of equity is higher. Moreover, it can be used to predict the effect of changes to BIS rules on LIBOR-repo spreads and hence on swap spreads. For example, a doubling of the capital ratio d should also result in a doubling of the LIBOR-repo spread.

In qualitative terms, the key results of this equation are that the LIBOR-repo spread is an increasing function of

- Level of interest rates
- Cost of equity (core capital) (relative to low-cost sources of funds, such as deposits)
- Capital ratio and risk weighting

A LIBOR-based asset swap can conceptually be considered as a LIBOR-repo basis swap over the life of the bond. Buying the bond, financing it in the repo market, and entering into a hypothetical LIBOR (minus X) – repo basis swap achieves the same cash flows as an asset swap of that bond versus LIBOR (minus the same X) (Huggins and Schaller 2013, p. 160). With the introduction of SOFR-based futures, the LIBOR–repo basis swap, which was a theoretical construct before, can now be traded, for instance, via SR3:ED strips.[7] On the other hand, at the same time that the theoretical modeling of LIBOR-based asset swaps via LIBOR–repo basis swaps became practically tradable, the switch from LIBOR to SOFR as reference rate has diminished the importance of LIBOR-based swap spread models.

While at the time of publication (Huggins and Schaller 2013) this model was able to explain most of the dynamics in the LIBOR–repo spread, a number of developments since then require additions. In general, the influencing factors described above remain important driving factors of the basis. Accordingly, the following model has the level of interest rates as one input variable. But unlike before, they explain only one part of the driving forces of LIBOR–repo spreads.

The increasing regulations in the aftermath of the financial crisis require banks to carefully assess the regulatory costs of each position relative to those of other possible positions. While without these constraints, each trade could be analysed separately, most market participants nowadays need to optimize their balance sheets under numerous capital and regulatory constraints.[8] This makes life difficult for analysts, as we will see in a moment, and also explains the occurrence and even persistence of market situations that would appear to present arbitrage opportunities in the absence of those constraints.

In the absence of balance sheet constraints, the LIBOR–repo spread can be modeled quantitatively via the formula above. Accordingly, unsecured rates trading below secured rates appear to be an anomaly and an arbitrage opportunity. However, as described in Chapter 1, in the presence of balance sheet constraints, there are costs associated with executing this arbitrage. For example, in some cases this may require the issuance of additional equity in order to maintain regulatory capital requirements. In this case, the advantage of repo versus LIBOR loans due to the different BIS treatment, which the formula captures, recedes.

The formula above models the secured–unsecured basis when the costs of balance sheet constraints are low. But when the costs of balance sheet constraints are relatively high, we observe situations that run contrary to the

---

[7]To be precise, as SOFR excludes most special bonds (see Chapter 1), the SR3:ED strip corresponds largely to a LIBOR–GC basis swap, which needs to be complemented with a GC–repo basis swap to replicate the asset swap spread of a specific bond.
[8]Institutions with fewer regulations (e.g., sovereign wealth funds) could be an exception.

intuition captured by this simple model. In fact, we sometimes observe situations in which relations that had been viewed as inequalities (e.g., *SOFR* ≤ *EFFR*) are violated. Thus, high costs of balance sheet constraints are the reason that repo rates exceeded Fed Funds, as depicted in Figure 4.3. Negative values in this graph correspond to repo rates trading above Fed Funds.

And as discussed in Chapter 1, the reaction of the Fed to SOFR spikes – the introduction of the standing repo facility – has resulted in the additional constraint that the overnight SOFR value should be less than or equal to the Fed's SRF rate.

It would be nice if the costs of balance sheet constraints in the banking sector could be modeled via a simple equation of the sort used above to characterize the relations between these various money market rates. But in practice, each bank has a unique balance sheet, which presents its own set of regulatory costs, and there's no way to build an industrywide model by aggregating these costs across the banking industry.

However, while it isn't possible to develop a quantitative *financial* model of these spreads from first principles, it may be possible to develop a quantitative *statistical* model. The insights into the financial reasons for the statistical relationships will not directly enter the quantitative equations anymore, but we at least can consider whether the statistical relations are consistent with our intuition, thereby minimizing the risk of relying on spurious correlations.

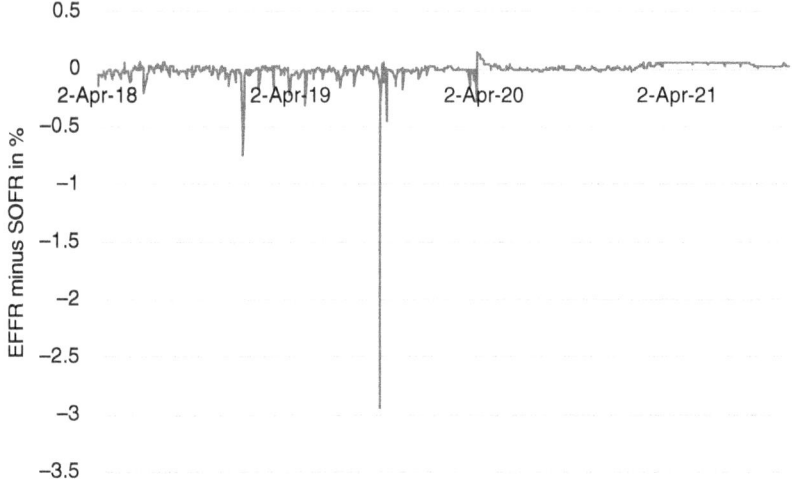

FIGURE 4.3 EFFR minus SOFR
Source: Authors, from data provided by the Fed (https://www.newyorkfed.org/markets/reference-rates/sofr) Disclaimer: These reference rate data are subject to the Terms of Use posted at newyorkfed.org. The New York Fed is not responsible for publication of the reference rate data by the Authors and Wiley, does not endorse any particular republication, and has no liability for your use

A MODEL FOR THE SECURED–UNSECURED BASIS, LINKING IT WITH OTHER BASES (CCBS)

Building on the previous considerations, we can ask which consequences are to be expected from stress in the banking sector, a broad term that may encompass higher cost of equity for banks, repatriation of funds from abroad to the US banking sector, etc. One would expect to observe this stress in several market segments, specifically:

- In a greater preference for secured lending (as given by the formula above for a higher g) and hence in a richening of SR3 versus ED futures.
- The model above has linked a higher secured–unsecured spread to a higher overall yield level and one would therefore generally expect increasing rates, though there have been historical instances when the basis has widened in an environment of decreasing yields.
- In greater volatility, both realized and implied.
- In wider (i.e., more negative) CCBS (Cross-Currency Basis Swaps) spreads,[9] since market participants tend to prefer keeping their funds in the US banking sector rather than in foreign countries in times of uncertainty.[10]
- In wider bank CDS (Credit Default Swap) spreads.

Given the causal links between these variables, it is reasonable to look at their correlations.[11] And indeed, the signs are as expected by the relationships already described. A higher spread of unsecured versus secured lending (as expressed by the SR3:ED future spread) is linked to a higher level of rates, a higher implied swaption volatility, a richening of the USD versus the EUR, higher (more negative) CCBS, and higher CDS for banks.

Especially high correlations exist with the level of interest rates as measured by SOFR (0.64) and to the CCBS. While the correlation with all

---

[9]An extensive discussion of CCBS is provided in Huggins and Schaller (2013), especially in chapters 13, 14, and 16.

[10]Empirically, this is even true in case the stress situation originates in the US, as during the subprime crisis. Following the beginning of this crisis, the CCBS became positive only for a few days, before turning significantly negative.

[11]Using weekly averages since the liquidity in some of the independent variables can be poor. Readers should keep in mind the structural break in all SOFR data series caused by the introduction of the SRF as discussed in Chapter 1. Hence, like all the others this analysis should also be considered as a hypothetical example only, to be repeated once enough data after the break will have become available.

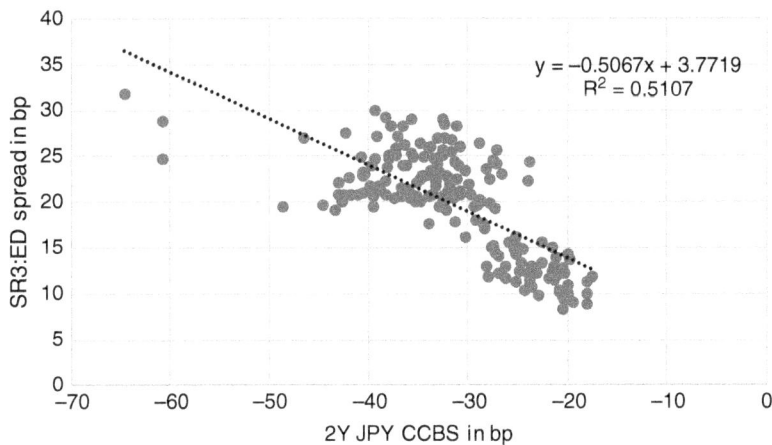

$$y = -0.5067x + 3.7719$$
$$R^2 = 0.5107$$

FIGURE 4.4   Regression of SR3:ED spread versus 2Y JPY CCBS
Source: Authors

TABLE 4.2   Multiple regression of the SR3:ED future spread versus SOFR and 2Y JPY CCBS

	Coefficients	Standard Error	*t* Stat	*P*-value
Intercept	4,825	0,991	4,869	2,43199E-06
SOFR	2,322	0,248	9,381	2,74488E-17
2Y JPY CCBS	−0,394	0,033	−12,121	3,86364E-25
R-square	0.67			

Source: Authors

maturities of both the JPY and EUR CCBS is significant, it is most pronounced for the 2Y JPY CCBS (–0.71), which is also relatively liquid. Figure 4.4 shows this specific regression.

A multiple regression of the SR3:ED futures spread versus the candidates for explaining variables listed above suggests that the rate level (SOFR) and the 2Y JPY CCBS have most explanatory power, as summarized in Table 4.2. Adding more explanatory variables does not lead to a significant improvement of the *R*-squared value. We therefore decide to use the regression from Table 4.2, i.e., to model the SR3:ED future spread via SOFR and the 2Y JPY CCBS.

FIRST APPLICATION OF THIS MODEL: PRICING SPREAD FUTURES

This statistical model allows pricing the SR3:ED future spread[12] as a function of SOFR and the 2Y JPY CCBS. Figure 4.5 illustrates the proximity of the model prediction to the actual value of the SR3:ED future spread in the past. Assuming the correlations will be stable in future as well,[13] one can predict the likely level of the SR3:ED future spread for a number of scenarios. Table 4.3 shows these predictions: The left side assumes a constant CCBS and calculates the effect of changes in the yield level on the futures spread, corresponding to a scenario in which Fed policy rather than stress in the banking sector drives market pricing. The right side assesses the opposite scenario of constant (low) interest rates for different CCBS levels, reflecting different levels of stress in the banking sector.

Of course, as statistically reflected in an R-squared below 1, there are other driving factors as well, which can at times overpower the ones captured

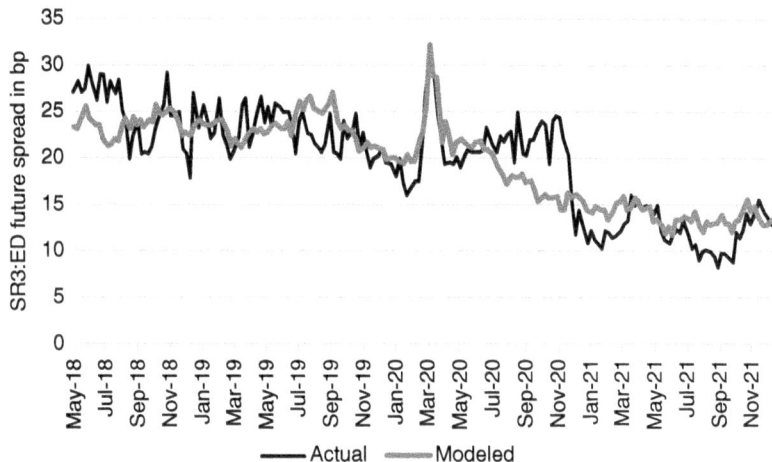

FIGURE 4.5 Actual versus modeled SR3:ED spread
Source: Authors

---

[12]It can easily be transferred to the SR1:FF as well by using this future spread as explained variable in the regression of Table 4.3. Following the switch of ED contracts to fallback rates, the SOFR–FF spread contracts will remain as only dependent variable for this analysis.

[13]Analysts should periodically confirm the accuracy of this assumption by repeating the regressions with updated data, particularly in light of the structural break due to the introduction of SRF. (See Chapter 1.)

TABLE 4.3 Model prediction of the SR3:ED future spread

SOFR in % 2Y JPY CCBS constant at −18.5 bp	Modeled SR3:ED future spread in bp	SOFR Constant at 22 bp 2Y JPY CCBS in bp	Modeled SR3:ED future spread in bp
0	12	−20	13
0.5	13	−40	21
1	14	−60	29
3	19	−80	37
5	24	−100	45

Source: Authors

by the model. Analysts are therefore well-advised to complement the model with other considerations. Unfortunately, as noted in Chapter 1, the missing accessibility of raw data makes some analyses impossible. For example, it would be interesting to know whether there are additional factors driving the secured–unsecured basis from the distribution of trades during the day.[14]

Returning to the classification at the beginning of this chapter, one can analyze the "horizontal" spread between 1M and 3M contracts via the method outlined in Chapter 2 for the SR1:SR3 futures spread and the "vertical" spread via the model for the basis described here. Combining both helps understand and predict most of the spreads in the STIR universe. For example, a trader expecting the yield curve to steepen 25 bp during the reference quarter could use the spreadsheet "3M versus 1M" of Chapter 2 to assess the effect on the SR1:SR3 futures spread. He can then go on and apply the model to analyze the effect of a repetition of the subprime crisis with a 2Y JPY CCBS at −80 bp on the SR3:ED future spread. And he can combine both to see what might happen to the SR3:FF futures spread if the yield curve steepening occurs together with a banking crisis.

SECOND APPLICATION OF THIS MODEL: REPLACING THE CCBS WITH SPREAD FUTURES IN SOME RV TRADES

The CCBS plays a vital role in many RV relationships: As it allows swapping cash flows in different currencies, it provides the foundation for comparing and trading global swap spreads against each other. It links all global

---

[14]For illustration, imagine a scenario in which rates tend to rise during the day and most repo takes place during the morning.

bond markets and enables comparing all bonds via a single number, i.e., the spread of the basis-swapped bond over USD LIBOR[15] and exploiting different swap spread levels for investing and funding, for instance, by issuing Samurai bonds.

Unfortunately, precisely due to its function of exchanging cash flows in different currencies, the CCBS suffers from high capital costs, regulatory burdens, margins, and transactions costs, which limit its practical use. Analysts often find themselves in a situation in which an RV relationship between global bonds seems out of line but cannot be exploited because the required CCBS is too costly to transact.

As our statistical model links the CCBS to the secured–unsecured basis, which has been introduced to the STIR universe (Figure 4.1) and can therefore be traded easily and cheaply (with margin offset), a major consequence could be the replacement of CCBS by SR3:ED spread positions. After ED futures trade on fallback rates, only SOFR–FF spread contracts remain as a possible replacement, which will then probably enjoy higher liquidity due to the migration from ED futures.

While the R-squared value of the regression shown in Figure 4.4 is only 0.51, significant moves in the CCBS seem to be well reflected in the futures spread. Moreover, the time series of the residual of this regression depicted in Figure 4.6 suggests that deviations are usually short-lived. Calibrating a simple mean-reverting process to this time series gives an estimated half-life of 3.7 weeks (Table 4.4). For comparison, a similar regression versus the CDS of Bank of America exhibits a trend and a slower speed of mean reversion, implying the SR3:ED spread is less suitable as a replacement for CDS than for the CCBS.

It appears therefore attractive to replace the expensive CCBS with cheaper SR3:ED spread futures whenever possible. This relationship allows execution of some of the arbitrage positions between global bond markets, which have been impractical due to prohibitively high costs of CCBS until now. Vice versa, the suitability of SR3:ED spreads to replace the CCBS in some RV trades should result in improved liquidity in the spread contracts covering the basis (Figure 4.2).

The question is, thus, in which trades can the CCBS be replaced by SR3:ED spread futures? In those trades which require the function of the CCBS to actually swap different currencies, it cannot be replaced by a financial product, which mirrors the behavior of the CCBS, but does not provide its cash flows. For example, a USD-based investor wanting to invest into

---

[15]And since the CDS also expresses all bonds via a single number, the two can be compared and traded against each other, as discussed in Chapter 16 of Huggins and Schaller (2013).

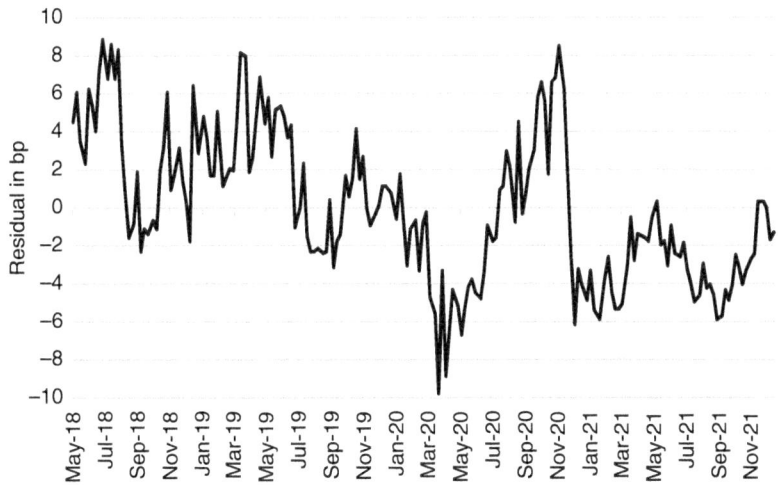

FIGURE 4.6 Regression residuals of the SR3:ED spread versus 2Y JPY CCBS
Source: Authors

TABLE 4.4 Mean reversion characteristics of the residuals from Figures 4.6 and 4.7

	Residual time series of a regression of the SR3:ED spread versus	
	2Y JPY CCBS only	2Y JPY CCBS and SOFR
Estimated mean (%)	−0,18	−0,09
Estimated speed of MR	0,19	0,27
Estimated sigma	5,60	5,48
Expected halflife (weeks)	3,70	2,56
Expected 90% performance (weeks)	12,31	8,52
One week Sharpe ratio for residual of 10 bp	5,37	7,68
One week Sharpe ratio for residual of 5 bp	2,80	4,03

Source: Authors

a JGB without taking FX exposure requires the currency exchanges of an
actual CCBS, particularly the exchange of the principal between USD and
JPY at the beginning and at expiration of the CCBS.[16]

---

[16]See Figure 16.1 of Huggins and Schaller 2013.

On the other hand, as the CCBS is the link between global bond markets, it is influenced by different valuations in different countries. For example, if basis-swapped 10Y Bunds trade at USD LIBOR-20 bp and 10Y USTs at USD LIBOR-50 bp, a USD-based investor judging both to be of the same credit quality may want to use the CCBS to invest his USD without FX exposure into basis-swapped Bunds. These flows support a narrowing (less negative) of the EUR CCBS. Hence, analysts of global bond markets seeing such a mismatch may want to position for the likely moves in the CCBS – without needing the cash flows from its FX swaps. They can therefore replace a CCBS position with a financial instrument that exhibits similar behavior without providing the cash flows. In summary, the CCBS can be replaced if the goal is to exploit its *moves* only, but not if it is important to obtain the CCBS *cash flows*.

From a conceptual perspective, the effects of introducing futures on secured rates to the STIR universe can be summarized as follows:

- They provide a market price for the LIBOR-GC basis swap, which is an important part of (LIBOR-based) swap spread models.
- They provide a cheap substitute for trading the moves of CCBS.
- Their link to the CCBS and rate level via the model is a new RV relationship and hence a new source for generating alpha, which is discussed in the next application.

THIRD APPLICATION OF THIS MODEL: NEW RV RELATIONSHIP

Figure 4.7 shows the residual of the regression from Table 4.2, i.e., of the SR3:ED spread future versus SOFR and the 2Y JPY CCBS. Table 4.4 exhibits the mean reversion characteristics of this regression residual and of the regression versus the CCBS only (shown in Figure 4.6) when modeled through a simple mean-reverting model (the Ornstein-Uhlenbeck process).

The new RV relationship of the model seems both optically and numerically attractive. For example, the Sharpe ratio of trading the residual of these two regressions at a level of 10 bp is expected to be 7.68 and 5.37 over the first week.[17]

However, due to the capital and transaction costs involved in trading the CCBS mentioned above, the residual may seldom be high enough to allow executing this RV relationship as a stand-alone trade. But it could still

---

[17]Assuming that immediately after the last data point of Figures 4.6 and 4.7 the residual becomes 10 bp.

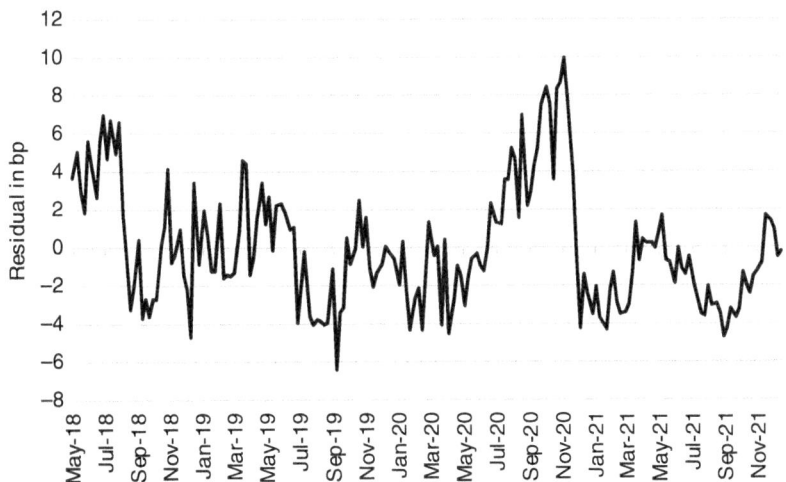

FIGURE 4.7 Regression residuals of the SR3:ED spread versus SOFR and 2Y JPY CCBS
Source: Authors

be incorporated as an additional and uncorrelated source of alpha in CCBS trading. Specifically, Figure 4.6 can be used as a guide, at which point in time replacements of CCBS with SR3:ED spread future positions are particularly attractive.

THE CCBS AND THE MODEL AFTER THE END OF LIBOR

The transition from unsecured to secured reference rates is a major event for financial products and their analysis. We have seen that the switch from LIBOR to SOFR as reference rate eliminates the basis inherent in LIBOR-based swaps. Following the final transition in June 2023, ED futures will trade on a fallback rate and therefore only FF–SOFR spread contracts will remain[18] to trade the "vertical" dimension of the basis and as *objective* of the model.

However, one should keep in mind that the unsecured–secured basis affects the CCBS due to exchanging different currencies. Hence, independent of the type of rate used in the basis swap (unsecured or secured), the CCBS should remain influenced by the unsecured–secured spread and therefore continue being usable in the model even after transitioning to SOFR as

---

[18]At the time of writing (Dec 2021), CME has expressed to the authors its commitment to maintain product choice and to continue ED futures as long as there is a need for them.

reference rate. One could say that the basis in the CCBS is *between* the two legs, not *in* the two legs. Actually, in case *both* legs switch from secured to unsecured rates simultaneously, it is possible that the effect on CCBS would be minimal – though it is of course advisable to re-run the regressions of the model in this case. If only *one* leg transitions from secured to unsecured, for instance, due to uncoordinated global regulations, the CCBS is likely to become more or less correlated to the unsecured–secured basis, depending on whether the transition occurs only in the US or only abroad.

In summary, while it is possible that the correlations of the model are affected by the transition of CCBS to secured rates, we are optimistic that the CCBS will remain correlated to the unsecured–secured basis and that the model built on it can still be used – though for the spread between SOFR futures and FF contracts only.

REMAINING PRODUCTS WITH EXPOSURE TO THE BASIS AFTER THE END OF LIBOR

In the course of the book, we have come across a few reasons for the reluctance of end users to embrace the transition to SOFR. In Chapter 1, we mentioned concerns about the lack of a level playing field with big banks. In Chapter 3, we described the tension between the reality of cash loan markets and the ideal SOFR arrangements envisioned by regulators. Here, we can add another reason for this reluctance: while loans on a LIBOR basis enable lenders to profit from a banking crisis as the widening unsecured–secured spread results in a higher reference rate, the switch to SOFR as reference rate eliminates this source of return. This may be another reason behind the perception that SOFR is a project forced on the market by regulators for the benefit of big banks by immunizing their funding rates (of the already outstanding loans with a fixed spread above SOFR) against increasing unsecured–secured spreads. Of course, one can counter this perception by arguing that banks as lenders face the other side of the coin, i.e., that they are unable to pass on their higher unsecured lending costs during a crisis via the reference rate.

But this argument also leads to the interesting question: Which instruments remain for a lender to profit from a widening of unsecured–secured spreads after the transition eliminates many products?

- Before the transition, lenders enjoyed a widening of the basis automatically via increasing LIBOR.
- After the transition to SOFR, lenders need to add a product to maintain exposure to a widening basis *after* entering into a SOFR-based loan. (If the basis widens *before* entering the loan, it should be reflected in higher spreads the bank offers over SOFR.)

- However, due to the transition to SOFR, most products providing this basis will disappear together with LIBOR. Asset swap spreads of government bonds, which incorporated the basis as long as they had LIBOR as floating rate, will no longer express the basis once they use SOFR as floating leg.

Hence, given these consequences of switching to a secured reference rate, products allowing to trade the unsecured–secured basis are likely to become rare. In this environment, CCBS could turn out to be a valuable exception. As we mentioned above, one can think of CCBS as incorporating the unsecured–secured basis *between* its two legs rather than *in* one of the two legs and hence to remain a proxy for the unsecured–secured basis even if both legs reference secured rates. And after the migration of ED futures to the fallback, when they become 3M SOFR contracts plus a spread, SR1:FF and SR3:FF spread contracts will be the only STIR positions covering the "vertical" dimension of the basis. Actually, these spread contracts could turn out to be the cheapest way to gain exposure to the secured–unsecured basis, which is likely to result in high demand from end users looking for a method to continue profiting from banking crises and thus increased liquidity.

SWAPS WITH SOFR AS FLOATING LEG AND ASSET SWAPS AFTER THE END OF LIBOR

Historically, swaps started with LIBOR as floating leg, i.e., an unsecured term rate, usually 3M. Under the impression of the financial crisis, the risk of an unsecured term rate was deemed to be unacceptably high and was mitigated by using OIS (overnight index swaps) with FF as floating leg, i.e., an unsecured overnight rate. Thereby, the unsecured exposure to banks was reduced from a (3M) term to overnight. In Figure 4.8, this corresponds to the horizontal dimension.[19]

The introduction of SOFR, i.e., a secured overnight rate, can be considered as further reduction of the risk to the lowest possible level. Conceptually, it adds the vertical dimension of secured rates as floating leg. Thus, a swap can now be based on overnight or term rates (horizontal dimension) and on unsecured or secured rates (vertical dimension). Whether SOFR term rates will someday be used as floating leg in swaps will depend on the evolution of the regulatory tension described at the end of Chapter 3. In that

---

[19]The dimensions are intentionally identical to those of Figure 4.1, allowing to identify the similarities and differences.

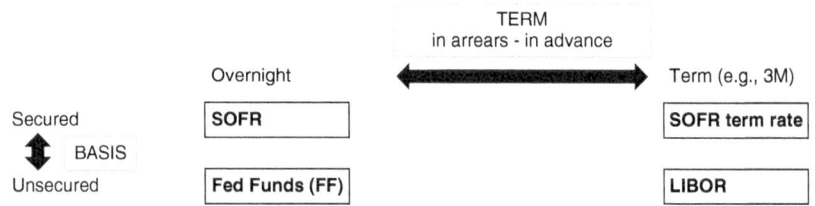

FIGURE 4.8   Relationship between floating legs of swaps
Source: Authors

case, the full matrix of Figure 4.8 would become available. Currently, there are only the three choices: secured overnight (SOFR), unsecured overnight (FF), and unsecured term (LIBOR).

The adjustments required for switching from LIBOR to SOFR as floating leg in a swap can therefore be classified along the two dimensions:

- The move from term to overnight requires the technical adjustment of moving from a rate determined in advance to a rate determined in arrears – and is familiar from the move from LIBOR to FF as the floating leg of OIS.
- The move from unsecured to secured has the fundamental effect of eliminating the secured–unsecured basis in asset swaps of government bonds.

In a swap with LIBOR as floating leg, the payment is determined at the beginning of each interest rate period but takes place at the end. In a swap with SOFR as the floating leg, the payment is determined at the end of each interest rate period, which could be the same time it takes place, depending on the specifications.[20] As a consequence, unlike in LIBOR-based swaps, when using SOFR as floating leg, the first payment is not known at the time of entering into the swap agreement. Moreover, the move from "in advance" to "in arrears" results in the problems discussed in Chapter 3, specifically, the issue of a short notice period. And the remedies outlined for cash loans, such as lookbacks, can also be applied in swaps. While OTC swaps allow the counterparties full flexibility to agree on a specification, clearinghouses may determine a particular remedy. For example, CME-cleared SOFR swaps use daily compounding with a two-day payment offset (CME Q4 2018, p. 7). The problems and possible solutions to adjusting swaps to an overnight floating rate are well known from the switch from LIBOR to FF and can be directly replicated for SOFR.

---

[20]Chapter 9 looks at the currently most common specifications in more detail.

By contrast, the switch from LIBOR to SOFR also contains the fundamental new feature of a secured rate as floating leg. Unlike the mere reduction of unsecured exposure by reducing the term from 3M to overnight (FF) in OIS, it eliminates the unsecured exposure and can therefore be considered as the final stage of the search for the least risky floating rate. It also eliminates the basis in asset swaps of government bonds. We have mentioned that a LIBOR-based asset swap of government bonds is conceptually the same as a LIBOR-repo basis swap over the life of the bond; replacing LIBOR with SOFR as floating leg, an asset swap of a government bond becomes conceptually the same as a SOFR-repo basis swap over the life of the bond. In other words, asset swapping a government bond with SOFR as floating leg results in exposure to the spread between SOFR and the specific repo rate of this government bond. If the repo rate of the bond were always the same as SOFR, the SOFR-repo basis swap and hence the swap spread of the bond should be zero. And the expected specialness of a government bond is (theoretically[21]) the only driving factor of SOFR-based asset swap spreads.

Repeating this argument in formal terms, LIBOR-based asset swaps of government bonds can be priced as LIBOR-repo basis swaps, which can be decomposed in a LIBOR-SOFR and a SOFR-repo basis swap, with SOFR usually being close to GC, as discussed in Chapter 1. The first part is driven by the unsecured–secured basis, while the second part is driven by the specialness of the specific bond. If the bond is not expected to become special – for example, because it is no benchmark anymore and has no chance of being the cheapest-to-deliver (CTD) of a bond futures contract, the SOFR-repo basis swap can be assumed to be close to zero. In this case – which is true for most bonds – all of the LIBOR-based asset swap is driven by the first part – and disappears when using SOFR as floating leg instead. Hence, while LIBOR-based asset swaps were mostly driven by the unsecured–secured basis (which we have suggested to assess through the model described above), SOFR-based asset swaps eliminate this basis and leave only the specialness (SOFR-repo basis swap) as driving factor. Except for benchmarks and CTD candidates, the expected specialness is typically small, resulting in a theoretical fair value of close to zero of the SOFR-based asset swaps of most government bonds.

As explained in Chapter 1, this theoretical consideration is likely to be influenced by regulation as well. If holding a government bond requires less capital than engaging in a SOFR-based swap, the prediction of SOFR-based asset swaps for government bonds to reflect their expected specialness (and

---

[21]For example, flows which affect the bond price but not its repo rate are not captured.

hence to be close to zero for most of them) will only materialize in times of little constraints from regulation, e.g., at a distance from leverage limits. If, on the other hand, the regulatory restrictions play an important role, for example, due to already high leverage, SOFR-based asset swap spreads of government bonds can deviate quite significantly from zero.

Vice versa, while the switch from LIBOR to SOFR eliminates the unsecured–secured basis in asset swaps for government bonds (funding at the secured repo rate), it introduces this basis in asset swaps for corporate issues, such as bank bonds. Combining the floating rates shown in Figure 4.8 with the different types (secured and unsecured) of fixed rates in asset swaps, one can therefore

- Asset swap government bonds without a basis by using SOFR-based swaps (and with a basis by using FF-based OIS).
- Asset swap corporate bonds without a basis by using FF-based OIS (and with a basis by using SOFR-based OIS).

Additionally, the horizontal dimension allows choosing a different term than overnight, currently for unsecured only.

It seems therefore likely that the asset swap market could evolve to a situation where SOFR is used for asset swaps of government bonds and FF for asset swaps of corporate bonds, allowing to exclude basis risk in both.

Both (asset) swaps and OIS using SOFR and FF in general are connected through the SOFR–FF basis, which can be hedged with future spreads as described above. Hence, one could foresee a future swap universe in which SOFR- and FF-based OIS take center stage for asset swapping government and corporate bonds respectively, and the spread between the two is actively traded via SR1:FF spread contracts.

HEDGING SOFR-BASED SWAPS AND GOVERNMENT BONDS WITH SOFR FUTURES

In broad conceptual terms, the transition from LIBOR to SOFR as a reference rate has led to SOFR future strips, SOFR-based swaps, and government bonds becoming very similar. All three can be considered as slightly different ways to compound a secured overnight rate into a term rate. (See Figure 9.1 for an illustration of this statement.) This fundamental link between the three markets, futures, swaps, and bonds, makes it possible to replicate and hedge each one with each other. And that is the conceptual foundation on which Chapter 9 will construct the hedges of swaps with SOFR as floating leg and of Treasuries with SOFR futures.

5
SOFR Future Options

The move from LIBOR to SOFR as reference rate implies a fundamentally new concept: Rather than using a term rate, we apply a daily rate. But SOFR futures combine the daily rates during their reference period into a (forward) term rate. Hence, when dealing with SOFR futures, the situation is similar to LIBOR; in a manner of speaking, one might say that SOFR futures transform the daily rates during their reference period into a term rate like LIBOR. And this is the reason behind the relatively easy transfer of concepts to the new reference rate. Via SOFR futures one does not need to deal directly with daily SOFR, but with the daily SOFR *aggregated* by the future.

However, once the SOFR futures contract enters its reference period, this aggregation ends and together with it the similarity to LIBOR and the direct transfer of concepts from the Eurodollar (ED) futures market. (Compare Figure 2.1.) As soon as the reference period starts, one needs to deal with daily SOFR values. When only the rate itself is concerned, this can be achieved by some straightforward adjustments for the front-month contract, discussed in Chapter 2 (e.g., for calculating the strip rate and executing the roll). But when volatility is also involved, the end of aggregation at the beginning of the reference period results in a completely new type of option. Before the reference period, options on SOFR futures have a forward term rate as underlying, as do options on ED contracts. But during the reference period, they depend on the path of daily SOFR values during the reference period. Thus, from one day to the next, at the start of the reference period, the same option on the same SOFR future, which used to behave like a standard American option on an ED futures contract, suddenly becomes an Asian option. In the manner of speaking used above, one might say that as SOFR futures enter their reference period, their aggregative function ends – and the options on them therefore transmogrify from standard options on a forward term rate to Asian options.

The fundamentally different concept of the new reference rate, whose practical consequences could be easily managed for futures, therefore manifests itself in a fundamentally different type of options on futures *as soon as the reference period starts*. From that point onward, one faces the mathematical challenge of pricing Asian options, which is further complicated by allowing jumps in the process. And both the markets using Asian options and the literature dealing with them have so far focused on Asian options of the European type only. Hence, the transfer from LIBOR to SOFR has resulted in a situation in which the options of the key money market (i.e., futures on the reference rate) are options without any pricing model available. From the perspective of options, the migration from LIBOR to SOFR can be considered as an uncontrolled[1] experiment: By bureaucratic fiat, the huge market for options on the reference rate is transferred from standard to highly exotic, from being accompanied by well-known pricing models to the absence of any pricing model. And one unintended consequence of the difficulties to price and hedge options on SOFR futures is their lesser suitability for hedging caps and floors – which may explain why market participants seem hesitant to migrate from ED to SOFR futures options.

However, all these challenges are absent *before the reference period starts*. The aggregation of daily SOFR via the future still works and hence options on SOFR futures are still standard American options with the forward term rate given by the futures as underlying. Since the trading in options on 3M SOFR futures ends before their reference quarter starts, they do not experience the final metamorphosis into exotic options. Hence, they can be priced and analyzed just as options on ED contracts. This allows the transfer of the realized and implied volatility analysis from the unsecured to the secured yield curve – just as Chapter 2 has transferred parts of the yield curve analysis itself. Moreover, the similarity of specifications between options on SOFR and on ED futures enables executing spread positions easily, thereby extending the basis trading from Chapter 4 to options.

Although the decision to let options on SOFR futures expire before they encounter the problem of becoming Asian during the reference period is one possible solution, it comes at the high cost of no options on futures being available until futures settlement. This means that it becomes impossible to hedge a cap or floor with a series of options on SOFR futures in the same manner as one can do with options on ED futures. In other words,

---

[1]From the public documents known to us, it does not seem that officials have given much thought to the implications of SOFR as underlying for the option market.

the problem of a missing pricing formula for the hedging instrument has been "solved" by the hedging instrument itself being missing. It is similar to healing a wound by amputation.

In contrast to the options on 3M SOFR futures, which end trading before the reference quarter begins, options on 1M SOFR futures end trading together with the underlying contract at the end of the reference month. Hence, these options are subject to the sudden switch to Asian option with American-style exercise. And to make matters worse, they apply the arithmetic average rather than the geometric average, which is even harder to tackle mathematically. On the other hand, while there currently exists no way to price this hedging instrument during the reference month, at least the hedging instrument exists.

In summary, the conceptual difference between a term rate (LIBOR) and an overnight rate (SOFR) is visible within the universe of SOFR futures in the break between the period before and during the reference period and within the universe of SOFR future options in the break between standard and exotic options. It also implies the break between options on 3M and 1M SOFR futures, with only the latter experiencing a sudden transformation during their lifetime. And finally, it implies the structure of this chapter:

- In the first half, we will focus on options on 3M SOFR futures only, exploiting the exclusion of the problem by their specifications. This allows providing an overview over option analysis and trading strategies in general and how they could be applied to SOFR future options – without needing to worry about exotic option pricing. Once more, the concepts can simply be transferred from the unsecured to the secured yield curve and allow new insights into the relationships between the realized and implied volatility along both, which can be exploited easily and cheaply by trading SOFR versus ED futures options spreads.

- In the second half, we will introduce options on 1M SOFR futures and together with them the Pandora's box of pricing American-style Asian options using an arithmetic average. After a brief review of the academic literature on this subject, we will describe the necessary steps toward dealing with these problems, but we will find ourselves without an exact pricing formula. Nevertheless, only by solving this formidable challenge can the full functionality of the key money market can be ensured – by providing options with a similar usability for hedging as the options on ED futures contracts offer. This would also support the liquidity in options on SOFR futures and hence the completion of the transition from the ED complex.

OPTIONS ON 3M SOFR FUTURES: PRODUCT SUITE AND SPECIFICATIONS

Since January 2020, a comprehensive suite of options on the 3M SOFR futures (SR3) has been available. The product suite is summarized in Figure 5.1 and graphically represented in Figure 5.3, while the main technical specifications are listed in Figure 5.2 (Kronstein December 2019).[2]

SOFR future options are linked to the contract month of the future, i.e., to the beginning of the reference quarter (as defined in Figure 2.2). Correspondingly, trading in options on 3M SOFR futures ends before the reference quarter begins. For instance, the last trading day for the options on the Sep 2022 SR3 future, whose reference quarter begins on Wednesday, 21 Sep, 2022 (included), and ends on Wednesday, 21 Dec, 2022 (excluded), is Friday 16 Sep, 2022. This avoids dealing with the metamorphosis into an

Expiries	
Standard Options	Quarterly Standard Options for each of the nearest 16 March Quarterly Months (Mar, Jun, Sep, Dec)
	Serial Standard Options for each of the nearest 4 months not covered by Quarterly Standard Options
1Y, 2Y, 3Y, 4Y and 5Y Mid-Curve Options	Quarterly Mid-Curve Options for each of the nearest 5 March Quarterly Months (Mar, Jun, Sep, Dec)
	Serial Mid-Curve Options for each of the nearest 4 months not covered by Quarterly Mid-Curve Options
3M, 6M, 9M Mid-Curve Options	Quarterly Mid-Curve Options for the nearest March Quarterly Months (Mar, Jun, Sep, Dec)
	Serial Mid-Curve Options for each of the nearest 2 months not covered by Quarterly Mid-Curve Options
1Y, 2Y, 3Y Mid-Curve Options	Weekly Mid-Curve Options for each of the nearest 2 Fridays not covered by the options above
Strikes	
First 4 quarterly and first 4 serial options	Intervals of 6.25 bp for a range of 150 bp around ATM
	Intervals of 25 bp for a range of 550 bp around ATM
Other options	Intervals of 12.5 bp for a range of 150 bp around ATM
	Intervals of 25 bp for a range of 550 bp around ATM
	(ATM being determined as the strike price closest to the future settlement price of the previous business day)

FIGURE 5.1   3M SOFR future options: product suite
Source: Authors, based on CME

---

[2]See also https://www.cmegroup.com/markets/interest-rates/stirs/three-month-sofr .contractSpecs.options.html.

Contract size	USD 25 per basis point (USD 2,500 per point per option contract)	
Style	American	
Exercise	By notification by 5.30 pm CT of the day of exercise Automatic exercise of ITM options after expiration	

**Trading venues
and hours**
	CME Globex: 5pm to 4pm, Sun-Fri with a 60-minute break each day
	    beginning at 4pm
	CME ClearPort: 5pm to 5:45 pm Sun-Fri with no reporting Monday-
	    Thursday from 5:45 p.m.–6:00 p.m.
	Open Outcry: 7:20 am to 2pm Mon-Fri	

Last trading day	Friday preceding the 3rd Wednesday of the contract month of the underlying future (i.e., the Friday before the beginning of the reference quarter)	
Minimum tick size	*Quarterly* Nearest	0.25 bp if premium not more than 5 bp; 0.5 bp else
	Second	0.5 bp
	Other	0.25 bp if premium not more than 5 bp; 0.5 bp else
	Serial	0.5 bp
Block trade minimum size	625 contracts	Asian Trading Hours (4pm–12am, Mon-Fri on regular business days and at all weekend times)
	1250 contracts	European Trading Hours (12am–7am, Mon-Fri on regular business days)
	2500 contracts	Regular Trading Hours (7am–4pm, Mon-Fri on regular business days)
Online resource	https://www.cmegroup.com/markets/interest-rates/stirs/three-month- sofr.contractSpecs.options.html	

FIGURE 5.2 3M SOFR future options: technical specifications
Source: Authors, based on CME

exotic option during the reference period. Like for options on ED futures, also options on SOFR futures always refer to a full 3M period of unknown rates, aggregated via the future into one single (forward) term rate.

Moreover, as the 3M SOFR future closely mirrors the specifications of the ED future (as discussed in Chapter 2), so the options on the 3M SOFR futures contract have been designed to closely resemble those on ED futures. Together with the margin offset, this facilitates spread trading between both, for example, for exploiting the differences between the volatility of secured and unsecured rates described below. And as part of the transition summarized in Figure Intro.1, options on ED futures "convert" into options on 3M SOFR futures by adding the ISDA spread adjustment to the strike of SOFR options (CME Group 2020).

However, the seemingly similar specifications contain one important difference. When options on ED contracts end trading together with their underlying, they cover the final 3M term rate, while options on SOFR futures

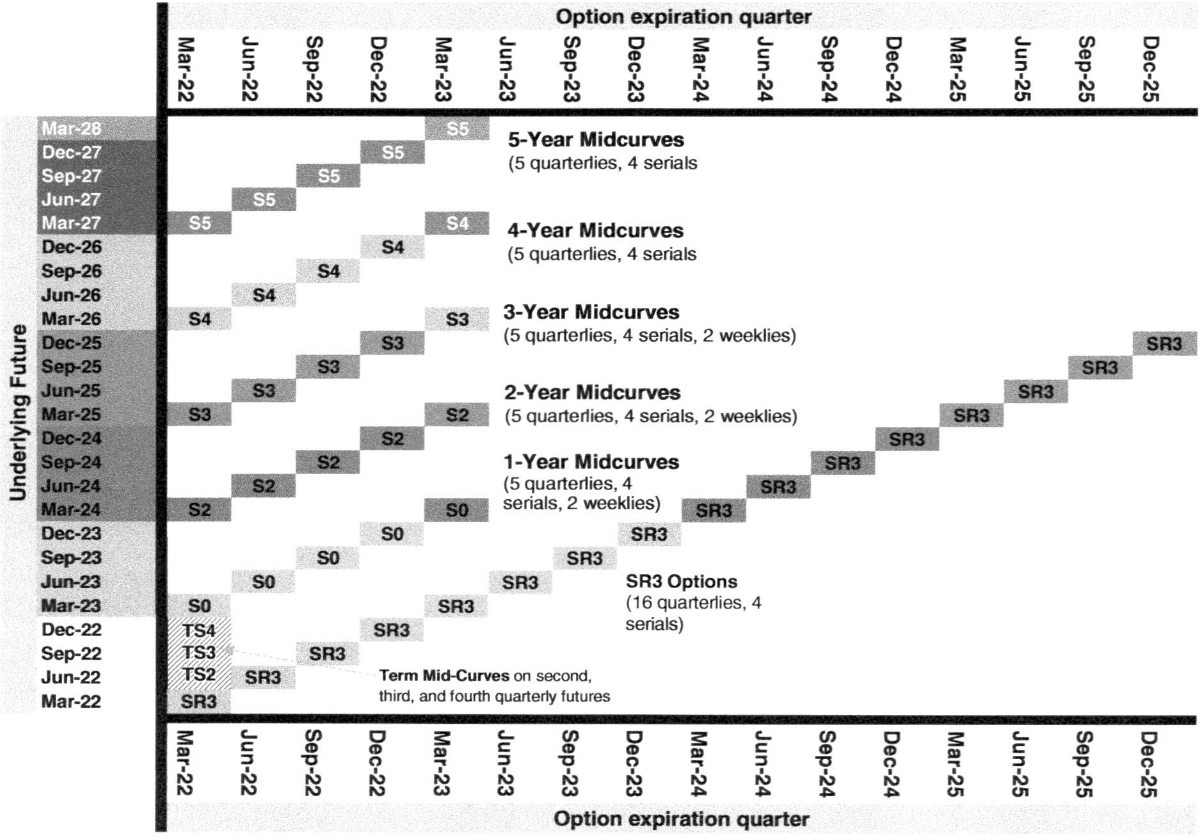

FIGURE 5.3 Options on SR3 futures

Source: CME (Kronstein, Trading SOFR Options, December 2019, Exhibit 1)

end trading before their reference quarters begin. To be more precise, options on SOFR futures end trading on the Friday preceding the third Wednesday of the contract month, while options on ED futures end trading on the Monday preceding the third Wednesday of the contract month – the day on which the SOFR value for Friday is published. As a result, options on SOFR futures end trading not only well before the underlying future ends trading (one business day before the end of the reference quarter), but also before its reference quarter begins, unlike options on ED futures, which end trading at the same time as their underlying contract and thereby cover the full period of the future strip.

This difference has major implications for the usability of future options for hedging caps and floors:

- When options on ED contracts end trading, they refer to the same 3M LIBOR term rate that is used in caps and floors. Hence, a LIBOR-based cap or floor can be easily and (more or less) perfectly hedged with a strip of ED future options, depending on how far the real situation is away from the ideal assumptions.[3] Unlike options on SOFR futures, which end trading at about the same time as options on ED contracts, they cover the 3M *term* rate underlying LIBOR-based caps and floors.
- When options on 3M SOFR contracts end trading, the reference quarter begins, which determines the value of the SOFR-based cap or floor. If volatility were to increase during the reference quarter, it would affect the value of the cap or floor – but there simply exists no option on 3M SOFR futures to hedge against this move anymore. Thus, even an ideal IMM SOFR-based cap or floor *cannot* be fully hedged with a strip of 3M SOFR future options. In fact, during the reference quarter determining the value of the cap or floor, a hedger could in theory only apply delta-hedging via the front-month contract but would remain exposed to changes in volatility, among other things. And if he uses other options, either other SOFR futures options or OTC derivatives, he incurs spread and model risk and/or high costs.

In general, when the analytic and hedging concepts can be easily transferred from LIBOR to SOFR (futures), SOFR-based products enjoy the easy and cheap hedgeability of LIBOR-products, with the low hedging costs for dealers translating into low transaction costs for end users. When this is not the case, however, the transition from LIBOR to SOFR results in greater hedging costs and thus greater transactions costs. As we have described

---

[3]In order to achieve a perfect match, in addition to matching dates as in an IMM cap or floor one would need to assume that the cap is an American option, which is usually not the case.

in Chapter 3 the higher hedging costs of the SOFR term-rate relative to LIBOR, SOFR-based caps and floors are likely to suffer from higher hedging costs than their LIBOR-based counterparts. While in the example of the ideal LIBOR-based cap mentioned above a dealer can make use of the cheap and liquid strip of ED future options for hedging and therefore offer tight bid–ask spreads for the cap, a dealer pricing a SOFR-based cap faces the problem of the 3M SOFR futures option market not offering a hedging instrument during the reference quarter. The dealer therefore either needs to accept unhedged exposure or engage in complex and costly hedging, for example, via OTC derivatives or via using options on 1M SOFR futures as well.[4] In both cases, higher hedging costs are likely to result in wider bid–ask spreads.

Moreover, the different ease of hedging SOFR-based swaps with SOFR futures versus the difficulty of hedging SOFR-based caps and floors with SOFR future options may explain why the liquidity in the former has been off to a much better start than in the latter. At the time of writing (Dec 2021), liquidity in options on SOFR futures was still very poor. Hence, while the comprehensive suite of options on ED contracts has been replicated for SOFR contracts (with the important exception of the last 3M), this was still a largely *theoretical* market, which could hardly be analyzed and traded in practice. During the editing process of this book in the first half of 2022, liquidity has started to pick up. The monthly Rates Recap published by the CME is a good source to obtain information about the current liquidity situation (CME February 2022).[5]

OVERVIEW OF GENERAL VOLATILITY ANALYSIS

Conceptually, one can classify option analysis and trading in two categories:[6]

- **Implied versus realized volatility.** The relationship between the two is achieved via delta hedging and used in the Black-Scholes formula. A consequence is that the current implied volatility quoted in the option market reflects (or, should reflect) the market consensus about the realized

---

[4]Resulting in a gap or overlap, as discussed below.
[5]The CME Group described the situation in February 2022, when the first meaningful trading in options on SOFR futures took place.
[6]Huggins and Schaller (2013) Chapter 17 contains a brief summary of option theory, and to which we will refer frequently. We assume familiarity with the basic concepts of options.

volatility of the underlying rate over the life of the option. A view that the realized volatility will be higher than implied can be expressed by buying the option (at the premium determined by the current implied volatility) and delta hedging it. This requires sufficient sensitivity (gamma) of the delta to changes in the yield level and is therefore only practical with options with a short time to expiry (e.g., 3M).

- **Implied versus implied volatility.** In contrast, options with a long time to expiry (e.g., 5Y) have a low gamma and are thus largely independent from moves in the underlying (hence unsuitable for delta hedging). In other words, options with a long time to expiry can be analyzed and traded almost in isolation from their underlying and its realized volatility. Taken together with their high vega, this makes them suitable for expressing views on the future *implied* volatility. For example, the expectation that implied volatility will increase over the next few months can be expressed by buying a straddle with 5Y expiry and unwinding it after a few months. The lower sensitivity of long expiry options to their underlying instruments also makes them suitable for analyzing and trading the relationships between implied volatility, for example, via a principal components analysis (PCA) on the volatility surface or cube (Huggins and Schaller 2013, p. 336).

In summary, options with short expiries are suitable for expressing views about the future *realized* volatility (relative to their price, i.e., their current implied volatility) via delta hedging; options with long expiries are suitable for expressing views about the future *implied* volatility (relative to their price, i.e., their current implied volatility). Correspondingly, *spreads* between options with short expiry are suitable for expressing views about the future *realized* volatility *curve* (i.e., for RV trades of the future realized volatility curve versus the current implied volatility curve); *spreads* between options with long expiry are suitable for expressing views about the future *implied* volatility *curve* (i.e., for RV trades of the future implied volatility curve versus the current implied volatility curve) (Huggins and Schaller 2013, p. 346).

When applying these general concepts to options on SOFR futures, we face the problem of low liquidity. Specifically, the first step for analyzing implied volatility is the creation of constant time-to-expiry and constant delta time series, for example, by calibrating an (SABR-)model to the volatility cube. One can then analyze the historical behavior and relationships between the implied volatility of different parts of the volatility cube and consider mismatches, e.g., PCA residuals, as candidates for trading opportunities. While options on futures are in principle a good area for this analysis due to their usually low transaction costs, the preconditions for this analysis are still lacking, since in the absence of a liquid market it could only observe its own assumptions rather than actual prices.

Given this situation, we focus first on analyzing the realized volatility of SOFR futures, which is independent of both the missing pricing model and the missing liquidity of options, and we describe the distribution of realized volatility over the secured yield curve and its evolution over time. We will then mention the connection of this analysis of realized volatility with implied volatility and describe possible trades. Since there exist some attractive trading strategies with options on SOFR futures, in particular spread positions versus options on ED contracts, this could support the migration to a liquid SOFR future options market.

DISTRIBUTION OF REALIZED VOLATILITY OVER THE SECURED YIELD CURVE

For analysts, the introduction of SOFR futures is a milestone in general, as they provide market prices for secured rates for consecutive 3M forward periods. This allows *repeating* the analytic methods developed for the unsecured curve (e.g., the ED future strip) for the secured curve and to *add* an analysis of the spread, i.e., the unsecured–secured basis. Applying this general idea to options, we will first *repeat* the analysis of realized volatility for the secured yield curve as given by 3M SOFR contracts and then *extend* it considering the *spreads* between realized volatility on the secured and unsecured yield curves.

The time series of SOFR futures has allowed us in Chapter 2 to extract a history of consecutive 3M forward rates for the secured yield curve and allows us now to calculate a history of the realized volatility curve for *secured* rates. While this has been possible for unsecured rates via ED futures for many years, the concentration of liquidity in the repo market on overnight market has until now prevented the transfer of this analysis to the market for secured lending.

Using the SOFR future data shown in Figure 2.5, we have calculated the evolution of the realized volatility curve (normal volatility, annualized) for secured rates over time and exhibit the results in Table 5.1. In more detail, we have divided the dates into approximate reference quarters, spanning from the 20th of March to the 20th of June, etc. The beginning of these 3M periods is indicated by "Jun-18" etc. in Table 5.1. We have then calculated the realized volatility for each of the SOFR futures during these 3M periods and thereby obtained the realized volatility curve for consecutive 3M forward periods. "3M," "6M," etc. in Table 5.1 refer to the approximate forward dates. For example, the first entry of 12 bp for "Jun-18/3M" refers to the

TABLE 5.1 Realized volatility in different parts of the secured rate curve over time (normal in bp, annualized)

	3M	6M	9M	12M	15M	18M	21M	24M
Jun-18	12	19	24	29	32	32	33	#N/A
Sep-18	13	22	28	35	39	42	44	45
Dec-18	23	36	45	54	60	64	67	67
Mar-19	24	53	68	77	83	85	85	83
Jun-19	68	85	91	99	102	104	104	104
Sep-19	38	55	64	73	78	81	84	85
Dec-19	92	84	79	76	76	78	81	83
Mar-20	13	17	19	22	26	29	35	39
Jun-20	6	8	8	10	11	13	16	16
Sep-20	5	6	7	9	10	11	13	15
Dec-20	7	8	8	7	9	12	19	28
Mar-21	7	6	6	8	15	21	29	39
Jun-21	6	6	9	16	23	33	44	53

Source: Authors, based on data from CME

realized volatility of the Sep 2018 SOFR future during the time period from 20 June 2018 to 19 Sep 2018, i.e., roughly during the period of the reference quarter of the *previous* contract.

Figures 5.4 and 5.5 slice through the two dimensions of Table 5.1. This corresponds to the slicing of Figures 2.6 and 2.7 for the level of consecutive 3M forward rates. Figure 5.4 depicts the evolution of the realized volatility in different consecutive 3M forward periods over time. Overall, realized volatility has increased as the Fed started to cut rates, but it reached its peak well before the Fed was done cutting. Unsurprisingly, realized volatility has been low across the curve as long as interest rates were expected to be anchored close to zero for an extended period of time. More recently, uncertainty about the future path of Fed policy has affected volatility in the longer part of the curve more than at the short end. The specific behavior of the shortest part of the curve, which has reached the peak well after the other parts, is remarkable.

Figure 5.5 shows the realized volatility curve at different points in time. With the exception of the period covering 20 Dec 2019 to 19 Mar 2020 (corresponding to the peak of realized volatility for the shortest part just mentioned), realized volatility curves have been upward sloping, reflecting uncertainty about Fed policy increasing with the forwards.

Chapters 2 and 5 have illustrated how SOFR futures allow transferring established analytic concepts from the unsecured to the secured yield

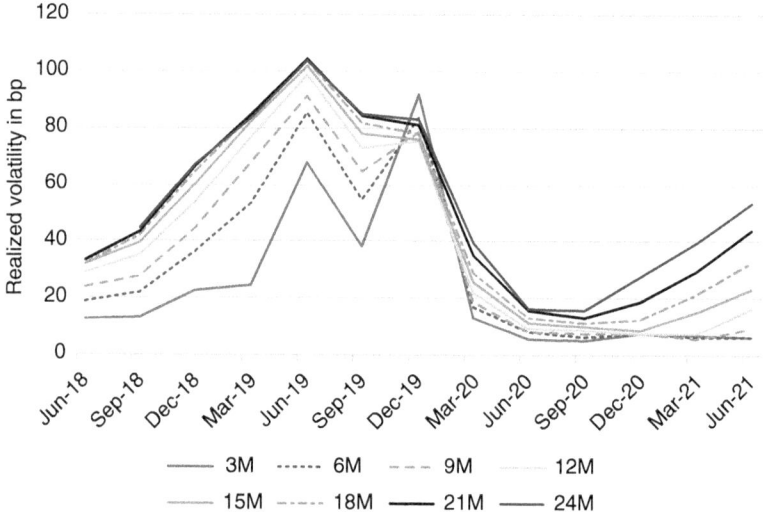

FIGURE 5.4 Realized volatility (normal in bp, annualized) of the secured rate curve
Source: Authors, from CME data

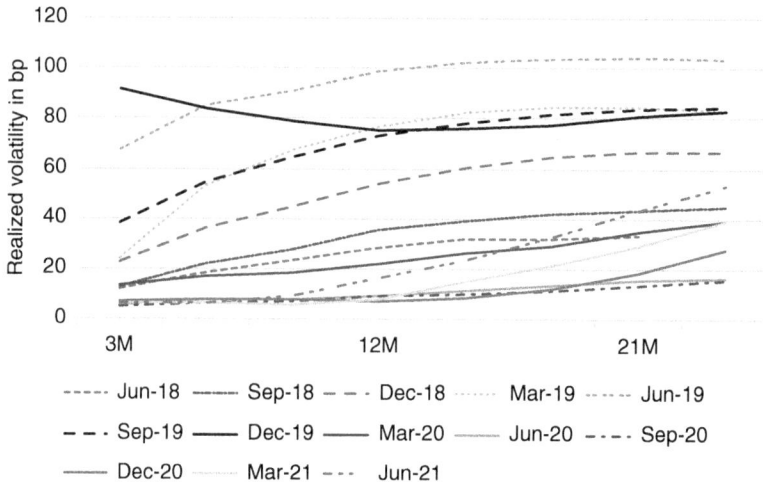

FIGURE 5.5 Realized volatility (normal in bp, annualized) of the secured rate curve
Source: Authors, from CME data

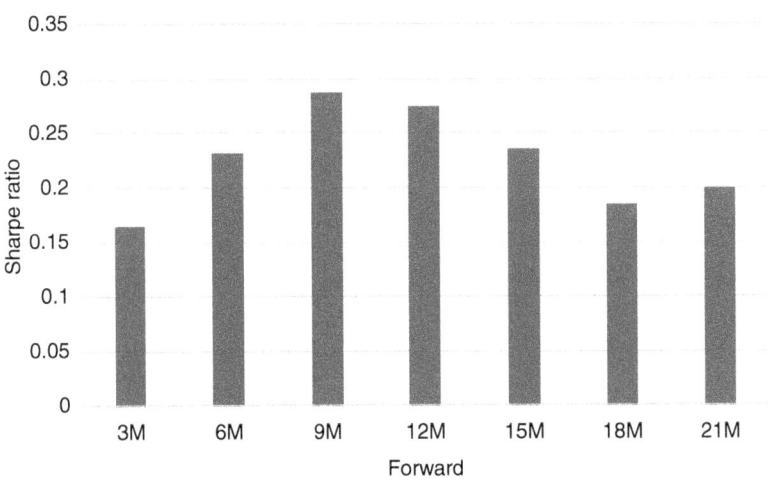

FIGURE 5.6 Average Sharpe ratios for the SOFR future curve
Source: Authors, from CME data

curve and its volatility. Combining both,[7] one can replicate the analysis from Burghardt (2011) and Ilmanen (1995) and calculate the historical average Sharpe ratios for investing in different consecutive 3M forward periods of the *secured* yield curve. Figure 5.6 shows the results of this exercise, i.e., the Sharpe ratio of holding a SOFR future corresponding to a specific consecutive 3M forward part ("3M," "6M," etc. in Table 5.1), taking the average over the 3M holding periods ("Jun-18," "Sep-18" etc. in Table 5.1). It appears that the Sharpe ratio is highest around the 9M forward point on the secured yield curve, which remarkably is quite in line with the results from Burghardt and Ilmanen from years earlier.

Given the short time period of available data, the results of these analyses should be considered to be preliminary, and they need to be repeated when a longer history – post SRF introduction – will have become available.

CURRENT IMPLIED VERSUS HISTORICAL REALIZED VOLATILITY

While an illiquid market prevents *historical* implied volatility analysis (e.g., via a PCA on the volatility cube), it is still possible to compare *current*

---

[7]The goal of this combination is the reason why we have used the same approximate reference quarters in Chapter 2.

implied volatility quotes, whenever they are observable, with the historical realized volatility. Graphically, this can be done by adding the current implied volatility curves in the chart (Figure 5.5) depicting the historical evolution of realized volatility curves. Figure 5.7 shows an example with the implied levels for ATM forward quarterly standard options observed on Dec 10 and 17, 2021.

This comparison allows assessing which historical realized volatility scenario is implied by the current market, both with regards to the overall level of volatility and to the shape of the volatility curve (Huggins and Schaller 2013, p. 327). If it turns out that the current implied volatility curve is extreme or abnormal relative to the range of historical realized volatility curves, it may be a candidate for an implied versus realized volatility (curve) trade via delta hedging, as described above. Also, analysts can use Figure 5.7 to assess which Fed policy scenario is currently implied in the SOFR future options market and, in case their view differs from the implied scenario, use these instruments to express their view via an option (curve) trade.

Again, the limited length of SOFR history still limits the strength of this analysis. In general, it is subject to the structural break due to the introduction of the SRF described in Chapter 1. In particular, the data of Figure 5.7 contain no realized volatility curve calculated during a period of sustained Fed rate hikes. In order to illustrate how this analysis could be performed

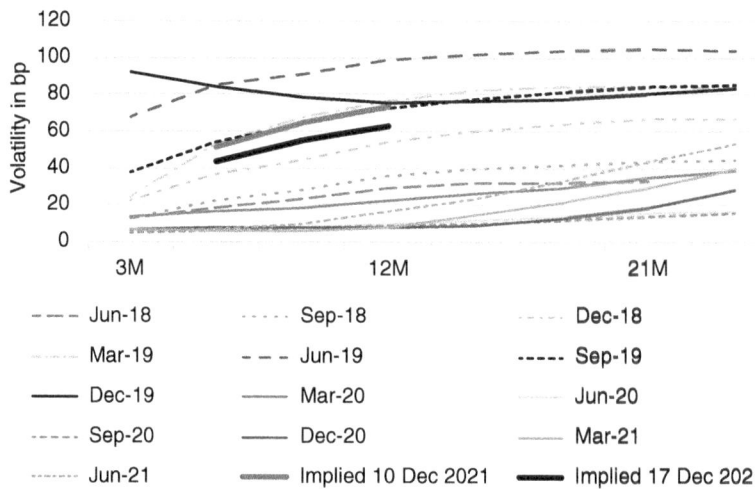

FIGURE 5.7 "Current" implied versus historical realized volatility along the secured rate curve
Source: Authors, from CME data

once enough (post-SFR) data will have become available, let us counterfactually assume that the range of historical realized volatility curve scenarios shown in Figure 5.7 was complete. One could then conclude that the implied volatility curve as of December 10, 2021, was both on a high level and steep relative to the range of historically observed realized volatility curves. If an analyst does not see a good reason for this (and speculation about Fed hikes could be such a good reason not reflected in the data yet), there are two possible trades:

1. **A position on the *level* of implied versus realized volatility.** This involves selling options on SOFR futures and delta hedging them, thereby obtaining the difference between the (high) current implied volatility and (expected lower) realized volatility as profit. In this case, the *shape* of the current implied volatility curve can be used for selecting the best (i.e., most overvalued) option for this trade. While the shape of the volatility curve is not directly traded, it influences the asset selection.

2. **A position on the *slope* of the implied versus realized volatility *curve*.** This involves selling 12M and buying 6M options on SOFR futures and delta hedging both of them, thereby obtaining the difference between the (high) steepness of the current implied volatility curve and the (expected flatter) realized volatility curve as P&L. This possibility directly trades the shape of the volatility curve.

Usually, the second alternative involves higher transaction costs, some of which can be mitigated by margin offsets, but also lower risk due to a (perhaps imperfect[8]) hedge of the exposure to the overall level of volatility. Which one of the two possibilities is best in a given situation can be assessed by calculating their Sharpe ratios (after transaction and delta hedging costs) in several different scenarios. When selecting the second alternative, the different expiries of the options also need to be considered, as delta hedging until (close to) the expiry of the shorter option is typically not practicable.

Figure 5.7 also contains the implied volatility curve for Dec 17, 2021, after a Fed meeting which clarified the future policy to a certain extent. As one would expect, the lower uncertainty has resulted in a lower overall level of implied volatility, while the implied volatility curve has remained steep. Under the counterfactual assumptions and caveats from above, on Dec 10, 2021, the first alternative might have been better (and performed well during

---

[8]Since the level of volatility can also affect the slope of the volatility curve. The hedge can therefore be perfected by accounting for this effect, e.g., by using PCA-weightings, as explained in Huggins and Schaller (2013, p. 339).

the first week), while on Dec 17, 2021, the second alternative might have offered the more attractive risk/return balance.

OPTIONS ON SOFR FUTURES VERSUS OPTIONS ON ED FUTURES

In the general discussion of the analytic implications of the introduction of a secured yield curve via SOFR futures to the universe of possible trades, we have claimed that, in addition to replicating the analysis for the unsecured yield curve (Chapter 2) and realized volatility curve (Chapter 5) for the secured yield curve, new analytic concepts between both have also become possible. Chapter 4 has provided the first steps for this new analysis of the secured–unsecured basis for the yield curve. This chapter extends it to the realized volatility curve.

The equation from Chapter 4 linking unsecured (LIBOR) and secured (repo) rates allowed the conclusion that the LIBOR–repo spread tends to increase when rates increase. This translates directly to an argument for higher (realized) volatility of LIBOR than of repo rates: When rates increase, LIBOR tends to increase more than repo; when rates decrease, LIBOR tends to decrease more than repo. Hence, LIBOR tends to move more than repo.

This argument has been used to explain the observation of (LIBOR-based) swaption volatility usually exceeding bond option volatility (Huggins and Schaller 2013, p. 325). Likewise, it can be used to explain the observation of ED future volatility usually exceeding SOFR future volatility visible in Figure 5.8.[9] However, as explained in Chapter 4, while the rate level remains an important factor driving the secured–unsecured basis (Table 4.2), it is not the *only* driving factor. Hence, whereas the argument is still valid, at times it may be overpowered by other influences. For example, the spikes in SOFR during 2019 may explain the "abnormal" period of realized SOFR future volatility exceeding realized ED future volatility.

Chapter 4 assessed the likely effects of the additional driving forces mentioned in Chapter 1 on the unsecured–secured basis. Translating the results in terms of realized volatility, an increase in the costs of executing the arbitrage between secured and unsecured lending rates gives more room for SOFR to

---

[9]In keeping with the method of Table 5.1, we have used a 3M rolling window for calculating the realized volatility, leading to the jumps in the time series. The (economically unjustified) jump at the end of the rolling window, i.e., 3M after the extreme move occurred, can be avoided by using an exponentially decaying weighting, as explained in Huggins and Schaller (2013, p. 329).

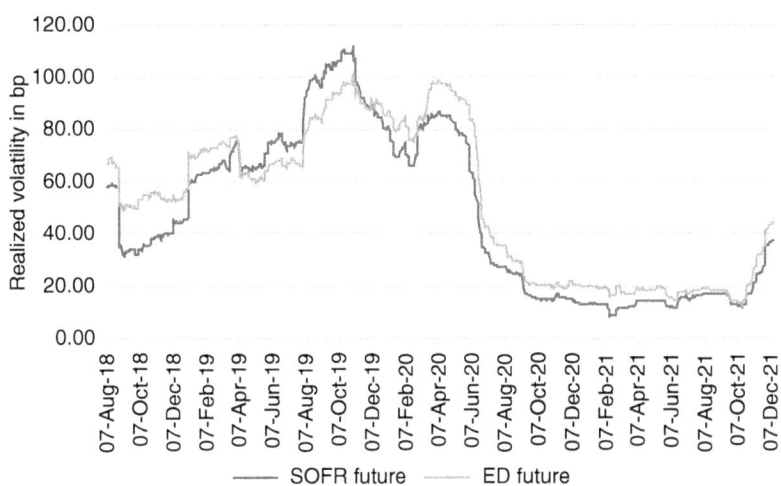

FIGURE 5.8 Realized volatility (normal in bp, annualized) of the Jun 2022 ED and SR3 futures
Source: Authors, from CME data

move. According to this analysis, when these costs increase, SOFR has more room to increase before hitting the arbitrage boundary. Hence, in times of high costs, for example, when the marginal bank faces balance sheet constraints, it is *possible* that the volatility in SOFR increases relative to the volatility of EFFR.[10] This may explain the atypical period of realized SOFR futures volatility exceeding realized ED futures volatility.

By contrast, the reaction of the Fed to these SOFR spikes of introducing the SRF has imposed an upper bound on SOFR but not on EFFR. In terms of realized volatility, the effect of this measure is therefore a reduction in realized SOFR volatility, both on an absolute level and relative to unsecured rates, which are not (directly) affected by the upper bound. In a certain sense, greater regulatory costs have relaxed the boundary for SOFR and the SRF has established a new boundary for SOFR. This may explain why, after the introduction of SRF, no atypical periods of realized SOFR future volatility exceeding realized ED future volatility have been observed.

---

[10] But this is not necessary. One can also read the relationship the other way round and state that when the costs of executing the arbitrage increase, EFFR has more room to fall before hitting the arbitrage boundary. Hence, an increase in capital costs can explain a general increase in realized volatility ("more room"), but not which of the two rates becomes more volatile. However, empirically the volatility of SOFR tends to increase relative to the volatility of EFFR in these instances.

Taken together, one might conclude that, while the argument for higher realized volatility of unsecured than secured rates based on the formula from Chapter 4 needs to be expanded with additional considerations, it is still largely valid.

Given the realized volatility relationship, a situation in which the implied volatility of options on SOFR futures exceeds the implied volatility of options on ED futures[11] can be considered as a potential trading opportunity, in particular if the Fed reaction to the SOFR spikes during 2019 is deemed sufficient to prevent repetitions.

In fact, analysts may want to monitor the STIR market for these additional opportunities provided by volatility spreads between secured and unsecured rates. Due to the significant margin offset between options on ED and SR3 contracts, future markets provide a much cheaper way to trade the general argument of the realized volatility of unsecured rates usually exceeding the realized volatility of secured rates than by trading swaptions versus bond options. And the suitability of options on SOFR futures for these RV trades versus options on ED futures may support the migration of liquidity toward the former.

OPTIONS ON 1M SOFR FUTURES: PRODUCT SUITE AND SPECIFICATIONS

Since May 2020, options on the 1M SOFR futures (SR1) contract also have been listed (CME April 2020). The product suite is summarized in Figure 5.9, while the main technical specifications are listed in Figure 5.10.

The key difference to the specifications of options on 3M SOFR futures is that both the 1M SOFR futures contract and the options on it end trading on the same day, i.e., on the last business day of the contract month. This difference in specifications has two major consequences:

1. Unlike options on 3M SOFR futures, options on 1M SOFR futures undergo the transmogrification into an exotic Asian option during their lives.
2. Unlike options on 3M SOFR futures, options on 1M SOFR futures provide a complete series of hedging instruments for caps and floors.

---

[11]After adjusting for the fundamental difference between standard and exotic options, for which task the missing pricing model for options on SOFR futures is required.

Expiries	Monthly Standard Options for each of the nearest 4 months
Strikes	Intervals of 6.25 bp for a range of 62.5 bp around ATM
	Intervals of 12.5 bp for a range of 125 bp around ATM
	(ATM being determined as the strike price closest to the future settlement price of the previuous business day)

FIGURE 5.9 1M SOFR future options: product suite
Source: Authors, based on CME

Contract size	USD 41.67 per basis point (USD 4,147 per point per option contract)
Style	American
Exercise	By notification by 5.30 pm CT of the day of exerise
	Automatic exercise of ITM options after expiration
Trading venues and hours	CME Globex: 5pm to 4pm, Sun-Fri
	CME ClearPort: 5pm to 4 pm Sun-Fri
Last trading day	Last business day of the contract month
	(i.e., on the same day as the underlying 1M SOFR future)
Minimum tick size	0.25 bp (USD 10.4175)
Block trade minimum size	250 contracts — Asian Trading Hours (4pm–12am, Mon–Fri on regular business days and at all weekend times)
	500 contracts — European Trading Hours (12am–7am, Mon–Fri on regular business days)
	1000 contracts — Regular Trading Hours (7am–4pm, Mon–Fri on regular business days)

FIGURE 5.10 1M SOFR future options: technical specifications
Source: Authors, based on CME

Thus, by virtue of the specifications of options on 1M contracts, at least there is a complete strip available for hedging purposes. But the tradeoff is that there is no pricing model. Extending the strip until the end of the life of the future closes the gap versus caps and floors – by extending the life of the options into the period when they become exotic.

When considering options on 1M SOFR contracts, the problem of dealing with Asian options cannot be avoided any longer, as it could be avoided by exploiting its exclusion by the specifications of options on 3M SOFR futures. And the choice of arithmetic averaging and American-exercise type in the specifications for options on 1M SOFR futures results in one of the most difficult pricing problems, which will be described below.

The other way around, the characteristics of Asian options can explain some of the behavior observed during the reference period of SOFR futures, specifically the decreasing volatility of the underlying future contract during its reference period due to the increasing number of SOFR values becoming fixed. (See Figure 2.5 and Chapter 9.) In fact, while options ending at the beginning of the reference period face the issue of unstable Greeks immediately before expiry, this problem is mitigated by the decreasing sensitivity of the underlying futures contract during its reference period. Intuitively speaking, while the gamma of an at-the-money (ATM) option goes toward infinity as the option approaches expiry, independent of whether the expiry is set at the beginning or at the end of the reference quarter, at the end of the reference quarter the volatility of the underlying SOFR future goes to zero, which might solve the problem. In the absence of a pricing model there is currently no way to quantitively express and to prove the intuition behind this argument (unless one relies on boundary conditions).

In Chapter 10, we will cover the second of these two major consequences in more detail and discuss hedging caps and floors with a combination of options on 3M and 1M SOFR futures. For the moment, we note that while it is possible in principle to hedge a cap or floor with calendar monthly resetting dates with a strip of options on 1M SOFR futures, the limited product suite limits the reach of this hedging method in two dimensions:

- As options on 1M SOFR futures are limited to the next four months (compare Figures 5.1 and 5.10), only very short caps or floors can be hedged with them alone. For longer caps and floors, a combination of options on 3M and 1M contracts must be used. But since the dates do not match, there will be either an overlap or a gap between the strip of options on 3M and the strip of options on 1M futures. And in the absence of a pricing model, it will be hard to assess and hedge the overlap or gap – leading to higher bid–ask spreads again.
- The strike prices of options on 1M SOFR futures do not cover a very large range. Thus, for hedging far out-of-the-money caps and floors, only the strikes of options on 3M SOFR futures can match the strikes – but not the period of the cap or floor to be replicated or hedged.

While the need to deal with Asian options is necessary if we want a complete series of hedging instruments, leading to an unavoidable mathematical complication of the transition from LIBOR to SOFR, some of the specifications seem to make the migration unnecessarily difficult:

- The product suite of options on 1M SOFR futures could be expanded to cover a wider range of periods and strikes.

- Applying daily compounding (rather than using an arithmetic average) also for 1M SOFR futures, which we recommended in Chapters 2 and 3 for different reasons, would also result in much easier pricing of the options, as discussed below. The ensuing difference to the specifications of FF futures could be solved by applying daily compounding to all STIR futures contracts.
- If options on 3M SOFR futures ended trading together with their underlying contract (as do options on 1M SOFR futures), there would at least exist a complete strip of hedging instruments for caps and floors. And since these involve daily compounding, the pricing problem seems to be somewhat easier to solve.
- This could also be an opportunity to consider European-style exercise rather than American-style exercise for options on both the 1M and 3M SOFR futures. For Asian options of the European type using geometric averaging, a pricing formula already exists. An additional advantage is the alignment of the hedging instrument with caps and floors, which usually are of the European type. And again, the ensuing difference to the specifications of FF and ED futures could be solved by switching all STIR contracts to the European-exercise type.

At the time of writing, liquidity in options on SOFR futures is still held back by both the absence of a pricing model and the absence of a complete product range for hedging caps and floors. In turn, the low liquidity of options on SOFR contracts seems to hold back the full migration from ED futures, since capped or floored loans can still be more effectively hedged with options on ED contracts. In order to complete the transition and to enjoy a functioning option market for the key money market rate after the switch to SOFR, a concerted effort of academics, market participants, and the CME seems necessary, with the specifications taking into account the current status and further evolution of pricing models.

OVERVIEW OF AVAILABLE PRICING MODELS FOR ASIAN OPTIONS

All pricing models for Asian options in the literature known to us treat the European exercise type only (Horvath and Medvegyev 2016 contains a relatively easy introduction). Applying them to the American type of CME's options on SOFR futures is therefore a general and presumably difficult problem.

Assuming continuous geometric Brownian motion and a geometric average as determinant of the payoff of the option, the Black-Scholes approach can be replicated to price Asian options fulfilling these conditions. From this starting point, Asian options that do not satisfy these conditions have been tackled in various ways:

- When an arithmetic average is used as determinant of the payoff of the option (which is more common in the market than a geometric average), there does not seem to exist a pricing formula. Instead, Monte Carlo simulations (applying the geometric average as control variate) (Kemna and Vorst 1990), Laplace transformations (Geman and Yor 1993), and approximations/boundaries (Vyncke, Goovaerts, and Dhaene 2003) have been studied.
- The second relaxation of the assumptions required for application in actual markets is the replacement of continuous with discrete processes. Vyncke, Goovaerts, and Dhaene (2003) present an analytic approximation for an arithmetic average over a discrete process. As the first and second moments match, the approximation allows calculating the Greeks. We have implemented and tested this model in the iron ore complex.
- Finally, and of key importance for money markets dealing with jumps, a wider variety of processes is allowed. Fusai and Meucci (2008) tackle Asian options on discretely monitored Lévy processes, which include mixed jump-diffusion models, and obtain (via Fourier transformations) a pricing formula for geometric averages and (via recursive integration) a formula for the moments for arithmetic averages.

Checking the available models for their suitability to price options on SOFR futures, we find:

- The general problem of American versus European type: Since all literature known to us assumes European type, either the literature needs to be transferred to the American type (which does not seem trivial), or CME needs to change the specifications to European (which seems to be the easier of the two possibilities).
- Options on 1M SOFR futures, which use an arithmetic average, are subject to the generally harder accessibility compared to the geometric average. The usual approach of the papers mentioned above is to transfer the results from the geometric to the arithmetic case, thereby needing to replace pricing formulas with approximations or simulations.
- Options on 3M SOFR futures use compounding according to the ISDA formula from Chapter 2. Unfortunately, the method of multiplying the SOFR value with the number of the days for which it is used (e.g., with three, in case of a weekend) results in the settlement rate of 3M SOFR

futures being theoretically different from a strict geometric average. Particularly at the current low interest rate level, however, it seems likely that this difference is negligible from a practical point of view. There is thus reason for optimism that options on 3M SOFR futures can be treated as settling to a geometric average, which is relatively easy to access, and for which pricing formulas exist in case of European-exercise Asian options.

▦ Taking into account the importance of jumps (due to Fed policy changes) in the money market, models only allowing for (geometric) Brownian motion seem rather unsuitable for our task. In Chapter 2, we surveyed a few possible processes for pricing futures, with a mixed jump-diffusion process (with drift) being the most general form. Fortunately, these processes are all covered by the Lévy process treated in Fusai and Meucci (2008).

A POSSIBLE ROAD MAP TOWARD PRICING OPTIONS ON SOFR FUTURES DURING THE REFERENCE PERIOD

Given the situation the practical dealer in options on money market futures has been put in by the migration from LIBOR to SOFR and the imperfect theoretical remedies available, the following describes steps for one possible way forward:

1. **The choice of model is fundamental.** As discussed at the end of Chapter 2, a mixed jump-diffusion process (potentially with drift) seems to be both conceptually reasonable (covering jumps from Fed policy changes and also unrelated volatility) and practicable. This process could be used to price both SOFR futures and their options, thereby avoiding mismatches from using different models for both. By contrast, this process is different from the simple jump-only step function used for CME's term rate. As discussed in Chapter 3, this is likely to result in mismatches between futures and options on one hand (priced via a jump-diffusion model) and the term rate (priced via a step function). However, as a pure step function is unsuitable to price options, this mismatch is unavoidable – as long as the CME sticks to its term rate calculation. If a trader is only concerned with pricing SOFR futures, he can consider using the same approach that CME applies for the term rate; once he also deals in options, he will encounter mismatches due to different models and can only choose where the discrepancy occurs – between futures and the term rate on one hand (both using jump-only) and options on the other hand, or between

futures and options on one side (both using mixed jump-diffusion) and the term rate on the other side.

Moreover, it needs to be determined whether the model should incorporate the spread between secured and unsecured rates by being calibrated to all STIR contracts at once. (See Chapters 2 and 4.) While this is advisable when focusing on the effect of the secured–unsecured basis on the relative pricing in the STIR universe, as we did in the last chapter, when applied to options, it would incorporate the spread between *standard* options on unsecured rates (ED and FF contracts) and *exotic* options on secured rates (SOFR contracts), i.e., add another layer of complexity to an already difficult task. Hence, for dealing with options, separate models for unsecured and secured rates seem to be more practicable. Here, the model tradeoff therefore is between the applicability for analyzing the secured–unsecured basis and the practicability for option pricing.

Finally, as mentioned in Chapter 2, a key consideration is the link between the jumps and the mean reversion (drift) in the model. For example, one needs to decide whether a rate hike should be treated as part of the mean reversion or not (and hence the mean being shifted to the same extent).

2. **Based on the model selection, the appropriate option pricing model needs to be developed by building on the available literature.** For our preferred process choice of a mixed jump-diffusion model, Fusai and Meucci (2008) seems to be a useful starting point, offering a pricing formula for geometric averages. Assuming 3M SOFR futures to be close enough to this assumption,[12] the only remaining major problem to be solved appears to be the adjustment from European- to American-style exercise. In the absence of a closed-form solution, numerical methods can be used to obtain an approximation.

3. **Finally, the pricing needs to work in practice.** This step requires data aggregation and encoding. In case of numerical methods such as Monte Carlo simulations being involved, the challenges and running time should not be underestimated (Horvath and Medvegyev 2016). Before being applied to actual trading, extensive testing is advisable. While at the time of writing, the illiquidity of the SOFR future options market prevents any testing, it is possible that by the time of publication, candidates for pricing models can be assessed against an actual market – and

---

[12]Recall that the compounding applied for 3M contracts can be considered to be close enough to geometric averaging for practical purposes.

vice versa enhance its liquidity by improving the usability of options on SOFR futures as hedging product.

Of these three steps, we will focus on the first one and assess in the next section the effect of model selection on the option prices – using our heuristic sheet from Chapter 2 in the absence of a pricing model.

IMPACT OF PROCESS SELECTION ON THE PRICING OF OPTIONS ON SOFR FUTURES

The first step of selecting a process is independent of the second step of selecting a pricing framework – and also independent of transition from standard to exotic options. In fact, the issue of choosing an appropriate process for modeling money market options is well known from pricing options on ED futures.[13] Under the realistic assumption of the Fed policy having a major effect on short-term rates, it makes sense to include jumps at the FOMC meeting dates (and maybe also around the quarter end) in the process. As described in Chapter 2, one may decide to use a combined jump-diffusion process or a spline with the FOMC meetings as external variables. The disadvantage of including jumps is that option-pricing models based on assuming continuous Brownian motion become unapplicable. Thus, one needs to build an option-pricing model accounting for the jumps. If one assumes that the rate is constant between the FOMC meetings (which is also unrealistic since it ignores all other sources of rate volatility), one can try and construct a tree. One problem with this approach is the unknown jump sizes, which could be addressed by allowing only 25 bp jumps, for example, resulting in a further move away from reality. And since high volatility often coincides with unscheduled FOMC meetings, this approach does not capture some of the biggest events for short rate volatility.

Similar to the way we used a similar spreadsheet in Chapter 2 to assess the influence of model and parameter selection on the pricing of SOFR futures, we can now expand this sheet to demonstrate the effects of different processes on the prices of options on SOFR futures. Again, we have simulated the evolution of SOFR via a Vasicek process with and without jumps. Of course, this approach can be subjected to the criticism we have just summarized in addition to the criticism from Chapter 2,

---

[13]In addition, the problem of options on ED futures being American while caps and floors are usually European options is also well known already from the LIBOR universe.

specifically the absence of a consideration of the link between the drift term of the Vasicek process and the jumps. Therefore, it should be considered as an initial heuristic attempt only.

The simulation is encoded in the Excel worksheet "Call simulation" accompanying this chapter, which is a slight modification and expansion of the sheet "SOFR future price simulation" from Chapter 2. We assume that on Jan 1, 2022, one wants to price a call on the Mar 2022 SR3 contract. During its reference quarter (from Mar 16 to Jun 15), there is one scheduled FOMC meeting, on May 4, 2022. Unlike in Chapter 2, we assume that there is zero probability for a change in Fed policy outside of this meeting, including on the two FOMC meetings before the start of the reference quarter.

Like in Chapter 2, column E defines the parameters for the Vasicek process and the probability distribution for the jump at the FOMC meeting(s). Based on this input, starting in row 15, the SOFR evolution is simulated, assuming the standard deviation to be the same for each calendar day. Again, we use only 200 simulations (in the columns), which is significantly too little. When used in a trading context, many more simulations, such as 1,000,000, are required. For each of the simulated paths, the payoff of a call (with the strike level being set in cell H1) is calculated – under the assumptions of a European-type option exercisable at the end of the reference quarter, i.e., the two changes to the specifications we have recommended above. The average payoff over all simulations is displayed in cell H4. Of course, this is not the option price as obtained via an option pricing model. The goal of the exercise is not to present a pricing model, but a heuristic framework to give a sense for the issues involved in process and parameter selection. In terms of the steps mentioned above, we try to get some sense for the process (step 1) to be used for building a pricing model (step 2).

Table 5.2 exhibits the results for a few different combinations of parameters for the jump-diffusion (and drift) process. For this table, we have only changed two parameters, the standard deviation of the diffusion process and the probability of the +25 bp jump at the May 4 FOMC meeting,[14] which allows displaying the results in the form of a matrix. The other parameters were kept stably at a SOFR start value on Jan 1, 2022, of 0.05%, a mean of 1.5%, a speed of mean reversion of 0.002, and a strike of 100.

---

[14]Assuming no probability for a cut; thus, if the probability for a +25 bp jump is shown as 80%, a probability of 20% was given to an unchanged Fed policy.

TABLE 5.2 Simulated average payoff of a call on the Mar 2022 SR3 future with a strike at 100 (annualized, bp)

		Standard deviation (ann)			
		0%	1%	2%	5%
Probability of a 25 bp hike	0%	0.0	1.9	6.3	20.2
	20%	0.0	1.8	6.1	19.2
	40%	0.0	1.5	6.0	18.3
	60%	0.0	1.3	4.8	17.6
	80%	0.0	1.1	4.5	17.0
	100%	0.0	1.0	4.3	16.6

Source: Authors

In line with the goal of this demonstration, we observe a high dependency of the results on the process and parameter selection:

- A pure jump process – under the assumption of no probability for a rate cut (and ignoring other considerations like margins) – results in an average payoff of 0.
- A pure diffusion and a combined jump-diffusion (with drift) process both assign a considerable value to a call with strike 100, with the value depending highly on the volatility parameter used for the Vasicek process.
- The difference between a pure diffusion process and a combined jump-diffusion (with drift) process can be assessed by comparing the first row of the table with the others. As anticipated, the pure diffusion process returns a higher average payoff for the call than the combined jump-diffusion process, since the latter also allows for a jump away from the strike. However, the impact of including a jump in the diffusion process, which is quite significant for low levels of the standard deviation (1%), fades away for higher numbers for the standard deviation (5%).

Hence, one can reach the same conclusion from Chapter 2 for SOFR futures for the options on these contracts as well. With the pricing being highly dependent on the choice of the process and its parameters, extensive research into step 1 is advisable before moving on to step 2 and building a pricing model. And even once the decision has been taken, it is useful to assess positions under different processes and parameters as well, for example, as a stress test. Imagine a trader using a pure jump process and coming up with a value of zero for the call priced above: Before selling these calls at negligible prices, he may want to look at their value in case of other sources for SOFR volatility apart from Fed policy via a glance at Table 5.2.

Moreover, while Table 2.2 may suggest that the diffusion term is not too relevant for pricing SOFR futures, and someone might argue that the drift from mean reversion can be captured to a certain extent in the jumps, Table 5.2 underlines the importance of the diffusion term for pricing options on SOFR futures. Hence, if the goal is to build a single model providing consistent pricing for both SOFR futures and options, using a mixed jump-diffusion process appears to be necessary. As mentioned above, this also means that the pricing model will be different from the one used for replicating and hedging CME's term rate.

After the process has been selected, the next step is to build a pricing model. To price the option during the reference period of its underlying future, the literature available for Asian options using that specific process needs to be surveyed. For our favorite process, a mixed jump-diffusion process (potentially with drift), Fusai and Meucci (2008) offer a good starting point. As they share the idealizing assumptions (European type expiring at the end of the reference period) of our simulation from above, the results from Table 5.2 can be compared with the numbers from Table 4 of Fusai and Meucci (2008). Given the unavailability of a pricing formula for American options, unless the reader is able to produce one, only numerical implementation is currently possible.[15]

By mandating the shift to SOFR as reference rate, regulators have – presumably inadvertently – posed a difficult theoretical problem for academics and a major practical problem for option market participants. We have tried to outline the three steps toward solving this problem and thereby enabling a liquid and functioning market in options on the key money market rate. We have also presented some evidence that a mixed jump-diffusion process could be the best choice in step 1.

There is some reason for optimism regarding step 2 given the amount of effort academics and market participants are currently putting in – with the size of money markets being a big motivation. During the editing process of this book, we became aware of several preprints with new contributions to the first two steps. While none of them appears to offer a complete solution, it is possible that by the time this book is published there will have been decisive progress and some clouds will have disappeared.

---

[15]Horvath and Medvegyev (2016) address some of the challenges involved.

6

Pricing Biases and SOFR Curve Building

Aprerequisite for a successful transition from LIBOR to SOFR is that market participants are able to construct a term structure of SOFR interest rates extending years into the future, making it possible to price SOFR loans, swaps, swaptions, caps, and similar instruments tied to SOFR rates over time. And given their relative liquidity, SOFR futures are an integral component in the construction of a SOFR term structure. In fact, for now, SOFR futures are often the only set of instruments used to construct a yield curve for the SOFR complex.

Market participants familiar with the LIBOR complex will be familiar with the key role that Eurodollar futures prices have played in the construction of LIBOR curves. And as part of that experience, they're likely to be familiar with the *convexity bias* attributed to Eurodollar futures. In particular, every quant worth his salt learns to adjust the prices of Eurodollar futures for this bias before using these prices as inputs to his LIBOR curve-building algorithm.

So before delving into the minutiae of SOFR yield curves, we'll consider whether SOFR futures might suffer from any similar biases that would require adjustment before using their prices to construct a SOFR term structure. And as a first step in that process, we'll review the situation for Eurodollar futures.

BIASES IN EURODOLLAR FUTURES PRICES

When considering potential biases afflicting SOFR futures prices, it's useful to remind ourselves of the biases present in their predecessor, the Eurodollar futures contract. These days, most academics and industry quants use the term *convexity bias* to refer to the difference between a Eurodollar futures rate and the forward LIBOR rate that covers the same period, often as embedded within a forward rate agreement. But this wasn't always the case.

The seminal paper on the difference between futures rates and forward rates is *The Relation Between Forward Prices and Futures Prices*, written by John Cox, Jonathan Ingersoll, and Stephen Ross, and published in the *Journal of Financial Economics* way back in 1981. Professors Cox, Ingersoll, and Ross (CIR) compared the relative prices of two contracts for forward settlement: a plain vanilla forward contract, and a futures contract. The only difference between the two was that the futures contract was subject to continuous margining while the forward contract was not.

In the event the futures price was positively correlated with the short-term interest rate paid on margin, the person who was long this contract would find that there was a tendency for him to earn a greater interest rate precisely when the balance in his margin account was greater and to earn a lower interest rate when the balance in his margin account was lower. Likewise, the person who was short this contract would find that there was a tendency for him to earn a lesser interest rate precisely when the balance in his margin account was greater and to earn a greater interest rate only when the balance in his margin account was relatively small.

Being averse to free lunches, people selling futures contracts require higher selling prices in exchange for being on the losing end of this proposition. And people buying futures contracts are willing to pay more for their positions, given their expectation that they'll be on the winning end of the proposition.

Note that we'd expect the situation to be reversed in the event the correlation between the futures price and the short-term interest rate were negative. In that case, the person holding the short position in the futures contract would find that he was benefiting from relatively greater interest rates precisely when the balance of his margin account was high, and he'd find that he was experiencing low interest rates precisely when the value of his margin account was low. Again, the person who was long this contract would experience the opposite effect. With the holder of the short position benefiting and the holder of the long position suffering, the two parties would be expected to transact at a relatively lower price than they would otherwise, to account for this effect.

One of the most important propositions in the CIR paper is that, *if* the short-term interest rate paid on margin is nonstochastic, *then* the futures price and the forward price should be equal. This would be the case trivially in the event that the interest rate was constant – or that there was no interest paid on margin at all.

More generally, if there were no correlation between the futures price and the short-term interest rate paid on margin, then the futures price and the forward price should be equal. This is trivially the case when the interest rate is nonstochastic.

The Eurodollar futures price is defined as 100 less the Eurodollar futures rate. And since the Eurodollar futures rate is positively correlated with the short-term interest rate paid on margin, the correlation between the Eurodollar futures price and the short-term interest rate is negative. And, following Cox, Ingersoll, and Ross (1981), we'd expect the futures price in that case to be *lower* than it would be otherwise, as a result of this financing effect. And with the futures price lower than it would be otherwise, we'd expect the futures rate to be *greater* than it would be otherwise.

Note that at no point in this argument did the concept of *convexity* make an appearance. These results are entirely motivated by the *financing* of profit and loss via the margining of the futures contract. And in the industry, that's precisely the term that was used to describe this effect – the *financing bias*. If the futures price is negatively correlated with the short-term interest rate, then the financing bias exists to balance the inherent advantage of the person who is short the futures contract.

In this case, how does convexity enter the picture?

NONLINEARITIES RESULTING FROM CONTRACT DEFINITIONS

Let's compare two instruments that derive their values from the same segment of a yield curve. And to abstract from extraneous issues, let's maintain the assumption that we're dealing with a riskless curve. In fact, we can assume that we're dealing with the SOFR curve. Finally, let's assume for the moment that there is no interest paid on margin, in which case the financing bias is equal to zero.

The first instrument will be a forward rate agreement (FRA), with the usual convention that the present value of the difference between R_S, the spot rate at time S (the expiration of the FRA), and φ_0, the FRA rate agreed at time 0, will be paid at time S. More specifically:

$$FRA\ payout = \frac{N\tau\left(\dfrac{\varphi_0}{100} - \dfrac{R_S}{100}\right)}{1 + \tau\left(\dfrac{R_S}{100}\right)}$$

This payout is meant to hedge the interest earned on the deposit, N, made at time S and held until time $T = S + \tau$. Adding this payout to the deposit of N (and simplifying), we see that the amount we have in our bank account at time S is given by

$$B_S = N + \frac{N\tau\left(\frac{\varphi_0}{100} - \frac{R_S}{100}\right)}{1 + \tau\left(\frac{R_S}{100}\right)}$$

The value of φ_0 is negotiated at time 0 so that the value at time 0 of the random FRA payout is equal to 0.

From this, the balance of our bank account at time T can be obtained by investing B_S at the rate R_S from time S to time T. Simplifying this, we have

$$B_T = N\left(1 + \tau\frac{\varphi_0}{100}\right)$$

From this equation, we see that φ_0 does indeed play the role of a forward rate, despite being paid at time S rather than time T – the reason being that it's the *present value* of $N\tau\left(\frac{\varphi_0}{100} - \frac{R_S}{100}\right)$ that is paid at time S.

The second instrument we'll consider will be styled after the Eurodollar futures contract – the only difference being that the final settlement price of the futures contract in this example will be $f_S = 100 - R_S$, where R_S is the term rate at time S for lending from time S to time T. Again, we assume that no interest is paid on margin balances.

The payout of this Eurodollar-style contract at time S is given by

$$Eurodollar\text{-}style\ payout = N\tau\left(\frac{r_0}{100} - \frac{R_S}{100}\right)$$

For example, if N is equal to USD 1 million and $\tau = 0.25$, then this payout is USD 25 per basis point difference between the futures rate, r_0, and the term rate at settlement, R_S, as is the case with the actual Eurodollar futures contract.

If we add this payout at time S to our cash investment of N at time S, we see that the balance of our bank account at time S will be

$$B_S = N + N\tau\left(\frac{r_0}{100} - \frac{R_S}{100}\right)$$

The balance of our account at time T can be determined by investing B_S at term rate R_S for the term $\tau = T - S$. In this case (and with some algebra), we have

$$B_T = N\left(1 + \tau\frac{r_0}{100}\right) + N\tau^2\frac{r_0}{100}\frac{R_S}{100} - N\tau^2\frac{R_S}{100}\frac{R_S}{100}$$

The first term in this equation, $N\left(1 + \tau\frac{r_0}{100}\right)$, is the amount we would want to have in our bank account at time T if r_0 were the forward rate at time 0 for lending from time S to time T.

The second and third terms, $N\tau^2\frac{r_0}{100}\frac{R_S}{100} - N\tau^2\frac{R_S}{100}\frac{R_S}{100}$, show the effect at time T of having the futures payout at futures expiry, time S, rather than at the end of the lending period, time T.

Figure 6.1 shows the all-in interest earned on the one-million-dollar deposit made at time S with the futures hedge and with the FRA hedge. In each case, the USD 1 million is invested at the prevailing term rate, R_S, along with the time S proceeds of the hedge, from time S to time T.

There are a few points worth noting.

1. The interest earned via the FRA hedge is not a function of R_S, the term rate at time S, because the payout at time S (the end date of the FRA and the settlement date of the futures contract) is the *present value* of the difference between the FRA rate and the term rate R_S (scaled by $N\tau$).

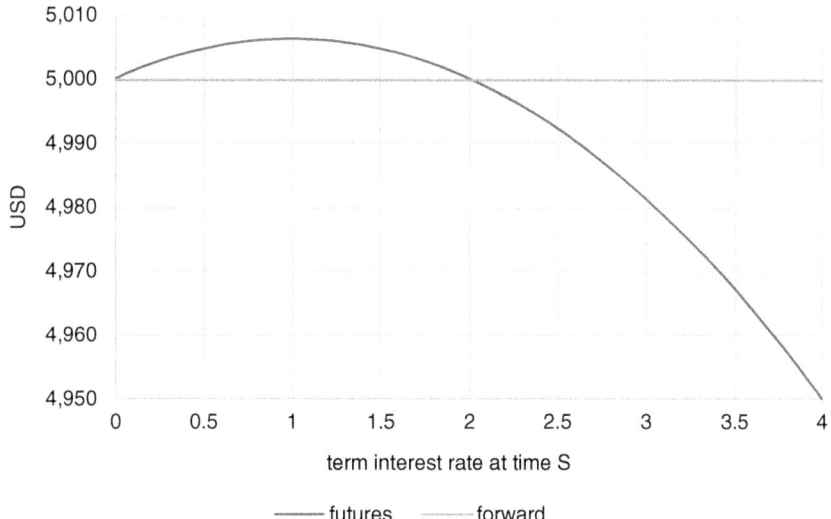

FIGURE 6.1 Time T values of all-in interest earned via futures and FRA hedges
Source: Authors

As a result, this is simply a constant (of USD 5,000 in this case, as the FRA rate was set to 2% in this example).

2. The interest earned via the futures hedge *is* a function of R_S, because the payout of the futures hedge gets reinvested at the rate R_S between times S and T.

3. Consistent with the formulae above, the interest earned through time T via the futures hedge is a strictly concave function of R_S. In fact, it's a parabola – i.e., it's quadratic in R_S.

We know from Jensen's inequality that the expected value of a concave function, $g(x)$, is less than or equal to the value of the function evaluated at the expected value of x. In algebraic terms, if $g(x)$ is a concave function of x, then

$$E[g(x)] \leq g(E[x])$$

Equality obtains in the event the standard deviation of x is zero.

Furthermore, the expected value of a concave function of $g(x)$ is a decreasing function of the standard deviation of x.

With this in mind, let's consider what that means for our concave function of R_S, shown in Figure 6.1.

First, the role of the market is to find a value for the futures rate so that the expectation of the value of the all-in interest as of time T is equal to the certain interest obtained in conjunction with the FRA hedge. When this futures rate is increased, this parabola shifts higher, increasing the expected value of the parabola, *ceteris paribus*. When the futures rate is decreased, the parabola shifts lower, decreasing the expected value of the parabola.

Second, the expected value of the parabola is a decreasing function of the standard deviation of R_S. When the standard deviation of R_S is large, the parabola needs to be higher than it would be in the event that the standard deviation of R_S is small.

The standard deviation of R_S is a function of two things. One is the amount of time that interest rates have been able to change since the trade was initiated at time 0. In particular, the standard deviation of R_S will be an increasing function of S (assuming the trade was initiated at time 0).

The other thing that affects the standard deviation of R_S is the volatility of rates generally and of R_S in particular. If rates are volatile, the standard deviation of R_S will be greater than it would be if volatility is low.

Taken together, all this implies that the required adjustment for nonlinearity is an increasing function of the time until the futures contract expires and an increasing function of the volatility of interest rates, everything else equal. (And as a reminder, we're still abstracting from the financing bias by assuming that no interest is paid on margin.)

From all this, we take away two main points:

1. There is a financing bias to consider, even when the contract in question is a simple, linear function of the interest rate underlying the contract. For example, if two counterparties decide to subject an FRA to standard futures-style margining, the FRA rate will be subject to a financing bias as well, assuming of course that the underlying FRA rate is correlated with the short-term interest rate paid on margin.
2. Even if we control for a financing bias (e.g., by considering a case in which there is no interest paid on margin), there is a nonlinearity involved when comparing an FRA rate with a Eurodollar futures rate. Because we compared the two rates at the *end* of the lending period they cover, the nonlinearity appeared to us in the form of the value of the futures payout being a *concave* function of the settlement rate, R_S.

Of course, the goal of this book is to understand SOFR futures rather than Eurodollar futures, so we won't go into any further detail concerning Eurodollar futures. (There's a considerable literature on this subject available for readers who would like to learn more.) But on the other hand, many people who approach the issue of biases in SOFR futures will attempt to apply their understanding of Eurodollar futures as a default template, so it's useful to review the issues here.

BIASES IN SOFR FUTURES

From the discussion of Eurodollar futures, we see there are two questions we should be asking about biases in SOFR futures.

1. Are SOFR futures prices subject to any biases due to nonlinearities?
2. Are SOFR future prices subject to a financing bias?

We'll see that the answer to the first question is *no* in the case of the three-month SOFR contract but *yes* in the case of the one-month contract. And we'll see that the answer to the second question is *yes, probably.*

Nonlinearities in the SOFR Futures Complex

The time T payout of a three-month SOFR futures contract is given by

$$3M \; SOFR \; payout = N\tau \left(\frac{R_0}{100} - \frac{R_T}{100} \right)$$

where

R_0 is the futures rate when the contract was purchased at time 0.

R_T is the settlement rate computed by compounding the daily SOFR values during the reference period.

and where N and τ are defined to be USD 1 million and 0.25 years respectively.

In addition to this payout from the futures contract, a person investing funds from time S to time T at the daily overnight SOFR values will see his balance grow from N to $N\left(1 + \tau\frac{R_T}{100}\right)$. Adding this balance to the funds obtained at time T via the futures hedge, we see that the combined value of his bank account at time T is given by

$$B_T = N\left(1 + \tau\frac{R_T}{100}\right) + N\tau\left(\frac{R_0}{100} - \frac{R_T}{100}\right) = N\left(1 + \tau\frac{R_0}{100}\right)$$

From which we see that R_0 indeed plays the role of a forward rate for the three-month SOFR futures contract. There is no nonlinearity involved that might require us to make an adjustment to the price of the contract before using it to construct a yield curve.

Unfortunately, the situation is not as straightforward when dealing with the one-month SOFR futures contract. In that case, the time T payout to the futures contract is given by

$$1M\ SOFR\ payout = N\tau\left(\frac{\gamma_0}{100} - \frac{\gamma_T}{100}\right)$$

where

γ_0 is the 1M futures rate when the contract was purchased at time 0.

γ_T is the settlement rate computed by *averaging* the daily SOFR values during the reference period.

Again, N and τ are defined to be USD 1 million and 0.25 years, respectively.

Again, a person investing funds from time S to time T at the daily overnight SOFR values will see his balance grow from N to $N\left(1 + \tau\frac{\psi_T}{100}\right)$, where ψ_T is the standard rate compounded during the one-month reference period:

$$\psi_T = 100\left[\left(\prod_{i=1}^{K}\left(1 + \frac{d_i}{360}\frac{r_i}{100}\right)\right) - 1\right]\frac{360}{D}$$

where

K is the number of business days in the one-month reference period.

d_i is the number of business days associated with the ith deposit.

r_i is the SOFR value for the ith business day.

D is the number of calendar days in the reference period.

Combining the funds earned via overnight lending and the funds received via the futures hedge, the total time T value of the account is

$$B_T = N\left(1 + \tau\frac{\psi_T}{100}\right) + N\tau\left(\frac{\gamma_0}{100} - \frac{\gamma_T}{100}\right) \neq N\left(1 + \tau\frac{\gamma_0}{100}\right)$$

We can write this expression in the form

$$B_T = N\left(1 + \tau\frac{\gamma_0}{100}\right) + N\tau\left(\frac{\psi_T}{100} - \frac{\gamma_T}{100}\right)$$

The second term on the right-hand side, $N\tau\left(\frac{\psi_T}{100} - \frac{\gamma_T}{100}\right)$, is a function of the difference between the actual futures settlement rate, γ_T, which is an arithmetic average of overnight SOFR values, and ψ_T, which is the futures settlement rate that would prevail in the event the one-month futures contract was settled the way the three-month futures contract was settled – i.e., with daily compounding rather than arithmetic averaging. In other words, if the one-month contract were settled the way the three-month contract was settled, the futures rate would be the forward rate corresponding to the one-month reference period. No adjustments would be required – at least no adjustments for nonlinearity. We'll get to questions of financing bias shortly.

What Can We Say about This Adjustment Without Making Use of a Specific Term Structure Model?

First, the daily compounded rate will be greater than the arithmetic average rate. To see this, we calculate the first derivative of the settlement futures rate as a function of each SOFR rate contained in the reference period. The first derivative of the settlement rate, R_T, with respect to one day's SOFR rate, r_k, is given by the expression

$$\frac{dR_T}{dr_k} = \frac{d_k}{D}$$

when using the simple arithmetic average, as in the case of the one-month contract. When using daily compounding, as per the three-month contract, the expression is

$$\frac{dR_T}{dr_k} = \left(1 + \frac{d_1}{360}r_1\right)\left(1 + \frac{d_2}{360}r_2\right)\cdots\left(1 + \frac{d_{k-1}}{360}r_{k-1}\right)$$

$$\times \left(1 + \frac{d_{k+1}}{360}r_{k+1}\right)\cdots\left(1 + \frac{d_N}{360}r_N\right)\frac{d_k}{D}$$

If all the rates are positive, then all the first derivatives are greater in the case of daily compounding. And if all the first derivatives are greater, then the settlement rate must also be greater. This result holds even in the case in which some of the SOFR values are zero, as long as none of the SOFR values are negative. (In the case in which all SOFR values are zero, the two settlement rates also will be zero.)

On the other hand, the difference between the rate calculated via daily compounding and the rate calculated via simple averaging is often quite small. Given the low levels of SOFR prevailing recently, the difference tends to be no more than a tenth of a basis point – and often less than that.

The differences do tend to increase with the level of simulated rates. For example, for simulated rate levels approaching 5%, the difference appears on the order of 1 basis point.

So our advice is to be aware of the issue and to use good judgment. If the purpose of the analysis requires a great deal of precision, we'd suggest running a simulation. If conditions are such that the difference appears to be of a magnitude similar to the bid–ask spread for the one-month contracts, we'd suggest making the adjustment.

The Financing Bias for SOFR Futures

If any futures contract is going to exhibit a correlation between the price of the contract and the interest rate paid on margin, the SOFR futures contract is it. In this case, the correlation between futures prices and the short-term interest rate is negative, so that the futures price should be less than it would be without the financing bias. And since the futures rate is 100 less the futures prices, the futures rate would be *greater* than it would be otherwise.

In theory, the bias could amount to quite a few basis points, especially when the correlation between the futures price and the short rate is high and when futures prices are volatile.

In general, the correlation with the overnight short rate is greater for shorter-dated futures at the front end of the curve than for longer-dated futures toward the back end. On the other hand, the financing effect has longer to operate when dealing with longer-dated futures, which would be expected to increase the influence of the financing bias.

Typically, quants calculate the required adjustments for each contract along the curve in accordance with the term structure model they're using to price other derivatives – an approach we recommend for the sake of consistency if nothing else. We won't go into those details here, except to note again the difficulty of identifying a term structure model that does a good job of capturing the dynamics of the SOFR term structure (including for the pricing of options on SOFR futures).

But we would like to raise two issues that may be relevant. First, the financing bias refers primarily to the effects of applying futures-style margining to an instrument. When the price of the instrument is correlated with the interest rate paid on margin, continual margining can add or subtract from the profits that otherwise would be earned on a trade. But most products these days are subject to margining, including FRAs, swaps, swaptions, caps, and floors. So if a futures contract and an otherwise similar FRA are both subject to futures-style margining, with interest paid on margin, it may not be critical to invest much time and effort making the adjustments, as the two products may well be adjusted by similar amounts.

Second, the effects of paying interest on margin only matter if the people whose trades are moving the markets are receiving interest in their margin accounts *and if that interest is making it into their P&L accounts*. As an anecdote, one of us (Doug Huggins) spent a number of years working as a proprietary trader at a bank and two hedge funds. At no time did anyone ever identify the interest paid or received on margin, for futures contracts or for anything else. There were times when the trades on the desk were of reasonable size (e.g., 10,000 Eurodollar butterfly spreads, involving 40,000 contracts, controlling a notional value of USD 40 billion). And we pored over every basis point along the curve. But we never included a financing bias in the analysis, because as far as we were concerned on the proprietary trading desk, we weren't paying or receiving any interest on margin. Someone clearly was, but it wasn't us. And as a result, we weren't interested in paying for something that didn't hit our P&L.

We don't know whether this experience was unusual – but it was the same in all three cases. So from our perspective, the size of the financing bias in any complex, including the SOFR complex, is probably best viewed as an empirical matter rather than as a theoretical matter. And if you believe market pricing incorporates a material financing bias, and you don't have margin interest incorporated in your P&L, then you have an opportunity to get paid for subjecting yourself to a bias that doesn't affect you. That's worth knowing, too.

BUILDING A SOFR SWAP CURVE FROM SOFR FUTURES

The discussion so far in this chapter has been somewhat academic. Let's see how these concepts can be put into practice in a real-world application – building a SOFR swap curve from a set of SOFR futures prices. In particular, we'll focus on three ways in which the construction of SOFR curves probably should differ from the construction of LIBOR curves.

Bootstrapping vs. Fitting

When building LIBOR curves, it's not unusual for people to choose as inputs a set of highly liquid instruments that cover nonoverlapping reference dates, with the result that it's possible for all input prices to be priced without error along a *bootstrapped* curve. Each instrument adds unique information about a specific portion of the curve, with the result that it's impossible for any of the input instruments to be arbitraged against one another.

When building SOFR curves, the basic building blocks tend to be steps delineated by FOMC meeting dates. There tend to be more of these meeting dates throughout the course of a year than are required to reprice the four three-month SOFR futures that cover the year. But there aren't enough FOMC meetings to reprice exactly all of the *one-month* futures contracts that cover the year. As a result, we tend to use a collection of one-month and three-month contracts when building a SOFR curve. And in this case, there certainly are more futures contracts to reprice than there are steps in the piecewise step function that defines the term structure of overnight forward rates. As a result, building SOFR curves tends to be an exercise in fitting a curve rather than bootstrapping a curve.

Price Adjustments

As already discussed, the prices of 3M SOFR futures contracts don't require any adjustments for nonlinearities, but they may require adjustment for a financing bias. The prices of one-month SOFR contracts in theory require adjustments for both issues. Again, we'd be a bit circumspect when making these adjustments. As noted above, the adjustments apparently required for the fact that the one-month contracts settle to an arithmetic average rather than via daily compounding amount to well under a basis point at the current low levels of rates. And the extent of the practical adjustment required for a financing bias is not as clear as for the theoretical adjustment, owing to the fact that there may be more than a few institutional market participants who don't feel the need to take a financing bias into account.

Discontinuities

When building LIBOR curves, we tend to avoid sharp discontinuities in forward rates, as the basic building block in a LIBOR curve tends to be the three-month rate, which changes only slowly when crossing a fixed date, such as the turn of the year, or an FOMC meeting date.

But the basic building block in a SOFR curve is the overnight rate, and it's natural to reflect sharp discontinuities, such as FOMC meeting dates, when constructing these curves.

An example should prove illustrative.

Example

Consider the construction of a SOFR curve given the settlement prices for one-month and three-month SOFR futures contracts on Friday, 25-Feb-22, shown in Table 6.1.

TABLE 6.1 SOFR futures prices as of 25-Feb-22

One-month SOFR futures		Three-month SOFR Futures	
Expiration Month	Settlement Price	Expiration Month	Settlement Price
Jan-22	99.95	Dec-21	99.9475
Feb-22	99.8	Mar-22	99.4975
Mar-22	99.635	Jun-22	99.02
Apr-22	99.37	Sep-22	98.635
May-22	99.225	Dec-22	98.345
Jun-22	99.095	Mar-23	98.095
Jul-22	98.935	Jun-23	97.95
Aug-22	98.875	Sep-23	97.91
Sep-22	98.735	Dec-23	97.92
Oct-22	98.585	Mar-24	97.995
Nov-22	98.475	Jun-24	98.06
Dec-22	98.395		
Jan-23	98.3		

Source: CME

In this example, we choose to model the term structure of overnight forward rates as a step function, with the discontinuities corresponding to FOMC meeting dates. Our task is to assign values to the overnight forward rates in each of these steps.

As of 25-Feb, there are only a few days left in the month of February, and we can use the settlement price of the Feb22 one-month contract to bootstrap the overnight forward rate for this period. The fitted value we obtain this way is 0.0525%.

The next FOMC date is scheduled for March 16, so we can use the value of the Mar22 one-month SOFR contract to identify the height of the step beginning on March 17. In this case, we obtain a value of 0.35733%.

The following FOMC meeting isn't scheduled until 4-May-22, so that the entirety of the Apr22 contract falls within the step defined by the two FOMC dates. So at this point we have a couple of choices.

If we want to continue with the bootstrap procedure, we can either skip the Apr22 contract, as we've already used the Mar22 contract to bootstrap the value of this part of the yield curve. Or we could use the Apr22 contract to determine the height of this part of the yield curve. In this case, the value of the overnight forward rates in this part of the curve would be 0.365%, slightly greater than the value we obtained using the Mar22 one-month contract.

Our other choice would be to give up bootstrapping and to switch to calculating a fitted curve, in which we minimize the sum of squared differences between observed prices and fitted prices, with no guarantee that we'll exactly reprice any of the futures contracts with zero error. For example, if we wanted to calculate a value for this part of the yield curve by minimizing the sum of squared pricing errors for the Mar22 and Apr22 contracts, our fitted value would be 0.36355% – a bit higher than the value we calculated via the bootstrap procedure using the Mar22 price, and a bit lower than the value we calculated using the Apr22 price.

For the sake of discussion, let's assume for now that we choose to stick with the bootstrap procedure, using the Apr22 contract rather than the Mar22 contract. As a result, the value we assign to the curve between the 16-Mar-22 and 4-May-22 FOMC dates is 0.365%.

In this case, the next segment of the yield curve we need to calculate is the segment between the 4-May-22 and 15-Jun-22 FOMC dates. We can bootstrap this value using the May22 futures contract; the figure we calculate in this case is 0.65574%.

The next value we need to calculate is the value of the overnight forward rates between the 15-Jun-22 FOMC meeting date and the 27-Jul-22 meeting date. We can use the price of the Jun22 one-month contract to bootstrap this figure. In particular, the value we calculate is 0.89426%.

The next value we need to estimate is the value of the overnight forward rates between the 27-Jul-22 and the 21-Sep-22 FOMC meeting dates. In theory, we could use the value of the Jul22 one-month contract for this purpose, but as there are so few calendar days in July after the 27th, we'll use the Aug22 contract for this purpose. In this case, we estimate a value of 1.00005%.

The next value we need to calculate is the value of the overnight forward rates between the 21-Sep-22 and 2-Nov-22 FOMC meeting dates. As the entirety of the Oct22 SOFR contract is within this interval, we'll use that contract to bootstrap this part of the curve. In particular, we obtain a value of 1.18833%. It's worth mentioning that the pricing error of the Sep22 one-month contract – which we skipped in our bootstrap procedure – is nearly seven cents – quite large relative to the pricing errors we've seen so far in this example.

And speaking of pricing errors, now that we've used the prices of one-month SOFR futures contracts to bootstrap a curve out to 2-Nov-22, we can check the pricing errors of the Mar22 and Jun22 three-month contracts. In particular, the fitted price of the Mar22 contract is 0.96 cents greater than the observed settlement price, while the fitted price of the Jun22 three-month contract is 1.75 cents greater than the observed settlement price.

For reference, at this point in our bootstrapping example, the average absolute pricing error of the first nine one-month SOFR futures contracts is 0.83 cents. And the average absolute pricing error of the Mar22 and Jun22 three-month futures contracts is 1.36 cents. The largest pricing error among the one-month contacts is 6.82 cents for the Oct22 contract.

If we priced the same part of the curve using the same futures contracts by minimizing the sum of squared differences between the observed prices and the fitted prices, then the average absolute pricing error for the first nine one-month SOFR futures contracts would be 1.10 cents, and the average absolute pricing error for the Mar22 and Jun22 three-month contracts would be 0.50 cents. The largest pricing error among the one-month contracts would be 4.44 cents for the Sep22 contract. The largest pricing error between the Mar22 and Jun22 three-month contracts would be 0.65 cents for the Mar22 contract.

It's not surprising that the prices of the one-month futures were, on average, more accurately priced using the bootstrap approach, as many of these one-month contracts were the contracts that were being bootstrapped. But even in this case, the maximum pricing error among the first nine one-month contracts was lower under the fitted procedure than it was under the bootstrap procedure. And the results for the Mar22 and Jun22 three-month futures contracts were uniformly better, as would be expected given that their prices weren't used in the bootstrap but were reflected in the fitted curve exercise.

Ultimately, the choice between bootstrapping a curve and fitting a curve depends on the application. If there are certain futures contracts for which the calculated prices absolutely must equal the observed market prices, then bootstrapping a curve with these futures providing inputs sounds like the best approach. On the other hand, if it's not critical to precisely reprice the values of certain futures contracts, we'd probably suggest fitting a curve – i.e., choosing values for the heights of the steps in the yield curve so as to minimize the sum of squared differences between calculated prices and observed market prices.

With this in mind, we apply the fitted approach to the yield curve out to the end of 2025. The resulting pricing errors for the one-month contracts are shown in Figure 6.2.

Note that the pricing errors are quite small for the first few contracts, for which the liquidity is relatively good.

The pricing errors for the three-month contracts are shown in Figure 6.3.

Note that the difference between market prices and calculated prices are almost nil starting with the sixth three-month contract, as there were no liquid one-month futures to include in this part of the curve. Otherwise, the first few three-month futures contracts along the curve were priced with very little error, while the fourth and fifth contracts, Sep22 and Dec22, had slightly larger pricing errors, consistent with the lower levels of liquidity in these contracts.

Figure 6.4 shows the piecewise step function that represents our fitted yield curve in this case.

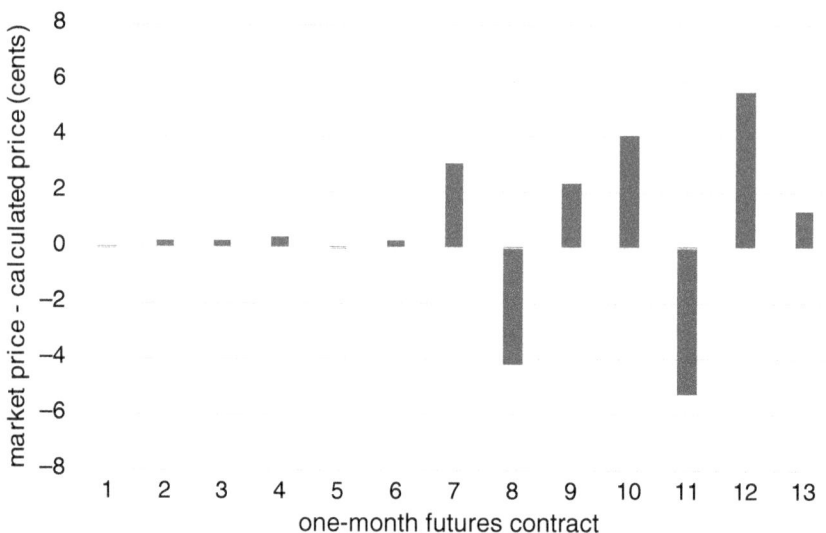

FIGURE 6.2 Fitted curve pricing errors for first 13 one-month SOFR futures contracts
Source: Authors

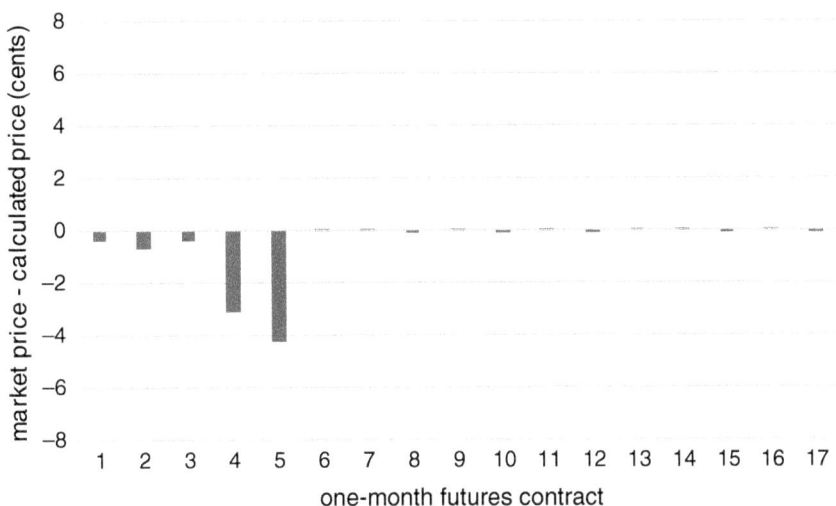

FIGURE 6.3 Fitted curve pricing errors for first 17 three-month SOFR futures contracts
Source: Authors

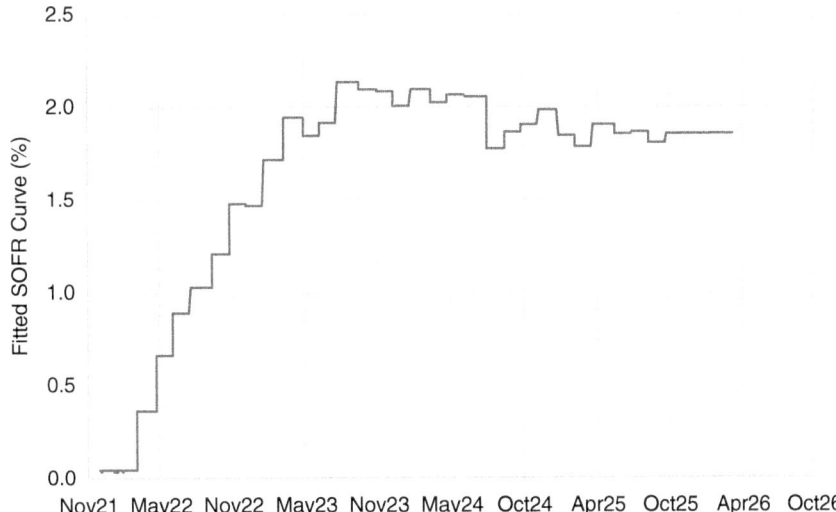

FIGURE 6.4 Fitted SOFR curve
Source: Authors

This curve strikes us as "noisy," in the sense that the term structure of fitted overnight forward rates appears to oscillate beyond about May 2023 – or at least to experience a series of frequent reversals during this period.

If this series of rate increases followed quickly by rate increases that are soon reversed is genuinely indicative of market pricing, a curve like this might be fine. On the other hand, our *a priori* belief is that this pattern is more likely indicative of noisy input data than of a series of policy rate reversals.

In an attempt to reduce this noise, we can introduce a regularity condition that increases the smoothness of the step function, where for this purpose we'll define *smoothness* as the sum of the squared butterfly spreads along the fitted curve.[1]

FIGURE 6.5 Fitted SOFR curve with regularity condition
Source: Authors

---

[1]The butterfly spread between three successive steps is given by $(2 \times r2) - r1 - r3$, where r1, r2, and r3 are the heights of the three steps. The butterfly spread is an approximation to the second derivative of the curve in the segment of the curve containing r1, r2, and r3. The absolute value of a butterfly spread (and hence its square) is relatively large in the presence of a reversal.

In particular, we'll choose the heights of the K steps, $\theta_1, \theta_2, \theta_3, \ldots, \theta_K$, so as to minimize the objective function:

$$Q = \sum_{i=1}^{N} (f_i - \widehat{f_i})^2 + \varphi \sum_{j=2}^{K-1} (2\,\theta_j - \theta_{j-1} - \theta_{j+1})^2$$

The first summation in this equation is simply the sum of squared differences between the N observed futures prices, f_i, and the K fitted futures prices, $\widehat{f_i}$. The second summation in the equation is the regularity condition that sums the $(K-2)$ squared values of the butterfly spreads along the fitted curve. This second summation is scaled by a number, φ, that controls the penalty for lack of smoothness.

In pushing the curve to be smoother, we necessarily worsen the quality of the fit between the prices of the futures contracts observed in the market and the prices computed along our fitted curve.

The penalty for lack of smoothness can be increased until we obtain a yield curve with an acceptable tradeoff between smoothness and fit. Figure 6.5 provides an example of such a curve.

The tradeoff between smoothness and quality is inevitable, and the choice is necessarily a subjective one for the analyst fitting the curve. But at least the formulation above gives the analyst a framework for assessing the alternatives in this regard.

Use Cases

7

Simple Examples of Hedging with SOFR Futures

In the first half of the book, we focused on the concepts underlying the SOFR futures and options complex, including the repo market, the construction of SOFR, and the specifications and characteristics of SOFR futures and options. In the second half of the book, we focus on practical applications of SOFR futures and options, with an emphasis on specific, worked examples.

In general, SOFR futures and options provide a useful way to manage SOFR risk. But as we consider specific examples, we'll see that it's particularly important in each case to define the terms *manage* and *SOFR risk*. For example, one money market fund manager may be interested in minimizing the standard deviation of the net asset value of his fund as of a specific target date, while another money market fund manager may be concerned only with minimizing the downside risk to the NAV of his fund. A corporate treasurer may be interested in using SOFR futures to convert daily rate risk to quarterly rate risk in a cash management program, while a hedge fund trader may be interested in maximizing the Sharpe ratio of a spread trade involving SOFR futures, without knowing the date on which he'll exit the position.

As we work through specific examples, we'll see that the term *SOFR risk* often entails a collection of risks that differ depending on the context. For example, a bank that wishes to use SOFR futures to convert the risk in a SOFR floating rate note from daily to quarterly may find that 3M SOFR futures provide only a rough approximation of the cash flow dates of the note. On the other hand, if this bank were to use 1M futures to better approximate the cash flows of the FRN, the exposure to rate volatility may increase, owing to the difference between the arithmetic average used in the 1M contract and the geometric average used in the 3M contract.

We'll start with three simple examples involving a corporate treasurer who wishes to convert part of a floating rate balance to fixed.

EXAMPLE 1: CORPORATE TREASURER CONVERTING FLOATING RATE EXPOSURE TO FIXED

Consider a corporate treasurer who had USD 100 million of working capital that he intended to deposit with banks, secured by US Treasuries, starting Wednesday, December 18, 2019, for three months – i.e., up to and including Wednesday, March 18, 2020. As Figure 7.1 suggests, overnight rates had been between 1.5% and 2% in recent months, but these had been trending lower, and there was concern that rates may decline further.

With that in mind, rather than investing the entire amount in overnight repo, he decided he'd like to effectively fix the interest rate he'd receive on half this amount – again, secured by US Treasuries via repo.

To accomplish this, on 18-Dec-19, he purchased three-month Dec19 SOFR futures contracts, expiring in March 2020.

The first thing the treasurer must do is to determine the number of contracts he needs to purchase. He starts with the fact that the CME SOFR futures contract is defined so that the value of a 1 bp change in price is USD 25. He calculates that a 1 bp change in the interest rate earned on a repo investment of USD 50 million over this 91-day period (using an actual/360 day count) is USD 1,263.89. To get this exposure via the three-month SOFR futures market, therefore, he needs to purchase 1,263.89/25 = 50.56 contracts.

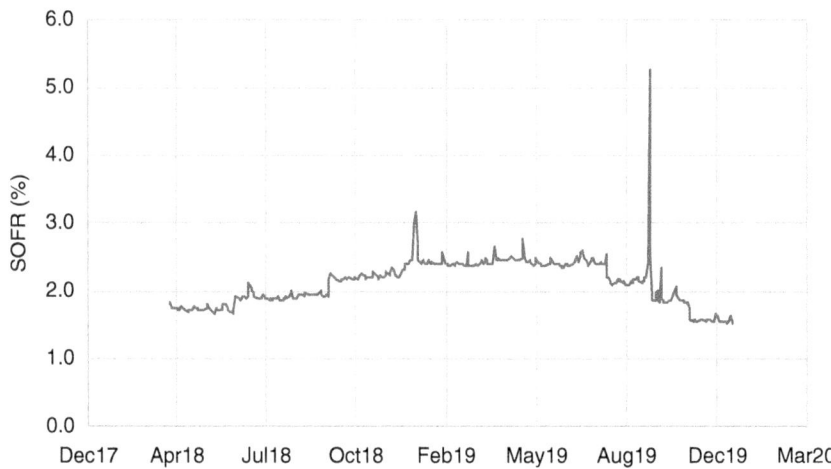

FIGURE 7.1   SOFR

Source: Authors, from Fed data (https://www.newyorkfed.org/markets/reference-rates/sofr) Disclaimer: These reference rate data are subject to the Terms of Use posted at newyorkfed.org. The New York Fed is not responsible for publication of the reference rate data by the Authors and Wiley, does not endorse any particular republication, and has no liability for your use.

In other words:

$$number\ of\ futures\ contracts = \frac{desired\ sensitivity}{actual\ sensitivity\ of\ the\ futures\ contract}$$

where the actual sensitivity of a 3M SOFR futures contract is USD 25 by construction; and the desired sensitivity is 0.01 × (d_i/360) × notional amount. In this case, d_i, the actual number of calendar days between the start date of December 18, 2019 (inclusive), and the end date of March 18, 2020 (exclusive), happens to be 91. And since the notional amount is USD 50 million in this case, we have: Desired sensitivity = 0.01 × (91/360) × USD 50,000,000 = USD 1,263.89. So the number of contracts our corporate treasurer needs to purchase is USD 1,263.89 / USD 25 = 50.56.

Let's see how this strategy fared in practice. Let's assume that on 18-Dec-19, the treasurer purchased 50 three-month SOFR futures contracts, expiring in 18-Mar-20, with a purchase price of 98.41. The implied SOFR rate is simply 100 − P = 100 − 98.41 = 1.59%. However, this is not the implied daily rate. To calculate the implied daily rate, we need to determine the single interest rate that would result in a final settlement price for the March 2020 futures contract of 98.41, assuming this rate were constant every day from 18-Dec-19 through 17-Mar-20. As it happens, in this case, that rate is 1.5869%.[1]

Had the SOFR rate been equal to 1.5869% on each day from 18-Dec-19 through 17-Mar-20, the starting value of USD 50,000,000 million would have increased to USD 50,200,956.00 by 18-Mar-20. But, as seen in Figure 7.2, the actual SOFR rate decreased toward the end of this period, such that, without any hedging, the initial deposit of USD 50 million actually increased to only USD 50,187,105.05 – i.e., USD 13,850.95 *less than* would have been earned had the daily SOFR rate been 1.5869%.

Given the actual SOFR value shown in Figure 7.2, the final settlement price of the Dec-19 three-month SOFR futures contract was 98.5175 – greater than purchase price by 0.1075. Given that the value of a basis point is USD 25 by construction, and given that the treasurer purchased 50 contracts, this change in the price of the futures contract resulted in a gain for the treasurer of 50 × USD 25 /bp × 10.75 bp = USD 13,437.50.

Adding this gain to the actual account balance of USD 50,187,105.05 results in a combined value of USD 50,187,105.05 + USD 13,437.50 = USD 50,200,542.55 – within USD 413.45 of the figure of USD 50,200,956.00 we calculated earlier.

---

[1] The daily implied rate is less than the implied simple term rate due to the effects of compounding.

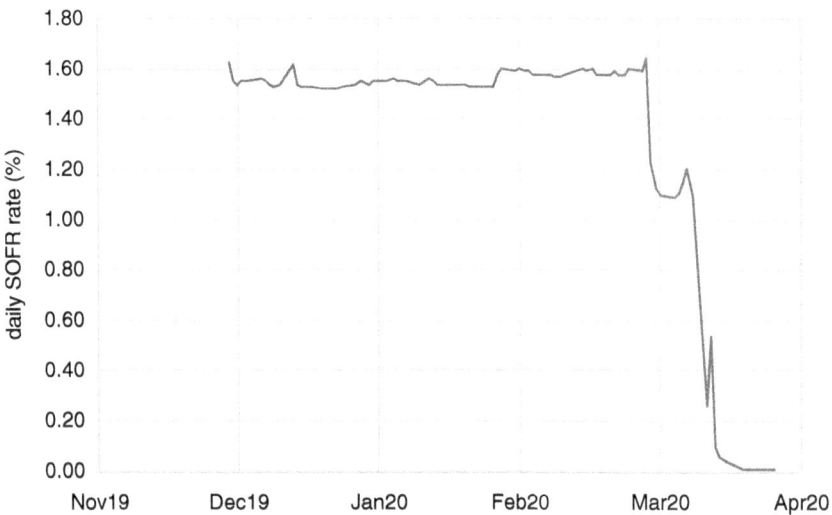

FIGURE 7.2   Actual and implied SOFR values
Source: Authors, from Fed data (https://www.newyorkfed.org/markets/reference-rates/sofr) Disclaimer: These reference rate data are subject to the Terms of Use posted at newyorkfed.org. The New York Fed is not responsible for publication of the reference rate data by the Authors and Wiley, does not endorse any particular republication, and has no liability for your use.

EXAMPLE 2: LOCKING IN AN INTEREST RATE WITH MISMATCHED DATES

What if our corporate treasurer were looking to lock in an interest rate for a somewhat different set of dates? For example, what if the lending period was 2-Dec-19 through 28-Feb-20?[2]

In this case, the treasurer has a bit of a conundrum, as the Dec-19 three-month SOFR contract covers a somewhat different period, namely 18-Dec-19 (inclusive) through 18-Mar-20 (exclusive). Figure 7.3 illustrates the nature of the problem. The lighter line represents the period for which our corporate treasurer wishes to lock in an interest rate, while the darker line represents the period covered by the Dec-19 three-month SOFR futures contract.

As we can see, there are 12 days at the beginning of the intended lending period that the Dec-19 contract doesn't cover. At the same time, the Dec-19

---

[2]1-Dec-19 and 29-Feb-20 were not business days.

23Nov19 07Dec19 21Dec19 04Jan20 18Jan20 01Feb20 15Feb20 29Feb20 14Mar20 28Mar20

——— lending period   ——— Dec-19 futures period

FIGURE 7.3 Intended lending period and period covered by Dec-19 3M SOFR futures
Source: Authors

contract covers an additional 12 business days that are outside of the treasurer's intended lending period. This is no longer a simple date-matching exercise. In this example, we need to make some additional assumptions.

When dealing with overnight rates, one of the most potentially important events is FOMC meetings. As it happens, there were a few FOMC meetings scheduled during the treasurer's lending period: 11-Dec-19, 29-Jan-20, and 18-Mar-20. So one assumption our corporate treasurer might make is the same assumption made when constructing a Term SOFR rate (as discussed in Chapter 8) – namely, that the term structure of daily SOFR rates can be assumed to be a stepwise function, with each step corresponding to a scheduled FMOC meeting. In this case, we'd have three steps:

1. From the beginning of the lending period, 2-Dec-19 through the first FOMC meeting on 11-Dec-19
2. From the day after the December 11 FOMC meeting through the second scheduled FOMC meeting on 29-Jan-20
3. From the day after the second meeting through to the end of the lending period on 29-Feb-20 (or through 18-Mar-20 when dealing with the three-month SOFR futures contract)

If we're going to make this assumption, we need to find some means of identifying the height of each step in our step function. In particular, we have

three unknowns – the heights of our three steps – so it would be ideal if we
had three observations we could use to identify these unknown step values.

As it happens, we can use the prices of the Dec-19, Jan-20, and Feb-20
one-month SOFR futures contracts as of 2-Dec-19, in this case 98.37,
98.375, and 98.425, respectively (using settlement prices).

To see the way in which fitted SOFR values can be obtained, consider
Table 7.1.

TABLE 7.1   Fitting a stepwise rate curve to one-month SOFR futures prices

	1M Dec	1M Jan	1M Feb
fitted SOFR	1.6300	1.6250	1.5750
fitted futures prices	98.37	98.37500001	98.42500001
settle price	98.37	98.375	98.425
(fitted price – settle price)^2	1.07776E-13	3.44146E-13	4.93929E-13

Source: Authors

In the fourth row, we show the settlement price of each contract. On the
fifth row, we show the squared difference between the settlement price and
the fitted price, where the fitted price is calculated from the fitted piecewise
step function, with the heights of the three steps as the independent variables.
More specifically, we choose the heights of the three steps to minimize the
sum of squared differences between the actual settlement prices and the fitted
prices derived from our fitted, stepwise overnight rate curve.

As can be seen in Table 7.1, we obtain a nearly exact fit with this method,
with the resulting rate curve shown in Figure 7.4.

In theory, we could have used the Dec-19 three-month SOFR futures
contract to help fit our stepwise rate curve. But in this case, we thought it
might be useful to see how closely the fitted price of this contract matched the
settlement price on 2-Dec-19. In this case, the settlement price was 98.395,
and the fitted price was 98.397. In our view, this difference of 0.002 is quite
encouraging, suggesting consistency across the settlement prices of these
futures contracts and our fitted stepwise rate curve.

Having built an assumed rate curve, we're in a position to calculate the
relative sensitivities of the ending value of our three-month corporate deposit
and our hedging instrument – in this case, the Dec-19 three-month SOFR
futures contract.

If we bump our fitted curve higher by 1 bp, the ending value of
our three-month deposit increases from USD 50,197,252.27 to USD
50,198,479.22, assuming an initial deposit of USD 50,000,000 – a gain of
USD 1,226.95. The corresponding change in the price of the three-month
Dec-19 SOFR futures contract is 0.01004. Given a point value of USD

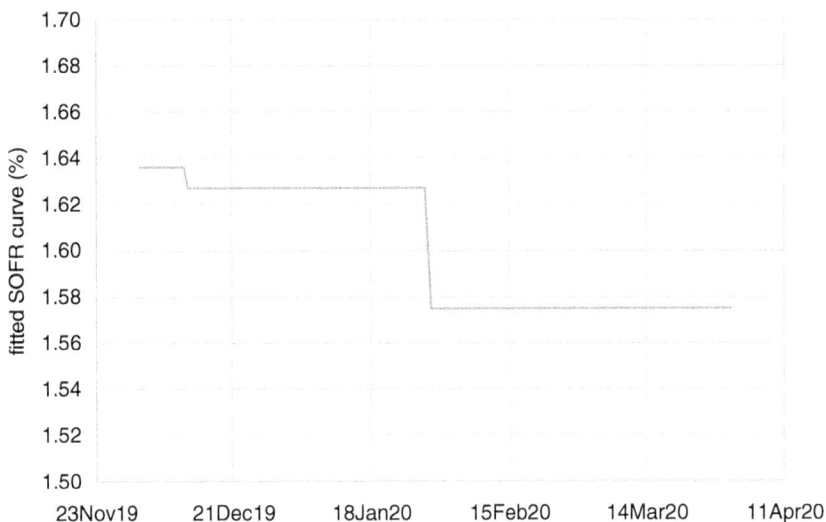

FIGURE 7.4 Fitted stepwise overnight SOFR curve
Source: Authors

2,500, the number of futures contracts required to equate the risk in this case is USD 1,226.95 / (0.01004 × USD 2,500) = 48.88.

Our corporate treasurer could round to 49 contracts without introducing much error. But for the sake of discussion, let's assume that he again fixed the number of futures at 50 and solved for the amount of the initial deposit he's going to lock in via futures. In this case, the figure is USD 51,141,741.

Note that the loan period targeted by the corporate treasurer is 89 days – slightly less than 90 days. So it's not surprising that the sensitivity of the ending loan value is such that more than USD 50 million in initial deposit is required to match the sensitivity of a 50-lot position in three-month SOFR futures contracts.

Let's see how this hedge performed in practice. The actual path of SOFR is shown along with our fitted curve in Figure 7.5.

Note that the actual SOFR rate decreased considerably relative to the overnight forward rates along our fitted curve, particularly toward the end of our lending period. As a result, the terminal value of the loan was only USD 51,336,755.08 – i.e., USD 6,742.88 less than our corporate treasurer was trying to lock in.

The final settlement price of the three-month SOFR futures contract was 98.5196, for a gain of 0.1246. Given a position size of 50 contracts and a point value of USD 2,500, this results in a gain of 50 × USD 2,500 × 0.1246 = USD 15,575.

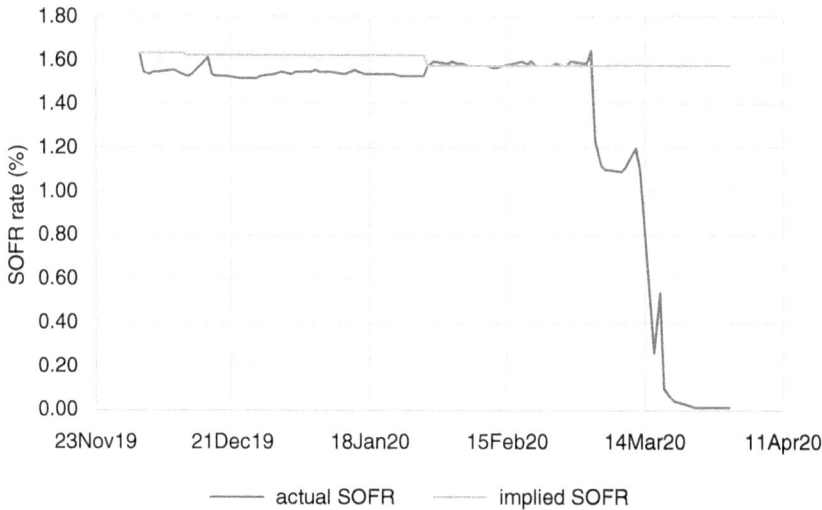

FIGURE 7.5 Fitted stepwise overnight SOFR curve and actual realized SOFR values
Source: Authors

In this case, the gain on the long position in the three-month futures contract was more than twice the shortfall in the ending balance of the deposit relative to the amount the treasurer was trying to lock in. So the futures hedge was helpful, but we can see that there is a fair amount of date mismatch risk when dealing with lending periods that don't match with the periods covered by the futures contract.

In this example, we assumed our corporate treasurer simply held the Dec-19 futures contract until expiration on 18-Mar-20. But in practice, someone in this position typically would be well-advised to sell the futures contract at the prevailing market price at the end of the lending period, since the additional days beyond the lending period are really just introducing noise.

In this case, the settlement price of the Dec-19 three-month SOFR futures contract on 28-Feb-20 was 98.47. Had the treasurer sold the futures hedge at this price, his gain would have been 0.075, resulting in a financial gain of USD 2,500 × 50 × 0.075 = USD 9,375. In this case, the gain on the futures still exceeds the loss of interest on the deposit by a considerable amount – but not by nearly as much as would have been the case in the event the treasurer held the position until expiration, since in this case the price of the Dec-19 futures contract continued to increase between the end of the deposit period (28-Feb-20) and the expiration of the futures contract on 18-Mar-20.

EXAMPLE 3: USING ONE-MONTH SOFR FUTURES AS A HEDGING ALTERNATIVE

In the previous case, the date of the single three-month SOFR futures contract didn't align perfectly with the reference period. In this case, we'll switch to one-month futures in an attempt to construct a more precise hedge.

As before, our corporate treasurer wishes to hedge half of his USD 100 million in overnight deposits from 2-Dec-19 through 28-Feb-20.

Using the term structure of overnight forward rates fitted in the previous example, we calculate that the treasurer's deposit of USD 50 million would grow to USD 50,190,659.93 if he could lock in all the overnight forward rates along this curve. The column, labeled "base curve" in Table 7.2, shows the sizes to which the deposit would grow by various dates in the event the overnight forward rates could be locked in. The next column to the right, labeled "bumped curve," shows the sizes to which the deposit could grow if the term structure of overnight forward rates were bumped higher by one basis point. The difference between these two values is shown in the next column to the right.

The next column, labeled, "difference," shows the difference per period. In other words, USD 403.27 of this cumulative difference accrues during the first period; another USD 432.26 of this difference accrues during the second period; and the remaining USD 391.42 accrues during the final period.

The next column in the table shows the basis point values for the one-month contracts considered in this example: Dec19, Jan20, and Feb20. As these are all one-month contracts, the basis point value in each case is USD 41.67.

The next column shows the ratio of the difference per period to the basis point value of each futures contract. This ratio gives us the number

TABLE 7.2 Calculations for a hedge of a simple deposit using one-month SOFR futures

	Base Curve	Bumped Curve	Difference	Difference per Period	Futures BPV	Contracts	Rounded
deposit on 2-dec-19	50,000,000.00	50,000,000.00	0.00				
deposit on 31-dec-19	50,065,693.08	50,066,096.35	403.27	403.27	41.67	9.678	10
deposit on 31-jan-20	50,135,873.19	50,136,708.72	835.53	432.26	41.67	10.373	10
deposit on 28-feb-20	50,197,324.48	50,198,551.43	1,226.95	391.42	41.67	9.393	9

of futures contracts we should purchase in order to hedge the size of our deposit. Finally, in the column to the right, we show the actual integer number of each contract to be used in the hedge.

How Did This Hedge Perform in Practice?

As we saw above, the actual SOFR values toward the end of this period were far below the overnight forward rates as of 2-Dec-19. As a result, the deposit would have grown only to USD 50,190,659.93 had it been left unhedged – a shortfall of USD 6,664.55 relative to the value consistent with the overnight forward rates as of 2-Dec-19.

At the same time, our futures hedge returned USD 6,379.68. With this gain, our *net* shortfall was reduced to USD 284.88 – a hedging error of 4.3%.

Note that the hedging error in this case was much lower than the hedging error in the previous case, in which the date mismatch between the interest period on the deposit and the reference period of the futures contract was material.

LESSONS TO BE LEARNED FROM THESE THREE SIMPLE EXAMPLES

From these three simple examples, we take away a few key lessons.

Hedge Ratios Are Relative Sensitivities

In all three examples, the thing we wanted to hedge (our hedge target) was the size of our cash balance at the end of the reference period. And the instruments we used to hedge were futures contracts: a three-month contract in the first two examples and a collection of one-month contracts in the third example.

But in each case, the strategy for calculating our hedge ratios was the same: to identify a state variable and then to make sure the sensitivity of our futures hedge to changes in that state variable were the same as the sensitivity of our hedge target to changes in that state variable. In the first example, the state variable was simply the final settlement rate of the futures contract (i.e., 1 – the final settlement price of the futures contract), since that rate determined both the gains from our futures contract and the size of our ending cash balance.

In the second example, the state variable was a parallel shift in the fitted yield curve. In particular, we did our best to make sure that a one basis point bump in the term structure of overnight forward rates produced a sufficient gain on our futures position to offset any shortfalls experienced in our ending cash balance. This was the approach taken in the third example, as well – though in the third example we had to contend with three hedging instruments rather than one.

But in each case, the strategy is first to identify a useful state variable and then to create a portfolio of futures contracts for which the change in net present value due to a change in the state variable offsets the change in the value of our hedge target (the ending value of our cash balance in these examples) due to the same change in the value of the state variable.

Dates Matter

In the first example, the reference period of our hedge corresponded with the reference period of our single hedge instrument, a three-month SOFR futures contract. And we saw that the performance of the hedge was relatively good.

In the second example, the reference period of our three-month futures contract didn't correspond particularly well with the reference period of our hedge, and despite our best efforts the performance of the hedge was relatively poor.

In the third example, we were able to regain a close correspondence between the reference period of our hedge and the reference period of our hedging instruments by using a collection of one-month futures contracts rather than a single three-month futures contract. And here again, we saw that the performance of the hedge was relatively good.

It's not always possible to choose hedging instruments with reference periods that correspond closely to the reference period of the target you wish to hedge. For example, if our deposit period ran from 15-Jan-20 through 15-Apr-20, neither a single three-month futures contract nor a collection of one-month futures contracts would provide a close correspondence between the reference period of our hedge instrument and the reference period of our target hedge. In those cases, we do our best, but we need to acknowledge that the performance of our hedge simply isn't likely to be as good in this instance as it would be otherwise.

Assumptions Matter

In the first example, we didn't need to make any assumptions about the behavior of the term structure of overnight forward rates, since the reference period of our hedge target was the same as the reference period of our hedge instrument.

But in the second and third examples, we needed to make assumptions, even if we weren't explicit about these assumptions at the time. In particular, in both examples, we assumed that the term structure of overnight forward rates moved in parallel, allowing us to assess relative sensitivities of our hedge target and hedge instruments simply by bumping the curve.

In practice, nobody believes this is truly the way the term structure moves. However, it may be a useful assumption in certain circumstances. More to the point, it may be a relatively useful assumption to make if the cost of making a more realistic assumption is likely to be large relative to the improved performance of the hedge under that assumption.

For example, in Chapter 8, we'll propose a method for precisely hedging forward CME Term SOFR values using a portfolio of one-month and three-month futures contracts. The assumptions underlying this approach may be more realistic (or at least less restrictive), though they do come with some additional computational costs, as we'll see in the next chapter.

8

Hedging the CME Term SOFR Rate

At some level, the secured overnight financing rate is an elegant concept, as it represents the most basic building block for yield curves. But as we have described in Chapter 3, there are a significant number of market participants for whom SOFR isn't ideal. For example, many corporate treasurers appreciate knowing the cash flows of their loans well in advance of those cash flow payment dates. And for these people, a plan vanilla SOFR loan simply isn't an attractive arrangement, due to the fact that the ultimate size of each interest payment is known only shortly in advance of the interest payment date.

In theory, secured financing rates for specific terms could be constructed the way the Fed constructs the secured overnight financing rate – i.e., by averaging each day the interest rates reported for repo transactions for specific terms, such as one month, three months, and six months. In practice, however, this is seen as problematic, as the volume of daily transactions with terms of three months, six months, etc., is considered to be insufficient for this purpose.

As an alternative, someone could organize a process in which banks are asked each day to provide the rates at which they would be willing to enter into repo transactions of various terms. And then these rates could be averaged and published at the same time each day. Of course, the problem with this approach is that regulators would be unwilling to sanction a process that they believe could be manipulated the way the LIBOR rate-setting process was manipulated.

So the market found itself facing a bit of a conundrum. The LIBOR rigging scandal precludes the use of a survey to determine secured term financing rates. And yet there aren't enough secured term repo transactions reported each day to create a robust averaging process.

In an attempt to address this issue, the Chicago Mercantile Exchange introduced Term SOFR,[1] for terms of one month, three months, six months,

---

[1] We appreciate the irony of the label "term secured overnight financing rate."

and twelve months. Term SOFR attempts to address the conundrum by converting a set of transactions reported in the SOFR futures market into a yield curve and then using this yield curve to calculate the values of spot rates with the desired tenors.

THE TERM SOFR METHODOLOGY

The inputs to the CME Term SOFR calculations are prices of one-month and three-month SOFR futures contracts. In particular, the methodology uses the first thirteen one-month contracts and the first five three-month contracts.

If the all the overnight values along the SOFR curve are allowed to differ from one another, then in general there will be an infinite number of combinations that will be exactly consistent with the prices of the eighteen futures contracts used as inputs to the process. More specifically, the yield curve will be underidentified – i.e., there won't be enough information to determine which of these yield curves should serve as the basis for calculating term rates.

In theory we could select a curve from this infinite collection of curves based on an additional criterion. For instance, we might select the smoothest of these curves according to some definition of smoothness. For example, in many applications the smoothness of a curve is measured by the integral of the square of the second derivative along the curve. In the case of SOFR curves we could define an analogous concept by summing the squared butterfly spreads along the term structure of overnight forward rates.[2]

THE CME TERM SOFR OBJECTIVE FUNCTION

However, the CME decided to take a different approach to the problem of an under identified yield curve. More specifically, the CME introduced an additional assumption – namely, that the term structure of overnight forward rates consists of a step function, with FOMC meeting dates defining the positions of these steps. In other words, the CME assumes that all the overnight forward rates between any two FOMC meeting dates have identical values. For example, all the overnight forward rates between the January and March FOMC meetings are presumed to have the same values, and all

---

[2]For example, if the term structure of overnight forward rates were as simple as 0.05, 0.04, 0.05, 0.06, 0.04, then this smoothness measure would be given by $(0.05 - 2^*0.04 + 0.05)^2 + (0.04 - 2^*0.05 + 0.06)^2 + (0.05 - 2^*0.06 + 0.04)^2 = 0.0004 + 0 + 0.0009 = 0.0013$.

the overnight forward rates between the March and May FOMC meetings are presumed to have the same values. The values of the forward rates in each segment generally differ from the values of the forward rates in other segments, but the values of the forward rates within each segment are presumed to be identical.

With this assumption, the degrees of freedom in the problem decline from a couple hundred to something on the order of 10 – and certainly to a number smaller than the number of futures contracts used in the process. As a result, this assumption takes us from having a yield curve that is underidentified to having a yield curve that is overidentified. In other words, our degrees of freedom are now *fewer* than the number of futures contracts whose prices we wish to match. In general, we won't be able to match all the input futures prices exactly.[3]

In order to identify specific, unique values for the heights of the steps in their stepwise yield curve, the CME specifies that step values should be chosen so as to minimize the sum of squared differences between the futures prices observed in the market and the futures prices produced by the fitted term structure of overnight forward rates. In particular, the CME (October 2021) chooses the heights of the steps in their stepwise yield curve so as to minimize the value of the objective function

$$f(\Phi) = \left[\sum_{m=1}^{13} {}_{m}^{1}w \left({}_{m}^{1}p - {}_{m}^{1}\widehat{p}(\Phi) \right)^2 + \sum_{q=1}^{5} {}_{q}^{3}w \left({}_{q}^{3}p - {}_{q}^{3}\widehat{p}(\Phi) \right)^2 \right]^{\frac{1}{2}} \quad (8.1)$$

where

- N is the number of steps.
- Φ is the vector of step values, $\{\varphi_k\}$, for $k = 1, 2, \ldots, N$.
- ${}_{m}^{1}p$ is the price of the mth one-month SOFR futures contract.
- ${}_{m}^{1}\widehat{p}$ is the fitted price of the mth one-month SOFR futures contract.

---

[3]If the yield curve is such that we are unable to match the prices of all the input futures contracts exactly, it may be tempting to conclude that an arbitrage exists – i.e., that we could obtain riskless profits by trading one set of futures contracts against another. However, this conclusion would be unwarranted. We're unable to reprice our input futures contracts in this case only because of the assumption that the term structure of overnight forward rates is a step function. If we relax that assumption, it will be possible generally to find a curve that reprices all the futures contracts precisely, consistent with the absence of arbitrage. In fact, as discussed, it generally would be possible to find an infinite number of such curves.

- $\frac{3}{q}p$ is the price of the qth three-month SOFR futures contract.
- $\frac{3}{q}\hat{p}$ is the fitted price of the qth three-month SOFR futures contract.
- $\frac{1}{m}w$ is the weight associated with the mth one-month futures contract.
- $\frac{3}{q}w$ is the weight associated with the qth three-month futures contract.

In theory, this criterion should be sufficient for identifying a stepwise yield curve from which to calculate term SOFR rates each day. But in practice, the stepwise yield curve fitted in this manner may exhibit undesirable characteristics at times. For example, depending on the FOMC meeting dates and futures expiration dates, it's possible this process could produce a curve in which the variability between successive steps is implausibly large.

In an attempt to prevent this, the CME adds an additional regularity condition – in this case a penalty function – to equation (8.1). In particular, this penalty function is given by the sum of squared differences between adjacent steps weighted by a number, λ, that scales this penalty function. As a result, the actual objective function used by the CME to determine the values of the steps in its stepwise yield curve is given by

$$
f(\Phi) = \left[\sum_{m=1}^{13} {}_{m}^{1}w \left({}_{m}^{1}p - {}_{m}^{1}\hat{p}(\Phi) \right)^2 + \sum_{q=1}^{5} {}_{q}^{3}w \left({}_{q}^{3}p - {}_{q}^{3}\hat{p}(\Phi) \right)^2 \right]^{\frac{1}{2}}
$$
$$
+ \lambda \left[\sum_{k=2}^{N} (\varphi_k - \varphi_{k-1})^2 \right]^{\frac{1}{2}} \tag{8.2}
$$

where λ is the weight associated with the penalty function.

If the value of λ is 0, then the penalty function has no effect whatsoever on the fitted step values. On the other hand, if the value of λ is large, then the fitted term structure of overnight forward rates will be horizontal.

Of course, the calculated term SOFR rates are a function of the fitted yield curve, so they're also a function of the value of λ. For example, Figure 8.1 shows the fitted 6M term SOFR rate as a function of λ, using data for 27-Jan-22.

As we can see from the figure, large values of λ can have very significant implications for the term SOFR rates published by the CME – on the order of 30 basis points for very large values of λ.

According to the CME, the value of λ currently is set to $\frac{1}{\sqrt{number\ of\ scheduled\ FOMC\ meetings}}$. As the number of scheduled FOMC meetings over the course of a year is typically eight or nine, the typical value of

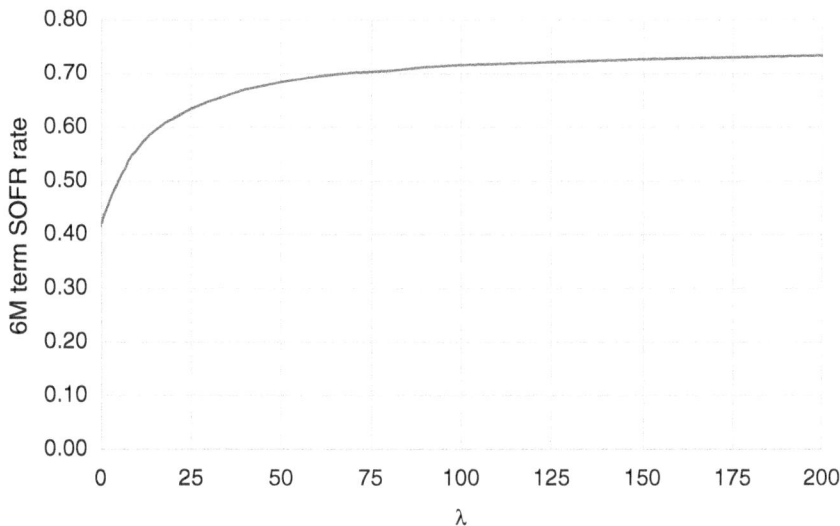

FIGURE 8.1 6M term SOFR rate as a function of λ for 27-Jan-22
Source: Authors

λ appears to be on the order of $\frac{1}{\sqrt{9}}$, roughly 0.33. In the present example, that's enough to increase the 6M term SOFR rate by slightly more than half a basis point relative to the term SOFR rate calculated when $\lambda = 0$.

Half a basis point doesn't seem like a large number. Of course, when it's multiplied by hundreds of millions or even billions of dollars, it starts to add up. And as the yield curve tends to be upward-sloping more often than downward-sloping, our sense is that the inclusion of this penalty function probably imparts an upward bias to term SOFR rates, favoring lenders and disfavoring borrowers. To be fair, however, we haven't analyzed this issue in any great detail, and more work would be required before we could determine whether this penalty function in fact does impart a systematic bias in published term SOFR rates.

This analysis does beg a few questions, however: *Who chooses the value of λ? What criteria are used in making this choice? Is this choice an objective decision or a subjective decision? To what reviews is this decision subject, and are these reviews made public?*

We don't mean to suggest there's anything amiss in this process. But for borrowers and lenders using CME Term SOFR rates as references, a lot of money is at stake, and we believe the market would benefit from even greater transparency into this issue.

OBTAINING FUTURES PRICES TO USE AS INPUTS TO THE TERM SOFR MODEL

In the preceding discussion, we simply assumed that an appropriate set of futures prices was available to serve as inputs to the term SOFR calculation methodology. In practice, the situation isn't that simple.

The CME has produced an involved methodology for determining each day's input price for each futures contract. This methodology isn't entirely straightforward, and the written explanation provided by the CME (October 2021) isn't sufficiently precise for their calculations to be checked and/or replicated by typical market participants (even if these market participants had access to all the necessary data).

But the gist of the approach is as follows (see also Figure 3.2):

1. The trading day from 7:00 a.m. to 2:00 p.m. Chicago time is divided into 14 intervals, each of 30-minute duration.
2. In each time interval, the CME will compute a volume-weighted average price (VWAP) for each of the 18 futures contracts used to produce the term structure of overnight forward rates.
3. The CME also will choose a random time during each of these 14 intervals to observe the bid–ask spread for each contract.
4. If the VWAP for each futures contract is within the observed bid–ask spread during an interval, then the VWAP is recorded as the futures price for that contract during that interval. If the VWAP for a futures contract is greater than the ask price (lower than the bid price), then the ask price (bid price) will be recorded as the futures price for that contract for that interval.
5. For each futures contract, the reference price for that day will be the volume-weighted average of the 14 prices recorded during each of the 14 time intervals, where the weights are the aggregate volumes of all the futures contracts traded in that interval as a fraction of the total volume of these 18 futures contracts during the day.

There are some further caveats, for example, to account for intervals in which no trading occurred – but this is the gist of the approach.

HEDGING TERM SOFR EXPOSURE

At the end of Chapter 2, we presented an approach to hedge with a portfolio of futures against changes in the step function determining *a* term rate. This relatively simple method could be considered as an approximate hedge for *the CME Term rate* as well. However, in case a more precise hedge of the CME Term rate is desired, the more complex method described below seems advisable. After presenting this method and experiencing the issues involved, we'll conclude that there is a tradeoff between the precision and the ease of the hedge.

Consider someone who borrows money for one year and who agrees to pay the 3M term SOFR rate at the end of month 3, month 6, month 9, and month 12. The first term SOFR rate would be specified at the start of the loan, so there is no need to hedge this rate. But in theory we could hedge the three remaining interest payments:

1. A payment at the end of month 6 of the 3M CME Term SOFR rate published at the end of month 3
2. A payment at the end of month 9 of the 3M CME Term SOFR rate published at the end of month 6
3. A payment at the end of month 12 of the 3M CME Term SOFR rate published at the end of month 9.

Let's assume that our borrower wishes to use SOFR futures to minimize the standard deviation of the sum of these random interest payments. What should he do?

A PRECISE APPROACH TO HEDGING CME TERM SOFR EXPOSURE

Consider a situation in which we're given a portfolio of stocks but without being told the quantities in which each individual stock is being held. But imagine further than we could learn the change in the value of the portfolio for a one-unit change in the value of each instrument. In that case, we could hedge the short-term change in the value of this portfolio by selling each stock in proportion to the sensitivity of the portfolio value to a change in the price of this stock. For example, if the portfolio increases in value by USD 100 when the price of IBM stock increases by one dollar, we should sell 100 shares of IBM as part of our hedging strategy. And if the value of the portfolio decreases by USD 50 when the price of Coca-Cola stock increases by one dollar, we should buy 50 shares of Coca-Cola as part of our hedging strategy.

We can apply a similar approach when dealing with our term SOFR exposures. For example, imagine that the 3M CME Term SOFR rate corresponding with our next interest payment increases by 5 bp when the price of the Dec22 one-month SOFR futures contract decreases by 10 bp. And let's imagine that the size of our loan is USD 10 million, such that a 5 bp increase in a quarterly interest rate corresponds to an increase in our interest expense of USD $10,000,000 \times 0.0005 \times (90/360) =$ USD 1,250. To hedge this, we want the value of our position in the Dec22 one-month SOFR futures contract to increase by USD 1,250 in response to a 10 bp decrease in the price of the Dec22 contract. Since a 1 bp price change is worth USD 41.67 per contract, a 10 bp price change is worth USD 416.70 per contract. So in order to experience a change in the value of our position equal to USD 1,250, we need to sell USD 1,250 / USD 416.70 = 3 Dec22 one-month futures contracts as part of our hedge portfolio. By repeating this calculation for each of the futures contracts that determine the value of the 3M CME Term SOFR rate, we can construct a portfolio that *locally* will hedge the exposures to CME Term SOFR rates in our loan. We say that our hedge portfolio will hedge the exposure *locally* because the sensitivities in this example may change as futures prices change and as time passes. We need to repeat these calculations regularly and adjust the positions in our hedge portfolio accordingly.

Let's consider a specific example in greater detail.

Consider a two-year loan, arranged on 27-Jan-22, which pays three-month CME Term SOFR rate every three months until the maturity of the loan, in two years. Assume that the amount of the loan is USD 100 million.

The first interest payment will be due on Friday, 27-Apr-22. But as the rate applying to the first period is known at the time the loan is arranged, this isn't something we can hedge.

The second interest payment will be due on Wednesday, 27-Jul-22, and as it will be set at the end of April, we can hedge this rate and the corresponding payment. The forward value as of 27-Jan-22 for this CME Term SOFR is 0.54850%, and the forward value on 27-Jan-22 of the associated interest payment[4] is USD 136,992.80.

The strategy for hedging this payment will be the same as in the simple example above involving shares of IBM and Coca-Cola. More specifically, we'll follow three steps:

1. Build a stepwise term structure of overnight forward rates, with the discontinuities corresponding to FOMC dates, just as the CME does when calculating CME Term SOFR values.

---

[4]In this exercise, we're calculating partial derivatives numerically, and to use the greatest precision possible, we will not be rounding values as per convention during these intermediate calculations.

2. Calculate the sensitivity of the forward-starting CME Term SOFR – and hence of the interest payment to be hedged – to a change in the price of each futures contract.

3. Construct a hedge portfolio of futures contracts so that the sensitivity of the value of the hedge portfolio to a change in the price of each futures contract is the *opposite* of the sensitivities calculated in step 2.

When we're done, the value of the combined position – i.e., the size of the payment being hedged plus the value of the hedge portfolio – should be insensitive to changes in the prices of any of the 18 futures contracts. In that case, we will have succeeded in immunizing the size of the payment from changes in the prices of any of the 18 futures contracts.

To see the calculations in greater detail, consider Table 8.1.

In the left-most column, we have the identifier codes for the 13 one-month SOFR contracts and the 5 three-month futures contracts used in this exercise. In the column immediately to the right, we have the settlement

TABLE 8.1   Calculations for hedge of 3M term SOFR starting 27-Apr-22, as of 27-Jan-22

#	Futures Identifier Code	Settlement Price	Payment (− 5 bp)	Payment (+ 5 bp)	Payment Difference	Value of 10 bp Change in Futures Price	Number Futures to Sell	Number of Futures to Sell (rounded)
1	SERF2	99.95	137,012.37	136,973.24	−39.14	416.70	−0.094	
2	SERG2	99.95	137,144.61	136,840.99	−303.62	416.70	−0.729	
3	SERH2	99.805	136,669.14	137,316.46	647.31	416.70	1.553	1
4	SERJ2	99.655	136,106.57	137,878.98	1,772.41	416.70	4.253	4
5	SERK2	99.485	132,868.35	141,117.34	8,248.99	416.70	19.796	20
6	SERM2	99.37	133,965.39	140,020.34	6,054.95	416.70	14.531	14
7	SERN2	99.265	135,744.63	138,240.96	2,496.33	416.70	5.991	6
8	SERQ2	99.155	137,035.21	136,950.38	−84.83	416.70	−0.204	
9	SERU2	99.105	137,023.18	136,962.41	−60.78	416.70	−0.146	
10	SERV2	98.995	136,994.69	136,990.90	−3.79	416.70	−0.009	
11	SERX2	98.905	136,992.89	136,992.73	−0.17	416.70	0.000	
12	SERZ2	98.825	136,992.75	136,992.83	0.08	416.70	0.000	
13	SERF3	98.76	136,992.77	136,992.83	0.06	416.70	0.000	
14	SFRZ1	99.95	137,071.22	136,914.38	−156.83	250.00	−0.627	
15	SFRH2	99.565	134,466.31	139,519.48	5,053.17	250.00	20.213	20
16	SFRM2	99.205	136,350.04	137,635.60	1,285.56	250.00	5.142	5
17	SFRU2	98.93	136,994.12	136,991.48	−2.65	250.00	−0.011	
18	SFRZ2	98.72	136,992.78	136,992.82	0.04	250.00	0.000	

Source: Authors

prices of these futures contracts as of 27-Jan-22. In the next column to the right, we have the size of the next payment according to a fitted curve in which the input price of each futures contract has been decreased from its actual value by 5 bp. In the column to the right of that, we have the size of the next payment according to a fitted curve in which the input price of each futures contract has been *increased* from its actual value by 5 bp. The next column to the right shows the difference between the values in the two columns immediately to the left. In other words, the values in this column show the change in the size of the next payment due to a 10 bp change in the input price of each futures contract. Now we need to compare the values in this column to the value of a 10 bp change in the futures rate associated with each contract. These are shown in the next column to the right. As a reminder, the value of a 10 bp change is $10 \times$ USD 41.67 = USD 416.70 for the case of a one-month SOFR futures contract and $10 \times$ USD 25 = USD 250.00 for the case of a three-month SOFR futures contract.

The next column to the right shows the ratio of the change in the value of each payment to the change in the value of each futures contract, due to a 10 bp change in the futures rate of each futures contract. The values in this column show the number of futures contracts we should sell to construct a portfolio that hedges the size of our next random interest payment, which is tied to the random value of the CME Term SOFR. The final column on the right shows these values rounded to the nearest integer.

Let's consider the composition of this hedge portfolio before rounding. The net number of one-month futures contracts we're to sell is 45, while the net number of three-month futures contracts we're to sell is 25. Let's think whether these figures make sense, even to a first approximation.

If the reference period of a one-month contract is 30 days, then a basis point value of USD 41.67 corresponds to a notional amount of USD 5 million. So if we're hedging a notional amount of USD 100 million for a reference period of one month, we'd expect to sell $100/5 = 20$ one-month contracts. And if we hedge a notional amount of USD 100 million for a reference period of three months, we'd expect to sell a total of $3 \times 20 = 60$ contracts – again, assuming we're using one-month SOFR contracts.

On the other hand, if we were using three-month SOFR futures contracts, and if the reference period were 90 days, then a basis point value of USD 25 corresponds to a notional amount of USD 1 million. So if we're hedging a notional amount of USD 100 million for a reference period of three months, we'd expect to sell 100 contracts – again, assuming we're using three-month SOFR futures.

In our hedge portfolio, we're using a combination of one-month and three-month SOFR futures contracts. In particular, we're using 45 one-month contracts and 25 three-month contracts. Since 60 one-month contracts have the hedging power of 100 one-month contracts, we can convert contracts in a mental accounting exercise. Since 25 three-month contracts have the hedging power of $25 \times 60/100 = 15$ one-month contracts, our combined hedge portfolio has the hedging power of $45 + 15 = 60$ one-month contracts, just as our intuition suggested it should have.

On the other hand, we also can convert the hedging power of our one-month contracts to the hedging power of three-month contracts at the same ratio – i.e., 60 one-month contracts for every 100 three-month contracts. In that case, our 45 one-month contracts have the hedging power of 75 three-month contracts. And adding this to the actual position of 25 three-month contracts gives us a combined hedging power equal to 100 three-month contracts – again, in accordance with our intuition.

So our hedge portfolio appears to provide the overall hedging power we'd expect. And looking carefully at Table 8.1, we can see that the composition of this hedge is focused on the period covered by our next random interest period – 27-April-22 through 27-Jul-22.

To get a feel for the performance of this hedge, we can manipulate the term structure of overnight forward rates and see whether our futures hedge portfolio offsets the changes in the forward Term SOFR value and the associated size of our next random interest payment.

For example, let's assume that all the overnight forward rates starting with the 16-Mar-22 FOMC date were to increase from their 27-Jan-22 fitted values by 25 bp. Then the forward Term SOFR value would increase from 0.54195% to 0.79222% – an increase of 25 bp. And the associated interest payment would increase from USD 136,992.80 to USD 200,256.20 – an increase of USD 63,263.40. At the same time, the value of our futures hedge portfolio would increase by USD 62,830.08 – within USD 433.32 of the increase in the value of our interest payment. In this case, the hedge performed to within seven tenths (0.7) of 1%.

If the values of the overnight forward rates after the 16-Mar-22 FOMC instead had decreased by, say, 40 bp, then the value of our interest payment would decrease by USD 101,167.61, which would be largely offset by a loss of USD 99,739.44 in the value of our futures portfolio. In this case, the performance of the hedge was to within 1.4% of target.

PRACTICAL CONSIDERATIONS

To calculate the sensitivity of the forward CME Term SOFR value to the input price of each futures contract, we needed to calculate the first partial derivatives of the forward CME Term SOFR value with respect to the prices of *each* of the eighteen futures contracts serving as inputs to the CME Term

SOFR algorithm. And because there is no closed-form solution for the forward CME Term SOFR value as a function of the futures prices, we needed to calculate these partial derivatives numerically. And because we wanted to obtain a high degree of accuracy, we used central differencing to calculate these partial derivatives, meaning we had to evaluate the objective function and calculate the forward CME Term SOFR value 36 times. And because each evaluation of the objective function required a numerical, nonlinear optimization, we needed to perform 36 of these. And that's just to hedge a single quarterly payment. To precisely hedge all the quarterly payments in a five-year loan would require hundreds of numerical, nonlinear, multidimensional optimizations. This isn't a task for the faint-hearted.

On the other hand, we did the calculations in this example in Excel. These calculations are tedious, and they're cumbersome – but they're also *feasible* without any special hardware or software. Having said that, we strongly suggest anyone who has a need to perform these calculations regularly and/or for a large loan book invest the time to automate these calculations.

The occasional hedger, who does not require a high degree of accuracy, may want to consider the approximate hedge (of *a* term rate) described at the end of Chapter 2 as an easier alternative. (See the Excel spreadsheet "Term rate hedge example" accompanying Chapter 2.)

Another issue to consider is the global nature of the algorithm for fitting a term structure of overnight forward rates. Looking carefully at the futures hedge portfolio detailed in Table 8.1, we see that the hedge portfolio contains one lot of the Mar22 one-month contract, even though the reference period for the Mar22 contract ends almost four weeks before the start date of our forward CME Term SOFR. And the hedge contains four lots of the Apr22 one-month contract, even though the overlap between the reference period of this contract and that of our forward CME Term SOFR is only a few days.

To help explain the composition of the hedge portfolio, it's useful to note that the fitted curve in this case is not bootstrapped, and the fitted curve depends on the inputs *globally*. For example, the curve-fitting algorithm may sacrifice the fit between observed and fitted futures prices in one part of the curve to improve the fit in other parts of the curve. Or the algorithm may allow the curve to become steeper in one region so that the curve can be flatter in another region. Such tradeoffs may be optimal when dealing with a global objective function that contains a global penalty function, but it means that changes in the prices of futures contracts that have no overlap with our CME Term SOFR value can still influence the CME Term SOFR value produced by the algorithm. We see the motivations behind designing an algorithm with this property, but it still makes us a little nervous. And it's certainly something that users need to keep in mind when implementing this curve-fitting methodology.

A bigger concern for us is that the process by which futures input prices are determined is not transparent. In fact, as this process involves collections of bid prices and offer prices taken at 14 random times throughout the day, it's fair to say that the process is opaque *by design*.

We're also slightly concerned by the fact that the CME Benchmark Administrator (CBA) doesn't make any of the input prices to the algorithm publicly available. We see no reason that this shouldn't be done, and we'd feel more comfortable if the input prices were published each day, along with the intermediate calculations that produced each input price.

The CME Term SOFR algorithm can be changed after consultation, and we understand that, in this event, the CBA will make an effort to inform *licensed users* of any changes to this methodology. But our view is that these CME Term SOFR values may well become part of the broader financial ecosystem, in which case a much broader community should be informed in advance of any changes to the methodology – *and at the same time that licensed users are informed of these changes*. For that reason, we'd like for the consultation process and any subsequent announcements regarding changes to CME Term SOFR to be made public.

9

Hedging Swaps and Bonds with SOFR Futures

The Convergence of Futures, Swaps, and Treasury Pricing Following the Transition to SOFR

In order to present the big – and beautiful – picture, let us ignore some ugly details like daycount conventions for a moment. One major consequence of the transition from LIBOR to SOFR is the fact that SOFR futures, SOFR swaps, and government bonds become conceptually very similar:

- 3M SOFR futures compound consecutive 3M forward periods of SOFR into a forward rate and hence the SOFR futures strip into a term rate.
- Swaps with SOFR as floating-leg exchange SOFR versus a fixed-term rate.
- Treasuries can be considered as exchanging their funding rate at (a level close to) SOFR for their coupon payments.

Hence, all three instruments – futures, swaps, and Treasuries – can be seen as (slightly different) ways to compound the same reference rate, daily SOFR values (or, in case of Treasuries, the repo rate, which is typically close to SOFR), into a term rate. Allowing for some imperfection in order to express the conceptual similarity, one could say that futures strips, SOFR-based swaps, and Treasuries all combine the same underlying SOFR into term rates. Abstracting from the technical differences, one might therefore consider all three instruments to be essentially the same – i.e., market prices for a certain future segment of daily SOFR.

Before adding the technical differences, let us contemplate the general consequences of this observation. With futures strips, swaps and Treasuries having become essentially the same, one can replicate and hedge one with another. Furthermore, one can establish arbitrage relationships between the three, which will provide additional sources of profit for relative value (RV) traders and enhanced liquidity in the interconnected instruments for every market participant.

These practical benefits, together with the conceptual beauty of three key markets converging toward essentially the same instrument, can be considered as a major advantage of the transition from LIBOR to SOFR. Expressing some aspects of this advantage more specifically:

- Before the financial crisis, LIBOR-based swaps used the same curve both for determining the cash flows and for discounting. The switch to discounting with another curve (Fed Funds and later SOFR) following the financial crisis resulted in the need to use dual curves when evaluating LIBOR-based instruments. Transitioning everything to SOFR reinstates the clean and easy situation of the old days: SOFR-based swaps usually[1] use the same curve – i.e., SOFR, both for determining the cash flows and for discounting. One consequence is that the present value of the floating side at inception is equal to 100.
- And the daily SOFR values are usually compounded for calculating cash flows and discount factors in the same manner as the settlement price of 3M future contracts. (See formula in Chapter 2.) Hence, the futures strip as defined in Chapter 2 applies the same calculation as SOFR-based swaps. In the following, we will use the futures strip rate as the discounting curve. It is easy to adjust this for other agreements, such as a two-day payment delay.
- Moreover, while the first floating payment of a LIBOR-based swap was usually known at the start of the swap (e.g., the current 3M LIBOR), the first floating payment of a SOFR-based swap refers to the reference period starting *after* entering the swap and is hence unknown. This rectifies the unintuitive feature that only nine months of a 12M LIBOR-based swap are unknown and hence affected by changes to the yield curve. For 12M SOFR-based swaps, the whole 12 months are unknown at the start of the swap. And this also aligns SOFR-based swaps with SOFR futures. The increasing portion of known values (see Figure 2.4) will result in an (almost) equal decrease of sensitivity to interest rate changes of both the swap and the future strip – a fact that stabilizes the hedge ratio of a futures strip.
- Regarding government bonds, we have explained in Chapter 4 that the migration to SOFR-based asset swaps eliminates the basis between

---

[1]Being OTC instruments, of course other agreements are possible as well.

unsecured and secured rates inherent in LIBOR-based asset swaps. Going one step further, with Treasuries being conceptually the same as a basis swap between their funding rate (individual repo) and their coupon rate, one immediately sees the link to a SOFR-swap between repo rates and the fixed rate. Assuming a Treasury always could be financed at SOFR (i.e., it never becomes special), and ignoring payment frequency and daycount differences as well as differences in regulatory treatment, the transition to SOFR allows us to consider swaps and bonds to be conceptually the same – an exchange of an overnight secured funding rate (SOFR) with a fixed rate. And the swap and bond markets are two different places to get a price for the same collections of future SOFR values (e.g., over the next two years). Another way to express this link is to say that, under these assumptions, the fair value of a Treasury asset swap spread is zero.

Unfortunately, one needs to add back the abstractions and simplifications, thereby introducing some complexities into this beautiful and clean picture:

- While the repo rate of individual Treasury bonds is usually close to SOFR, differences are possible due to specialness effects. As SOFR excludes most of the specialness and can be considered as a general collateral (GC) rate, the financing rate of a specific Treasury could be special, for example, because it is a benchmark or cheapest-to-deliver (CTD) into a bond futures contract. In this case, the compounded expected daily financing rates of a Treasury bond, i.e., its yield, should be lower than the compounded expected SOFR (i.e., the futures strip rate, *ceteris paribus*, including daycount and payment frequency). However, in the range of the yield curve covered by SOFR futures, specialness is usually absent due to the absence of its main causes, benchmarks, and CTDs. It is even possible that on days with a particularly large share of special repo rates – e.g., due to high transaction volume in a 10Y benchmark – not all of this effect is excluded during the SOFR calculation and that thus SOFR would be below the repo rate of a specific Treasury. In summary, for shorter Treasuries, it should usually be fine to assume SOFR ≈ Repo and hence equality of the foundation in Figure 9.1.
- Regarding the integration of the daily rates (SOFR and individual repo) into term rates, a variety of different technical features complicates the task of comparing the three markets. Among these are different payment frequencies (e.g., 3M for futures and 6M for treasuries) and daycount conventions (usually actual/360 for money market and actual/actual for

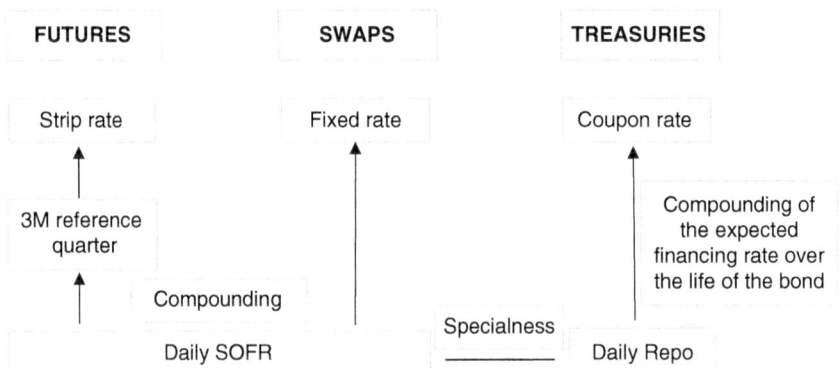

FIGURE 9.1 Integration of SOFR into a term rate in the future, swap, and Treasury markets
Source: Authors

Treasuries). Moreover, as an OTC product, the swap counterparties can agree to all sorts of discounting curves and payment times. For example, SOFR-OIS cleared by the CME have a two-day payment delay. On top of all this comes the issue of date mismatches, highlighted in Chapter 7.
■ And also the impacts from the regulatory side need to be considered. As mentioned in Chapter 4, it can be beneficial for a bank to hold Treasuries rather than engaging in swaps from the perspective of capital costs. The extent of this benefit – and hence the premium the bank is willing to pay for Treasuries – depends on the proximity of balance sheet constraints, which is hard to observe and to quantify. (See Chapter 1.)

Despite these caveats, however, the close link between the three markets introduced by the transition to SOFR can still be used as the basis for replicating and hedging, in particular with SOFR future strips. Figure 9.1 illustrates these links and the remaining part of this chapter will further investigate and exploit them. First, we will provide empirical evidence for the conceptual similarity of SOFR futures and government bond markets. Then, we will apply the return to the good old days of a single curve to replicate the hedging of LIBOR-based swaps with ED futures strips for hedging SOFR-based swaps with SOFR futures strips. Finally, after exploiting the proximity between swaps and Treasuries to transfer this method to hedging Treasuries with SOFR future strips, we will follow one specific Treasury hedge over time and discuss its management and actual performance.

In contrast to the convergence of the markets for swaps and *government* bonds, the transition from the unsecured funding rate LIBOR to the secured funding rate SOFR has caused a divergence of the markets for (SOFR-based) swaps and *corporate* bonds. Actually, hedging a corporate bond with a SOFR-based swap now involves the same unsecured versus secured basis (credit risk) that was involved in hedging government bonds with LIBOR-based swaps (Burghardt, Belton, Lane et al. 1991, p. 110). Hence, we do not recommend hedging corporate bonds with SOFR-based swaps or futures – unless to intentionally express a view on the unsecured versus secured basis – but rather to use ED or FF futures as mentioned in Chapter 4.

TREASURIES VERSUS SOFR FUTURES STRIPS

Building on Chapter 4, we have just argued via Figure 9.1 that, due to the proximity of the financing rate (i.e., the repo rate of the individual Treasury) to SOFR, the asset swap spreads of Treasuries should usually be close to zero (when the swap uses SOFR as floating leg), or equivalently, that the Treasury yield should usually be close to the SOFR futures strip. Intuitively, both the Treasury yield and the SOFR futures strip can be thought of as slightly different ways to compound the expectations about very similar daily financing rates into a term rate.

In order to provide some empirical evidence for this argument, we have calculated the 1Y and 2Y SOFR futures strip rates at the beginnings of the last four reference quarters (Dec 2020, Mar, Jun, and Sep 2021), using the same simplifications[2] as outlined in Chapter 5 and the formula for the strip rate calculation from Chapter 2. This strip rate compounds the daily SOFR values into a term rate using money market daycount conventions; in order to compare it with semiannual bond yields, the following formula has been applied:

$$\left(\left((S - 1) \times \frac{365}{360} + 1 \right)^{\frac{1}{2n}} - 1 \right) \times 2$$

where

- S is the strip yield as calculated in Chapter 2, i.e., by compounding all daily SOFR values.
- n is the number of years (1 or 2).

Figure 9.2 shows the difference between the constant maturity Treasury (CMT) yield as published by the Federal Reserve Economic Data (FRED)

---

[2]For the goal of an overall comparison, these simplifications seem acceptable. For the specific hedge example below, we will use the actual reference quarters.

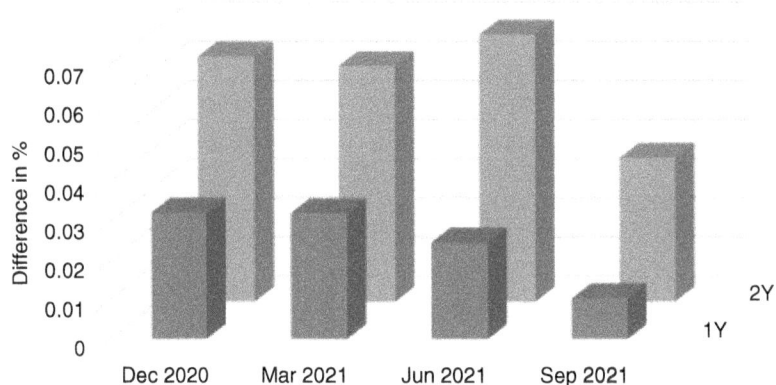

FIGURE 9.2   CMT minus future strip yields
Source: Authors, from CME and FRED data

database and the SOFR futures strip rates as calculated in the manner above. Overall, the differences are small – in line with the goal to validate the argument above. This proximity is also the basis to replicate and hedge Treasuries with SOFR futures strips.

The positive differences visible in Figure 9.2 mean that the CMT yields have been slightly above those of the futures strips. This could be explained by the following factors:

- As usual, specialness has been largely absent from 1Y and 2Y Treasuries. Hence, specialness of 10Y benchmarks, for example, might have caused SOFR to quote below the individual repo rates of short Treasuries (see above).
- Due to the low interest rate environment and easy access to funding, leverage restrictions have played no major role for the pricing during the last year. In terms of Chapter 1, the regulatory cost affecting RV relationships has been close to zero and hence the preference for Treasuries for regulatory reasons has been negligible.
- Effects from the simplification of the reference quarters and from the calculation method of the CMT could also be involved.

When trying to extend this analysis further back, we face the issue of less liquidity in the SOFR futures, especially in the later part of the 2Y strip. Abstracting from these problems (and from those of the simplifications), the general picture provided by Figure 9.2 still holds: slightly positive spreads of a few basis points and more so for 2Y maturities than for 1Y maturities. And we also observe an instance of negative spreads during the period of spikes in SOFR. In March 2020, during the sharp drop in interest rates, there was a period of exceptionally cheap Treasuries relative to the futures strip. We will choose this period intentionally for the analysis of the performance of a Treasury hedge with futures; the discrepancy will show up as a gap between the lines of Figure 9.4.

HEDGING SOFR SWAPS WITH SOFR FUTURES

This section starts by exploiting the move back from dual curves to a single curve to replicate the hedging method of swaps with LIBOR as the floating leg and as discount curve with ED contracts in the ideal case of an IMM swap. We will then consider the adjustments required in less ideal and more realistic circumstances as well as for the recent evolution of the typical conventions for SOFR swaps, ending with an example of hedging of what might currently be the most common SOFR swap.

Due to the novelty of SOFR swaps and their conventions, most of the material in this chapter – and in some other chapters as well – is original and has not been subjected to years of practical application in the market. It is therefore likely that additional aspects not covered here will surface over time when using our approach. The methods and formulae should therefore be considered only as a conceptual starting point, which the reader will probably need to adjust when applying to actual hedges, for example, to reflect further evolutions of the conventions. This comes on top of the necessary adjustment for his specific hedging goals, as mentioned in Chapter 2 and in the introduction to section 2.

As a starting point, let us assume that the SOFR swap replicates the typical conventions of an IMM LIBOR swap:

- The fixed side pays quarterly coupons using bond conventions (30/360).
- The floating side also pays quarterly rates using money market conventions (Actual/360), with the 3M LIBOR being replaced by the compounded SOFR during the 3M reset period (using the ISDA formula from Chapter 2).
- The same compounded SOFR is used as discount factor.
- The reset periods of the swap coincide with the reference quarters of the SOFR futures, as is the case with IMM swaps.
- The payment dates of the swap match those of the futures, i.e., there are no payment delays.

The perfect match of the conventions between futures and swap markets achieves the goal of demonstrating the ideal case in the sense of the conceptual discussion above; the replication of the conventions of LIBOR swaps achieves the goal of demonstrating the link to the hedging method with ED futures. We are aware that both assumptions are rather unrealistic given the current typical conventions for SOFR swaps (with a payment delay and money market conventions also on the fixed side, among others) and will address the necessary adjustments after presenting this artificially ideal case.

In a nutshell, the hedge of such a swap using SOFR as floating leg with SOFR futures can be done in the same manner as Burghardt, Belton, Lane et al. (1991, p. 98) describe hedging a swap using LIBOR as floating leg with ED contracts: Determine the sensitivity of the swap to each forward rate and hedge it with the corresponding ED future, thereby obtaining immunity against movements in all parts of the forward curve. This is possible since both the cash flows and the discounting curve are the same (SOFR) again.

In more detail, assume a 1Y swap starting on Jun 16, 2021, and exchanging on the contract dates (Sep 15 and Dec 15, 2021, and Mar 16 and Jun 16, 2022) of the 3M SOFR futures a fixed rate of 1% (quarterly 0.25%) versus the floating rate as defined by the compounded SOFR values during the previous swap period, which is assumed here to match the reference quarter of the contract. IMM swaps, which have been constructed according to the specifications of their hedging instruments, fulfill this assumption, which makes hedging with futures easy. Also assume that the payments in the swap occur at the same time as the future settlement, i.e., without an offset like for CME-cleared SOFR OIS. Under these ideal assumptions, the floating payments in the SOFR-based swap are exactly the settlement payments of the SOFR futures strip.

The present value of this swap[3] (for receive fixed, pay floating) is given by:

$$\frac{C}{4} \times \sum_{i=1}^{4} \frac{1}{\prod_{j=1}^{i} \left(1 + R_j \times \frac{D_j}{360}\right)} + 100 \times \frac{1}{\prod_{j=1}^{4} \left(1 + R_j \times \frac{D_j}{360}\right)} - 100$$

where

- C is the annual fixed coupon, in this example assumed to be 1%.
- R_j is the (forward) rate for the jth period of the swap, in this example matching the reference quarter of the jth future in the strip, thus $R_j = 100 - $ price of the jth future.
- D_j is the number of calendar days in the jth period.

---

[3] Assuming money market conventions for discounting and bond conventions for the fixed payment, i.e., without adjusting the quarterly coupon payments for the actual length of the reference quarters.

It is instructive to compare this formula with the one from Burghardt, Belton, Lane et al. (1991, p. 98):[4] Unlike for LIBOR swaps, the first floating payment is unknown for SOFR swaps, resulting in the present value depending on the first rate as well. Also note that the term −100 at the end of the expression is the present value of the floating side in this ideal circumstance, where both the floating payments and the discount curve are calculated by exactly the same compounding formula.

Based on this formula, one can now calculate the sensitivity of the present value of the swap to each rate period of the futures strip. This can be done analytically by differentiating the formula by R_j or numerically by recalculating the present value after bumping a specific R_j by 1 bp and taking the difference. The latter method is encoded in the sheet "Swap hedge with strip" accompanying this chapter: The effect of a 1 basis point (bp) increase in the R_j from column D is calculated in cell D12 and pasted into column I. One can then immunize against the effects of changes in each forward rate (R_j) by selling the corresponding futures contract. The hedge ratio is obtained by dividing the change of present value (for a given notional, in this example USD 100m in cell C14) (column J) by the basis point value (BPV) of the futures contract, USD 25. This results in a hedge of short 102 Jun 2021, short 102 Sep 2021, short 101 Dec 2021, and short 101 Mar 2022 SR3 contracts (column K). The money market conventions explain the fact that more than 100 futures are needed for each period. The decreasing discount factor (column G) explains the fact that the number of futures decreases with an increasing forward horizon.

This result suggests that a good approximation for the hedge could be obtained by an easier method: Calculate the change of present value of the swap in USD for a *parallel* curve shift (rather than for each individual consecutive forward rate), divide the result by 25 to get the total number of futures, and divide it *equally* over the futures contracts in the strip. The condition for this approximation to work well is that the discount factors are all close to 1, which is the case in the example above. However, for higher rates and/or longer tenors of the swap, the discount factors will be less close to 1 (and to each other) and thus the simpler method will produce a less accurate approximation for the hedge against moves in any consecutive forward rate.

---

[4]The formula in Burghardt, Belton, Lane et al. (1991) seems to apply bond conventions for discounting, which would result in the present value of the floating side being different from 100 and may need to be corrected.

Moving from the ideal to the real world, we now consider the necessary adjustments for more typical conventions and less perfect matches between the dates. Regarding the conventions:

- Using money market conventions (Actual/360) for both the fixed and floating leg seems[5] to be the current norm for SOFR swaps. This results in the position of the discrepancy between bond and money market conventions moving from within swaps (between fixed and floating leg) to the external relationship between bonds and swaps. As long as bonds do not apply money market daycount conventions, the discrepancy will not disappear, for example, from asset swaps, but rather than being located between the fixed and floating leg of the swap, it now occurs between the bond and the fixed leg of the swap.

  This change can easily be incorporated into the present value formula above and hence into the hedge based on it by multiplying C with 365/360.

- SOFR OIS cleared by the CME use a two-day payment delay for the floating side (and of zero or two days for the fixed side) according to CME (Q4 2018, p. 7) (see Chapter 3 for more background). This can also easily be incorporated into the formula by extending the time frame for calculating the discount factor accordingly. If only the floating side uses the payment delay, two different discount factors need to be applied. And this introduces a mismatch between the floating payment and the discount factor again, resulting in the present value of the floating side becoming different from 100 even at inception. While the discrepancy is usually not as high as in cases of using dual curves with a basis between them, the term for the present value of the floating side becomes more complicated than the simple –100. Moreover, moves in SOFR after the start date of the swap result in a deviation of the present value of the floating side from 100 even in the ideal case of a perfect match at inception.

- Most SOFR swaps appear to apply annual payments for both the fixed and the floating leg. Accordingly, rather than discounting each individual quarterly payment as above, the netted payment is discounted

---

[5]Being OTC products, there are no firm specifications like for future contracts. Hence, we need to base our statements on sources from clearinghouses like CME (Q4 2018) or https://www.cmegroup.com/trading/interest-rates/cleared-otc .html and anecdotal evidence.

annually. For the hedging method, this means that the "natural" decomposition of the discount factors into the segments of the SOFR futures strip needs to be "artificially" created. But with this little trick, shown in the formula breaking down *S* below, the same approach can be used.

And regarding date mismatches:

- If the start date of the swap does not correspond to the start date of a reference quarter (unlike for the ideal IMM swap considered above), the first SOFR futures contract used for hedging is already in its reference quarter. This can be handled by applying the techniques presented in Chapter 2. In fact, the artificial decomposition of the discount factor mentioned above and expressed mathematically below will then have $R_{unknown}$ as first segment.

  The further the start date of the swap falls behind the start date of the reference quarter, the more SOFR values are already known. This results in a lower sensitivity of the SOFR futures contract to changes in the SOFR level, since they only affect the remaining reference quarter. But the same is true for the sensitivity of the swap, which also depends only on the unknown part of SOFR values. In an ideal case, the decreases of sensitivity of the swap and its hedging instruments are equal, allowing us to keep the hedge ratio stable even as the front-month contract progresses through its reference quarter (only adjusting the hedge ratio for the increase of the discount factor over time). Depending on the conventions (and the level of known SOFR values) it is theoretically possible that the passing of time affects the sensitivity of the swap and the futures hedge unevenly. But the results of the examples shown below suggest that simply keeping the hedge ratio of the front month stable until settlement seems to work usually well in practice.

  We lack experience about the practicability of maintaining the hedge during the last days of the reference quarter into settlement, though; after applying these concepts in the actual market, it may well turn out that rolling the hedge with the front month into the first deferred contract month, for example, three days before it expires, works better.

- If the end date of the swap does not correspond to the end date of a reference quarter, the last SOFR futures contract used for hedging will cover a period going beyond the swap term. If no FOMC meeting falls between the two end dates, it is usually[6] acceptable to continue

---

[6]Apart from FOMC meetings, a quarter end may be considered as problematic. On the other hand, the SRF (discussed in Chapter 1) could be seen as mitigating this problem.

using the futures strip without adjustment. If an FOMC meeting takes place between the two end dates, however, the adjustment techniques described in Chapters 2 and 7 need to be incorporated, for example, by calibrating a jump(-diffusion) process.

Figure 9.3 illustrates the date mismatches at the beginning and at the end of the futures strip covering the swap and the approaches to dealing with them.

Let us now try and combine all these adjustments (with the exception of a mismatch at the end date) into a possible hedge of what is likely to be the most typical SOFR swap with a strip of SOFR futures. Reflecting the currently most common conventions described above, we assume that the 1Y SOFR swap, still starting on Jun 16, 2021, and ending on Jun 16, 2022, exchanges yearly payments of a fixed versus a floating rate, i.e., just once at its end. We further assume that both legs apply money market conventions and a two-day payment delay, i.e., that the payment takes place on Jun 17, 2022. And we calculate the hedge at an arbitrary point in time during the reference quarter of the first contract (Jun 2021), not necessarily at the start date of the swap. As a consequence, we will encounter a different term than −100 for the present value of the floating leg.

For this case, the netted payment is given by the difference of the fixed rate and the compounded SOFR values over the year, both using money market conventions, i.e.:

$$
C \times \frac{365}{360} - \left[\prod_{i=1}^{n} \left(1 + \frac{\frac{SOFR_i}{100} \times d_i}{360} \right) - 1 \right] \times 100
$$

where

- C is again the annual fixed coupon.
- n is the number of business days during the swap period, i.e., i starts on Jun 16, 2021, and ends on Jun 14, 2022.

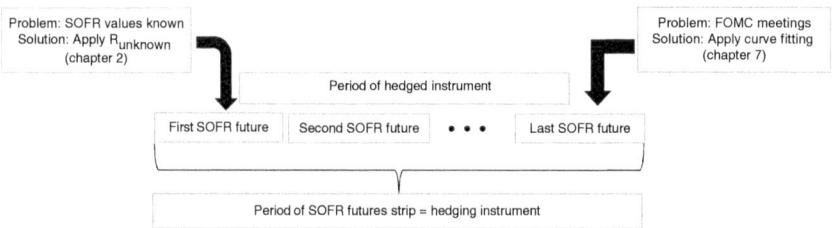

FIGURE 9.3　Date mismatches between the hegded instrument and the SOFR futures strip used for hedging
Source: Authors

- $SOFR_i$ is the SOFR for day i (published on the next business day).
- d_i is the number of calendar days for which $SOFR_i$ is used.

The discount factor is determined by the strip rate S from Chapter 2, starting at the present day, in this case assumed to be any day during the reference quarter of the Jun 2021 contract, and extending two business days after the end of the swap, i.e., until the actual payment date. Breaking down S into the segments of the strip, one can write the discount factor in the following form:

$$\prod_{j=1}^{n_{unknown}} \left(1 + \frac{\frac{SOFR_j}{100} \times d_j}{360}\right) \prod_{j=n_{unknown}+1}^{n_2} \left(1 + \frac{\frac{SOFR_j}{100} \times d_j}{360}\right)$$

$$\times \prod_{j=n_2+1}^{n_3} \left(1 + \frac{\frac{SOFR_j}{100} \times d_j}{360}\right) \prod_{j=n_3+1}^{n_4} \left(1 + \frac{\frac{SOFR_j}{100} \times d_j}{360}\right) \prod_{j=n_4+1}^{n_4+2} \left(1 + \frac{\frac{SOFR_j}{100} \times d_j}{360}\right)$$

where

- j starts at the present day.
- $n_{unknown}$ is the number of business days during the unknown (future) part of the reference quarter of the first contract, as defined in Chapter 2.
- n_k is the number of business days between the present day and the last day of the reference quarter of the kth contract.

Dividing the netted payment by the discount factor, i.e., both expressions, returns the present value for the more realistic case. While it looks more complicated than the ideal case described at the beginning, the same idea can be applied to calculate the hedge ratios: Rather than bumping each R_j and observing the impact on the present value, now every $SOFR_j$ during each reference quarter needs to be changed. And unlike in the easy case above, this shift now also affects the floating payment, i.e., both the numerator and the denominator of the present value formula.

As starting values for the bump, it seems reasonable to use the known values for SOFR (as in the sheet "Strip" from Chapter 2) and the unknown SOFR values implied by the futures strip. With this adjustment, the same method described above can be applied: Calculate the effect of a 1 bp bump in each of the individual reference quarters on the present value of the swap and obtain the number of futures by dividing by the effect of a 1 bp bump during its reference quarter on the present value of the futures contract. Specifically for the front-month contract, the effect of a 1 bp bump to all SOFR values during the (remaining part of the) reference quarter can be different from the effect of a 1 bp bump to the futures price. Hence, the divisor cannot simply be assumed to be 25 anymore but needs to be calculated as well.

The Excel sheet "Swap hedge with strip 2" encodes this approach toward hedging. We assume the hedge is calculated on the "present day" of June 23, 2021, i.e., one week after the start date of the swap, and incorporate the relevant part from the sheet "Strips" from Chapter 2 to deal with the known part of SOFR values. We use the actual SOFR values for the known part and the SOFR values implied by the futures market of Jun 23, 2021 (column H), for the unknown part (column K).[7] For this case, the implied daily SOFR values are extremely close to the future rates.

As a complication, an FOMC announcement is scheduled for June 15, 2022. While this does not affect the futures anymore, it has an effect on the discount curve, which extents two days longer: The SOFR for June 14 is the last value used for calculating the floating rate payment and the prices of the hedging instruments; but the SOFR values for June 15 and 16 are involved in the calculation of the discount factor, and at least the latter is affected by the FOMC decision published on June 15. This is also a good example of the effect that seemingly small convention details like a two-day payment delay can have on the pricing and hedging models. It introduces a new variable (for the Fed policy change on June 15) into the equation, which could be calculated by the jump process fitting method. For this specific case, given the current price of the Jun 2022 contract and the fact that only one or two days are affected, one might decide to not further complicate the sheet by assuming no policy change at the June 15 meeting.

Inputting the same values for C (1%) and the notional (USD 100 m) as before, column K performs the calculations from the formulae above, showing the future rates, the fixed and floating payments, the discount factor, and the present value for the swap for the specific SOFR values (column C). These SOFR values can now be bumped segment-wise via column L. The resulting changes in the present value of the swap and the future rate are displayed in columns M and N, respectively. We note that our expectation, that the sensitivity of the first future contract and the swap decreases to an equal extent as more SOFR values become known, is validated. Using the same method as

---

[7]Using the method presented in the sheet "Strips," which is not encoded again in this sheet.

before, the number of futures required to hedge against those segment-wise changes in the SOFR strip is calculated in column O. For this example, the hedge consists in selling 101 of each of the four contracts, Jun, Sep, and Dec 2021 as well as Mar 2022.

Comparing the results with the easy hedge from the beginning, there is only a marginal difference. Before jumping to the conclusion that the efforts of incorporating all adjustments add little value, the reader should keep in mind that the situation is likely to change when the yield curve is not flat and close to zero anymore.

HEDGING TREASURIES WITH SOFR FUTURES

Exploiting the close link between the three markets described at the beginning and illustrated in Figure 9.1, the approach to swap hedging can be easily adjusted to hedging government bonds with a SOFR futures strip as well. This section starts by describing the modifications before demonstrating a possible hedge for a concrete example. It will then follow the evolution of the hedge over time, discuss the necessary management, and assess its performance.

For a Treasury with semiannual coupon payments, the present value is given by

$$\frac{C}{2} \times \sum_{i=1}^{n} \frac{1}{S_i} + 100 \times \frac{1}{S_n}$$

where

- C is again the annual coupon.
- n is the number of coupon payments until maturity.
- S_i is the strip rate until the payment date of the ith coupon (as defined in Chapter 2).

As above, the same little trick of decomposing the strip rate into the segments defined by the reference quarters of 3M SOFR futures can be applied. Once the hedging problem is set up in this form, it can again be approached by extracting a curve of daily SOFR values from the current SOFR future prices,[8] bumping all daily SOFR values during a specific reference quarter,

---

[8]Using the adjustment for the known SOFR values during the reference quarter for the first future and the techniques for accounting for FOMC meetings during the reference quarter of the last future once more (see Figure 9.3).

observing the effect on the present value of the bond (and the futures contract), and calculating the hedge ratio by dividing the two. Repeating this
exercise for every futures contract in the strip returns the hedge portfolio.

The Excel worksheet "Bond hedge with strip" encodes this approach
and is hence similar to "Swap hedge with strip 2." It calculates this hedging
possibility for the 1.5% US Treasury note maturing on Sep 30, 2021. In
order to describe the evolution of the hedge over an interesting time with
big rate moves (and in order to include a problematic phase with widening
swap spreads as well), we have chosen Jan 2, 2020, as the "current" day for
initiating the hedge. On this date, the remaining cashflows of the bond were
covered by the strip of 3M SOFR futures starting with Dec 19 and ending
with Sep 21 (column G). Thus, the SOFR values from Dec 18, 2019, until
Jan 1, 2020, were already known and are treated as in the sheet "Strips"
from Chapter 2 again. The last reference quarter extends quite long after
the maturity date of the bond (until Dec 15, 2021). In the reference quarter
of the Sep 21 SOFR future, two FOMC meetings are scheduled, one on Sep
22, 2021, the other on Nov 3, 2021.

While the first falls before the maturity date of the bond and therefore
also affects the bond pricing, due to the different length of the period affected
(about a week of the bond versus about six weeks for the future), its impact
on the future is significantly larger. And the Fed policy announcement on
Nov 3, 2021, occurs after the Treasury has matured and therefore affects
the Sep 21 contract only. In principle, this situation requires the application
of curve-fitting techniques in order to adjust the sensitivity of the hedging
instrument to Fed policy to the one of the bond to be hedged. However,
with the price of the Dec 21 futures contract being very close to the one
of the Sep 21 futures contract (only 1.5 bp different), the market did not
price in a Fed policy change at the two FOMC meetings in question. If the
hedger agrees with this expectation, he could skip the curve-fitting exercise
and simply assume a constant SOFR during the reference quarter of the last
future in the strip (as we do in the Excel worksheet).

As above, we have used the daily SOFR values (column C) during each
reference quarter as implied by the current market prices (in column H, as of
Jan 2, 2020) as starting points for the shifts (column C).[9] It should be noted
that this discount curve from the futures market results in a present value of
the bond (100.42), which is 0.20 above the market price – and in line with the
positive spreads observed in Figure 9.2. Hence, one could adjust the starting
points by this spread, i.e., shift all daily SOFR values by 11 bp; however,
in this case the influence on the results is negligible. Based on this discount
factor curve, cell K19 encodes the formula above to calculate the present

---

[9] Also in this case, the implied daily SOFR values were almost the same as the future
rate.

value of the bond. And then again, by bumping the segments of the SOFR curve corresponding to the reference quarters of the contracts (column L), the effect on the present value of the bond (and of the futures contracts) can be obtained (column M), leading to the hedge portfolio with the futures strip (column O), shown in the first column of Table 9.1. Let us highlight again the equal decrease in sensitivity of both the first futures contract and the bond due to the SOFR values already known. By contrast, at the end of the strip, the last future is significantly more exposed to changes in SOFR during its reference quarter than the bond, which matures already a few days into the reference quarter; this is reflected in the correspondingly lower amount of Sep 21 contracts in the strip. Apart from the edges of the strip, the somewhat higher rate level compared to the examples above translates into a slightly more pronounced decrease of the discount factors and hence also of the hedge ratios.

As a first check of the hedge just calculated, let us assume that immediately after initiating the position, i.e., on Jan 2, 2020, all SOFR values increase by 1 bp, i.e., the yield curve shifts up. In the Excel worksheet, this can be simulated by bumping all segments via column L by 0.01%. This move results in a decrease of the present value of the bond (cell L20) by USD 17,568 and in an increase of the value of the hedge portfolio by USD 17,517.[10]

TABLE 9.1 Evolution of a hedge of a Treasury note with a SOFR futures strip

3M SOFR contracts	Jan 2, 2020: start of hedge	Mar 18, 2020: rehedge	Jun 17, 2020: rehedge
Dec 19	−101	0	0
Mar 20	−101	−103	0
Jun 20	−100	−103	−103
Sep 20	−100	−102	−103
Dec 20	−100	−102	−103
Mar 21	−99	−102	−102
Jun 21	−99	−102	−102
Sep 21	−17	−18	−18
Sum	−717	−632	−531

Source: Authors

[10]Keep in mind that the simple multiplication of the number of contracts (717) with the BPV (USD 25) does not work for the 101 front-month contracts. Hence, the P&L of the hedge portfolio is obtained by (717 − 101) * 25 plus 101 * 0.8384 * 25 (see cell N3).

These hedges are not static and in theory require daily rebalancing. In practice, longer rehedging intervals could turn out to be acceptable, with the precise length depending on the level of rates, among other things. This is due to the following changes as time passes:

- The discount factors increase and therefore require an increasing number of futures to maintain the hedge of the present value of the swap. Obviously, this effect is more pronounced in higher rate environments and also depends on the shape of the yield curve.
- Considering the first contract in the strip, every day an additional SOFR value becomes known (and needs to be added to column C of the Excel worksheet). And at the end of its reference quarter, the futures contract settles and is dropped from the hedge portfolio. This results in a big change in the absolute number of contracts in the hedge portfolio at the turn of each reference quarter. However, as the front-month contract loses sensitivity each day during its reference quarter, it is actually a smooth transition. This is a contrast to ED futures strips and can be considered as an advantage when hedging with SOFR futures strips.

Let's see how the rebalancing might look in the specific example of the Treasury note, which has been hedged according to the leftmost column of Table 9.1 on Jan 2, 2020. If one decides to recalculate the hedge at every turn of the reference quarters, the following changes are visible in the next columns of Table 9.1:

- As the first contracts, Dec 19 and Mar 20, settle, they simply drop from the hedge portfolio.
- During the period considered, the yield curve has become lower and flatter. The overall decrease of rates is reflected in an increase of the number of futures contracts required for the hedge (for each of those contracts which are still part of the hedge portfolio). And the flattening of the yield curve resulted in a more equal distribution of the number of futures contracts across the strip.

Finally, we consider the actual performance of this hedge in an environment of a sharp drop of rates. Assuming no rebalancing (also not on Mar 18, 2020), Figure 9.4 compares the profit of the bond position with the profit of the futures strip used as a hedge.[11] At first, until March and also

---

[11]For ease of comparison, the P&L of long positions in both the note and the futures strip are depicted; of course, in the actual hedge, a long position in the bond is hedged with a short position in the futures strip, as shown in Table 9.1.

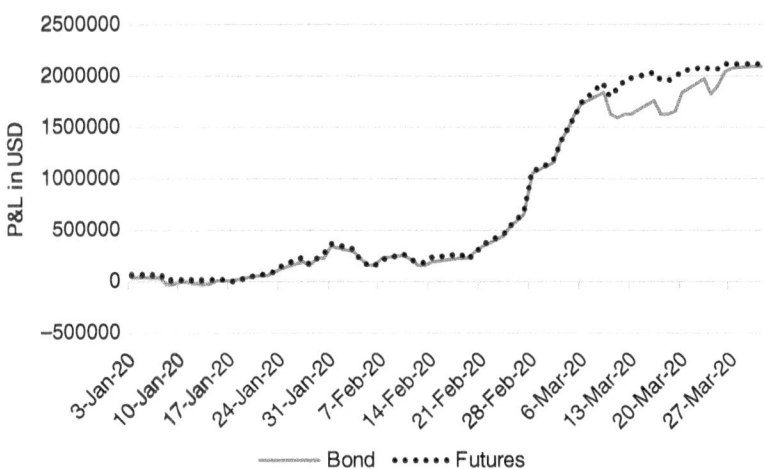

FIGURE 9.4 Evolution of the Treasury and of the hedging futures portfolio
Source: Authors

during the rate decrease, the performance of the hedge was almost perfect. For example, two months after initiating the hedge (i.e., on Mar 2, 2020), the bond had gained USD 1,162,500, while the futures portfolio had lost USD 1,158,325.

During March, there was a period of larger discrepancies: For example, at the end of the reference quarter of the Dec 19 contract (when the rebalancing from Table 9.1 was calculated), the hedge portfolio established on Jan 2, 2020, and maintained without adjustment had suffered a loss of USD 1,959,518, while the note had returned a profit of USD 1,631,250, resulting in a loss of the hedged position of USD 328,268. This corresponds to about 20% of the overall move.

Investigating the reasons for the poor performance of the hedge during this period, with the asset swap spread (using a swap with SOFR as floating leg) of the Treasury note becoming more positive, it appears as if its pricing has been ephemerally influenced by the corporate bond market. Hence, the foundation of the whole hedging concept of constant spreads (Figure 9.1) has been violated. As a consequence, the markets, which should be linked by the argument at the beginning of this chapter, have decoupled, and thus the hedge based on the assumption of constant asset swap spreads has not performed as well as before. This example can also serve as illustration of the risk of mis-hedging with futures strips if the fundamental link does not hold, for example, when applied to a corporate bond or in times of changes in the effect of capital costs on the relative pricing between futures and government bonds.

Putting a happy ending to the story, the decoupling turned out to be ephemeral indeed, and by the end of March, the gap was closed again. For example, on Mar 31, 2020, the bond had gained USD 2,100,000 versus a loss on the future portfolio of USD 2,113,099, bringing the mismatch down to less than 1%. If confirmed by a larger number of cases, the experience of this example points to two conclusions:

1. This approach to hedging seems to work in practice as long as its theoretical foundation (Figure 9.1) holds firm. When the foundation shakes, for example, due to changes in the leverage situation driving the asset swap spreads (with SOFR as floating leg) of government bonds away from zero, the hedge built on it is also at risk.
2. If mismatches of the hedge are considered to be ephemeral, a hedger could simply maintain it and wait for the discrepancy to disappear, as in this example. And a relative value trader might even consider the brief periods as arbitrage opportunities in the framework of the links between the three markets from Figure 9.1: Buying the bond versus selling the hedge portfolio of futures on Mar 18, 2020, at a spread of USD 328,268 would have returned a profit of USD 315,169 until Mar 31, 2020. Obviously, this "arbitrage" is based on the condition of the foundation holding and the mismatches being short-lived.

Regarding the implementation of these hedges in software programs, Excel worksheets are not practical for recalculating the hedge ratio every day, let alone for managing a whole portfolio of hedges or for monitoring the market for a large number of potential arbitrage opportunities. Readers should therefore budget time and money for the IT-implementation and back-testing both of the possible approaches to hedging described here and of alternatives which may fit better to their specific goals.

Hedging Caps and Floors with SOFR Futures Options

We highlighted in Chapter 5 the interconnected problems of a missing theoretical pricing approach and of missing market liquidity for options on SOFR futures. The first problem makes it impossible to simply transfer the hedging concepts from Eurodollar (ED) futures options. While in Chapter 9 we described how to hedge a SOFR OIS with a strip of SOFR futures in the same manner as one hedges a LIBOR-based swap with a strip of ED contracts, that approach requires major modifications for hedging a cap or floor on SOFR. The second problem makes it impossible to test any hedges constructed with options on SOFR futures in the same manner as we did for the bond hedge with a SOFR futures strip (Figure 9.4), among others.[1]

Despite these problems, this chapter intends to give some practical advice for hedging caps and floors with options on SOFR futures. While one cannot expect the hedge to be as easy and well-fitting as in case of LIBOR-based products, one can try and make the best of a difficult situation by dividing the hedging strategy conceptually according to the two fundamentally different stages explained at the beginning of Chapters 2 and 5:

- *Before* their reference period starts, SOFR futures function as aggregators of daily SOFR values into a (forward) term rate and hence the options on them work just like those on ED contracts. Here, the concepts can again be simply transferred to caps and floors based on the new reference rate.

---

[1]During the editing process of this book in the first half of 2022, liquidity in options on SOFR futures has started to increase.

■ But as soon as the reference period begins, the difficulties begin. At that point, the options on 3M SOFR futures have stopped trading altogether, so in order to hedge the corresponding caplet or floorlet until the end, one needs to switch to options on 1M SOFR contracts. While these cover the period until payment of the floorlet, they undergo a metamorphosis into arithmetic Asian options, for which pricing models are generally unavailable. Among others, this makes it impossible to manage the date mismatch in the switch from 3M to 1M and to calculate the Greeks needed for the hedge ratios.

Like Chapter 5, Chapter 10 is structured according to this break: It starts by applying the concepts for hedging with a strip of options on ED contracts to hedge caps and floors based on SOFR and encounters no hurdles – until the reference periods start. While options on ED contracts cover the same 3M LIBOR term rate, which is also used in caps and floors, options on 3M SOFR futures stop trading, leaving only those on 1M SOFR contracts available (and face the date mismatch between both). Simultaneously, in the absence of a pricing model, only basic hedging strategies are possible. Hence, at this point in time, Chapter 10 presents an overview of elementary replication and hedging strategies for options on 1M SOFR futures, which do not require a pricing model. Of course, once a pricing model exists for options on 1M SOFR futures, these simple strategies can be collapsed into delta hedging or floating strikes.

This chapter ends by considering a further complication from the recommendation of the ARRC to apply the floor in some loans on a *daily* basis: This results in options on 1M SOFR futures not only being currently impossible to price due to the underlying being an arithmetic average of daily SOFR values, but also that their underlying is different from the floor to be hedged. We will apply our heuristic spreadsheet for a last time in order to get a first impression of the severity of the mismatch and conclude that this is another question whose answer is heavily dependent on the process selected.

While we have tried throughout the book to make the transfer from LIBOR to SOFR despite its conceptual differences as easy as possible for market practitioners, we need to finish by stating that the intrinsically higher complexity of the new reference rate inevitably manifests itself when applied to hedging caps and floors. This seems to be a casualty of the transition.

HEDGING WITH OPTIONS ON 3M SOFR FUTURES BEFORE THEIR REFERENCE QUARTER STARTS

Expanding Figure 2.1, Figure 10.1 illustrates the situation of hedging a SOFR-based floor (with two 3M floorlets being shown) with options on SOFR contracts. Each point represents one daily SOFR value; like the reference periods of the futures, the underlying rates determining the payoff of the floorlets can be considered as aggregations of these daily values into (forward) term rates.

If the hedge is executed on a day *before* the reference periods of the 3M SOFR futures start, it can be constructed, priced, and analyzed just as in case of hedging a LIBOR-based floor with options on ED contracts. If one assumes that the dates and strikes match (i.e., that we're dealing with an IMM floor), then the hedge is as easy as the one for an IMM swap described in Chapter 9. In fact, the payoff of the floor can be hedged with a strip of calls on 3M SOFR futures with a strike at 100 minus the level of the floor.

And if the dates or strikes do not match (as in Figure 10.1) and/or a hedge against additional variables (such as implied volatility or time value) is desired, the models available for options on ED futures can be transferred:

- The method from Burghardt et al. (1991) could be copied, applying linear algebra to maintain neutrality in the Greeks in certain manually defined scenarios. However, given that this method ignores both the slope of volatility curves and the smile, it appears outdated.
- The current state of the art would be to fit a term structure model (or, in the absence of liquidity in the futures option market, to estimate its parameters, perhaps from other option markets), allowing to address mismatches both of dates and of strikes appropriately.
- If the floor is European, as is usually the case, the difference to the American option on SOFR futures needs to be considered. For options on ED contracts, this is typically done via numerical simulations, which can be applied in the SOFR universe as well.

MANAGING THE HEDGE DURING THE REFERENCE QUARTER

Shortly before[2] the beginning of the reference quarter of the first 3M SOFR future, its options stop trading. Hence, if one does not react to this early end

---

[2]On the Friday before the 3rd Wednesday of the contract month. See Figure 5.2 for more details.

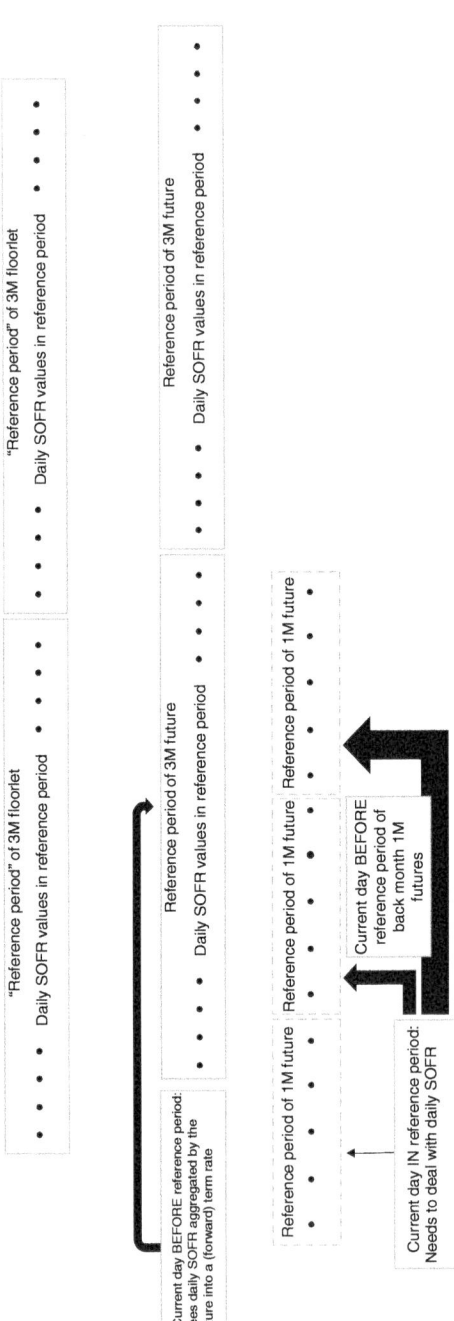

FIGURE 10.1 The aggregation of daily SOFR via the future before the reference period starts and via floorlets

Source: Authors

of trading, each floorlet remains unhedged after this event. In case of an IMM floor, it would be unhedged for the full 3M period plus a few days. In terms of Figure 10.1, this corresponds to deleting the 3M futures options as possible hedging instruments a few days before the beginnings of their reference quarters. Under the likely assumption that a significant unhedged period is not acceptable, one therefore needs to consider other hedging instruments still trading:

- In case exposure to the secured–unsecured basis (see Chapter 4) is acceptable, one might think of options on ED futures. However, this does not lead to a decent solution: The option on the ED future covering the same period ends trading on the next business day (Monday), and the option on the following ED contract in the strip has a different period as underlying.
- This only leaves options on 1M SOFR futures as replacement for the expired option on 3M SOFR futures. When the option on the 3M SOFR future stops trading, the "current" day (Figure 10.1) lies somewhere in the middle of the reference period of the front-month 1M SOFR contract. Hence, to cover the whole period of the floorlet, one would need to use a combination of an exotic Asian option (front month) and of standard options (back months) on 1M SOFR contracts. As one progresses through the period underlying the floorlet, these standard options also will become exotic as soon as their contracts enter their reference months.

Since there are only options on 1M SOFR futures left as reasonable hedging instruments without a basis,[3] the practical hedger will now be confronted with the problem of a missing pricing formula for Asian options using arithmetic averaging (and of the American type, to make it even more complicated). While the early end of trading in options on 3M SOFR futures spares him encountering this difficulty with 3M future options, in case he wants to maintain his hedge, he will face it when looking at 1M future options as a replacement.

In the absence of a pricing formula (or an approximation with the same first two moments, as explained by Vyncke, Goovaerts, and Dhaene (2003)), the Greeks cannot be calculated. Thus, a possible reaction to this problem could be to only hedge the payoff of the floorlet with a series of options on 1M SOFR futures, but keep exposure to changes in implied volatility,

---

[3]Apart from OTC products, which are costly and only pass on the pricing problem without solving it.

for instance, after the option on the 3M SOFR contract has expired. The next section describes how this could be done without using any (nonexisting) option pricing formula. This approach is risky, if the hedge needs to be unwound before the payment date of the floorlet.

In order to obtain some hedge against changes to the implied volatility (and thereby reduce the risk in case of unwinding the hedge early), one could use options on back-month 1M SOFR futures (in Figure 10.1, this would be the second and third boxes in the row representing 1M SOFR contracts). Since these are still standard options, one can calculate the Greeks both for the floorlet and the future options and thereby the hedge ratios needed for immunity against changes to implied volatility, for example. Of course, this "hedge" is far from perfect (already due to the date mismatches), requires constant adjustments – and ends when the last 1M SOFR future in the floorlet period (third box in Figure 10.1) enters its reference month and the Greeks cannot be calculated anymore. That method therefore only shortens the period of unhedged exposure from about 3M to about 1M.

Without a pricing model (step 2 from Chapter 5), it is impossible to assess, compare, and address the mismatches involved in different hedging approaches theoretically. And without a liquid market, it is impossible to test them empirically (step 3). Unlike in Chapter 9, we can thus neither offer a simple method to deal with mismatches nor look at their magnitudes (as in Figure 9.4). One needs to accept that the current situation does not allow easy or perfect hedges of SOFR-based caps and floors with options on SOFR futures.

Though we can provide neither mathematical proof nor empirical evidence, a practicable hedging strategy for a SOFR-based floor could consist of the following elements:

- Use options on 3M SOFR futures as long as they trade.
- Once they expire, switch to the basic hedging strategy of the payoff of the next floorlet described below.
- If there is a possibility that the hedge needs to be unwound early, reduce the period of unhedged Greeks by using options on back-month 1M SOFR futures as long as this is possible. In this case, it may be advisable to switch from 3M to 1M futures options some days before the former expire in order to avoid the instability problem.

BASIC REPLICATION STRATEGIES OF CAPS AND FLOORS WITH 1M FUTURE OPTIONS

The shift to SOFR has incorporated into the life of options a sudden jump into unknown territory, deprived of the support of a pricing model, leaving only basic approaches available. An analogy could be a researcher being thrown by a plane crash into an untouched (exotic option) world, who needs to rely on elementary techniques for survival until help (from a pricing model) arrives. We will briefly review some of these basic replication and hedging methods, which do not require a pricing formula.

The most straightforward method to ensure earning a minimum interest rate is to simply buy a floor at that minimum rate and to hold it until expiry. As this does not involve any (delta) hedging, no pricing model (or an approximation for calculating the Greeks) is needed. The same can be obtained by buying a series of calls on consecutive 1M SOFR futures at a strike of 100 minus the minimum interest rate desired. Given the early end to trading of options on 3M SOFR futures, options on 1M futures are preferable. But given the limited number of expiration dates listed, this only covers the next three to four months and does not provide strikes far-out-of-the-money. (See Chapter 5.) For example, a floor on the average SOFR from January to March 2022 at 0.2% can be achieved by buying calls with a strike of 99.80 on each of the three 1M SOFR futures from January to March 2022. Similarly, a cap at 0.2% can be obtained by buying puts with a strike at 99.80.

Hence, one can consider a series of options on consecutive SOFR futures as replications of caps and floors and use them as a basic hedge. For instance, a dealer short the floor from the example above could buy the series of calls on 1M SOFR futures as an approximate hedge. This is a crude method, of course, which does not take into consideration any different impact of changes in the implied volatility on the (standard) floor and the set of (exotic) futures options. If the hedge needs to be unwound before expiry, this can result in significant losses.

Moreover, while the method of buying a series of calls on consecutive 1M SOFR futures at a strike of 100 minus the minimum interest rate desired will achieve the goal of guaranteeing that minimum interest rate (just like buying a floor), it is quite likely that it costs more than necessary. Imagine that an investor wants to earn at least 0.1% interest during the month of February 2022 and therefore purchases a call with strike 99.90 on the 1M Feb 2022 SOFR future, and that during the first two weeks of February, the daily SOFR values have been 0.2%. By looking at the settlement formula using an arithmetic average, the investor figures out that he is going to achieve his goal of earning at least 0.1% in case the average SOFR during the remaining two weeks exceeds 0.0%. Hence, he can sell his call with strike 99.90 and buy a cheaper call with strike 100.00, thereby reducing the cost of his hedge while still ensuring to meet his goal.

Formalizing this idea, as more and more SOFR values become known, it is possible to adjust the strike accordingly by using the formula

$$S = \left(S_t - A\frac{n_k}{n_t}\right) \times \frac{n_t}{(n_t - n_k)}$$

where

- S is 100 minus the adjusted strike for the day when n_k days of the reference period are known.
- S_t is 100 minus the strike over the whole reference period.
- A is the arithmetic average over the known SOFR values.
- n_k is the number of known days of the reference period.
- n_t is the total number of days of the reference period.

In the example above, S is 0, S_t is 0.1%, and A is 0.2%. Also note that for $S_t = A$, it follows that $S = S_t$.

By adjusting the strike of the call via this formula, theoretically every day, it is possible to ensure receiving a minimum interest rate without paying too much.[4] For longer periods, the formula can be expanded to cover a series of options on 1M SOFR futures. Using the case from above, where a floor on the average SOFR from January to March 2022 at 0.2% is desired and assuming that the average of SOFR during January and February was 0.3%, a call with a strike at (about[5]) 100.00 on the March 2022 contract would be sufficient to achieve this goal.

Figure 10.2 shows an example of this cost-minimizing strategy for the month of June 2018, during which the daily SOFR values first dropped from 1.81% to 1.69%, before increasing to more than 2%. Applying the formula above for daily strike adjustments, to achieve a floor at 1.8%, the strike of the call needs to be adjusted downward (resulting in a loss) to a level of 98.15 on June 14, before the increase in SOFR values allows an adjustment upward (resulting in a profit), ending at 98.55. In contrast, to achieve a floor at 1.9%, the strike of the call needs to be constantly adjusted downward, since the daily SOFR values were quite a bit below 1.9% at the beginning of the month and even their increase toward the end of the month could not bring the average toward 1.9%. As a consequence, this strategy required a significant strike adjustment in the later period, ending at a strike of 97.05 – while the loss was mitigated by the low time value.

---

[4]From the perspective of setting the strike level of the option on the 1M SOFR future. Of course, it is possible that there are cheaper alternatives from using other options.
[5]Ignoring the different number of days in these three months.

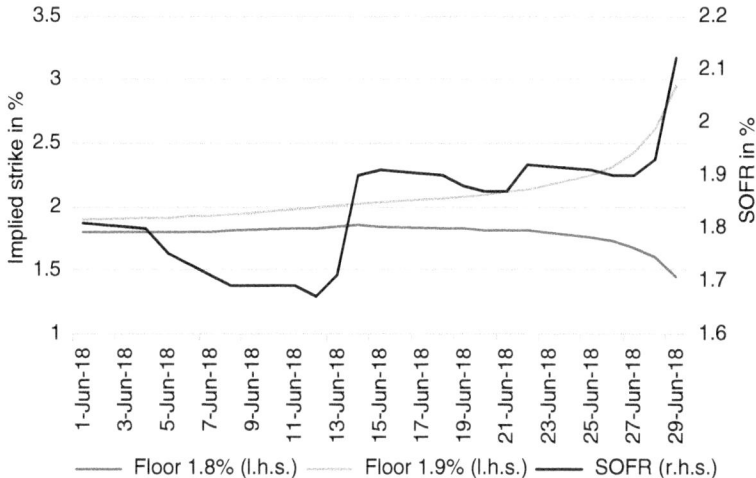

FIGURE 10.2 Implied strikes for obtaining a 1.8% and a 1.9% floor during June 2018
Source: Authors, from CME data

It is tempting to compare this strike adjustment strategy with similar observations from options trading:

- Like the Black-Scholes approach transfers the P&L from a payment at expiry to P&L from delta hedging before expiry, so does this strategy to P&L from strike adjustments before expiry.
- Like some Greeks (such as gamma for ATM options) converge toward infinity immediately before expiry, so does the adjusted strike level.
- Moves in the underlying cause the P&L of delta hedging as well as of the strike adjustments. But in the latter case only, the skew matters, too. In fact, close to expiry, exposure to the skew can become substantial due to the large adjustments required.

Together with the fact that all variables used in the formula above will also occur in any option pricing formula, these similarities make it likely that the basic strike adjustment strategy will collapse into model-based option trading, once it is available. While the precise form of this integration will depend on the precise form of the pricing formula, two possibilities seem conceivable:

- A collapse into delta hedging along the approach of Black-Scholes. For this to become possible, only the Greeks need to be known, for which approximations along the lines of Vyncke, Goovaerts, and Dhaene (2003) are sufficient.

- A collapse into Asian option pricing with floating strikes. Once such a model will be available, this appears to be a natural integration for the elementary strike adjustment strategy.

DEALING WITH DAILY FLOORS

Another problem arises from the recommendation of the Alternative Reference Rates Committee (ARRC) to apply the floors of some loans to each daily SOFR value rather than the SOFR compounded over the reference period. Due to the early-repayment option of the borrower in business loans, ARRC argues for flooring the daily SOFR values (Federal Reserve Bank of New York 2020a; Federal Reserve Bank of New York 2020b). In this case, the floor has a different underlying than the options on SOFR futures, which refer to the SOFR compounded or simply averaged over the reference quarter. This leads to a further mismatch between the floor and the options on SOFR futures as potential hedging product, resulting in even more risk and/or higher hedging costs. In fact, if a perfect hedge is the goal, options on SOFR futures cannot be used for hedging floors following the ARRC recommendation, even if a pricing formula existed. Figure 10.3 illustrates this additional problem.

Conceptually, a floor based on ARRC's recommendation is a set of standard options, while the options on SOFR futures used for hedging are exotic

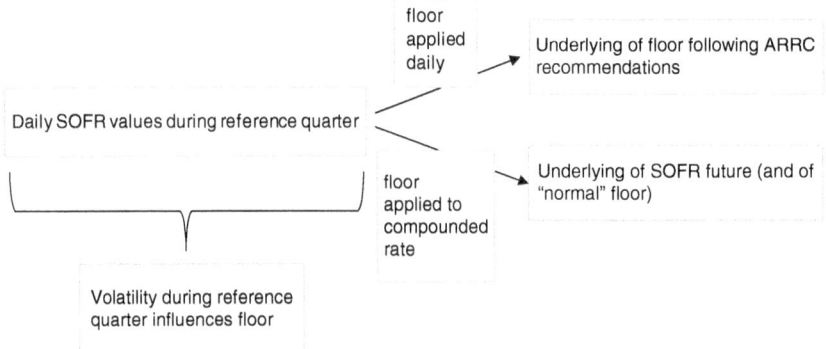

FIGURE 10.3 Underlying of SOFR-based floors and options on 3M SOFR futures
Source: Authors

options. Even after a pricing model for the latter will have become available and hence the difference between standard and exotic options will be assessable, the difference between a collection of daily options and an option on the arithmetic average or compounding of these daily values will continue to exist. At this future stage, one could try to tackle this difference by a theory for the spread between an (exotic) option on a portfolio and (standard) options on each of the components of the portfolio, consisting in this case of the daily SOFR values and hence of highly correlated variables.

At the current stage, however, we can only provide a first impression about the magnitude of the mismatch between a floor on daily SOFR values and a floor on SOFR compounded over the whole reference quarter by further expanding the simulation sheet (used for step 1 toward a pricing model in Chapter 5). As before, this should be considered as an initial attempt only: Since ARRC's recommendation has introduced a completely new feature, our goal is to provide some basic intuition about the potential severity and driving factors of the mismatch. In order to avoid the problem of the missing pricing formula for options on SOFR futures, we look at the difference between a (standard European) floor over the whole 3M period versus daily (also standard European) floors.

The simulation is encoded in the Excel spreadsheet "Floor simulation" accompanying this chapter, which is a slight modification and expansion of the sheet "Call simulation" from Chapter 5. Again, we assume that on Jan 1, 2022, one wants to price a floor on SOFR during the reference quarter of the Mar 2022 SR3 contract (Mar 16 to Jun 15). During the reference quarter, there is one scheduled FOMC meeting, on May 4, 2022; and – unlike in Chapters 2 and 5 – one can add an unscheduled meeting on Jun 1, 2022, to the simulations. By contrast (also unlike in Chapter 2), we assume that there is zero probability for a change in Fed policy outside of these two meetings, including on the two FOMC meetings before the start of the reference quarter. Of course, one can also run the simulation without this rather unrealistic assumption, but the added complexity of further multiplying the possible parameter combinations is not needed for our current goal, since the difference between the two types of floors depends mainly on the Fed policy changes occurring *during* and not *before* the reference period.

As in Chapters 2 and 5, column E defines the parameters for the Vasicek process and the probability distribution for the jump at the FOMC meeting(s). For each of the simulated paths, the value of a floor (with the level of the floor being set in cell H1, just as the strike of the call has been set in Chapter 5) is calculated both for the daily floor as recommended by ARRC for loans with a prepayment option and for the floor on the whole compounded 3M period. The average floor values over all simulations and the premium for daily floor application (in percentage terms) are displayed in column H. For example, if the value for the daily floor is 11 bp and for the floor over the whole period 10 bp, a premium of 10% is shown in cell H5.

Table 10.1 summarizes the results of this simulation for a number of different input parameters. The key observation is that the premium can be significant if a jump process is used,[6] but is limited when a diffusion process is applied. For a pure jump process with the scheduled Fed meeting on May 4 only, the premium for the daily floor over the floor for the whole period is 44% if one assumes an equal probability distribution for a 25 bp hike, no action, and a 25 bp cut. If a second Fed meeting takes place on June 1 with the same probability distribution, the premium increases to 72%. This can be explained intuitively by imagining the paths of SOFR entering the reference quarter at 5 bp (for a pure jump process, this is the case for all paths) and dropping to –20 bp at the first meeting. As the compounded 3M rate is still above 0%, the floor applied to the whole period expires out-of-the-money, whereas every day with an SOFR at –20 bp contributes to the payoff of the floor applied daily. Taking this to an extreme, if the Fed was certain to cut by 25 bp on May 4 and hike by 25 bp on June 1, the premium for the daily floor would increase to 129%.

For a pure diffusion (with drift) process, on the other hand, the premium is much less pronounced. It seems to slightly increase with the speed of mean reversion, and it clearly decreases when the level of the floor increases. Combining both processes to a jump-diffusion (with drift) process, the premia lie between the high levels of the jump process and the low levels of the diffusion process, as one would expect. For the parameters shown in Table 10.1, the premia of the jump-diffusion process are much closer to the ones of the pure diffusion (with drift) process. However, this could change when the overall contribution to the floor value from the jumps becomes relatively larger (e.g., due to more FOMC meetings and/or larger jumps).

Overall, one could be tempted to conclude preliminarily that in case of a diffusion process, the premium introduced by the ARRC recommendation to apply the floor daily is limited; one might deal with it by first calculating the usual hedge ratio for normal floors (covering the whole period) and then

---

[6]In the Excel spreadsheet, this can be obtained by using very small numbers in cell E2, such as 0.000001. Using 0 as parameter will not work due to the set-up of the simulation.

TABLE 10.1 Simulated premium of daily versus compound caps in %

MAIN CASE 1: ONLY JUMP(S), start value 0.05%, floor at 0%

Subcase 1a: Only FOMC meeting on May 4

Probability of +25 bp Jump	Probability of 0 bp Jump	Probability of −25 bp Jump	Premium
50%	0%	50%	44%
50%	50%	0%	0%
33%	34%	33%	44%

Subcase 1b: Also unscheduled FOMC meeting on June 1

May meeting			June meeting			
Probability of +25 bp Jump	Probability of 0 bp Jump	Probability of −25 bp Jump	Probability of +25 bp Jump	Probability of 0 bp Jump	Probability of −25 bp Jump	
50%	0%	50%	50%	0%	50%	47%
33%	34%	33%	33%	34%	33%	72%
0%	0%	100%	100%	0%	0%	129%

(Continued)

TABLE 10.1 (*Continued*)

MAIN CASE 2: ONLY DIFFUSION AND DRIFT

Start value	Standard Deviation (ann)	Mean	Speed of Mean Reversion	Floor	Premium
0.05%	2%	1.50%	0	0%	7%
0.05%	5%	1.50%	0	0%	7%
0.05%	2%	1.50%	0.002	0%	10%
0.05%	5%	1.50%	0.002	0%	10%
0.05%	2%	1.50%	0.002	1%	3%
0.05%	5%	1.50%	0.002	1%	5%

MAIN CASE 3: JUMP-DIFFUSION (AND DRIFT)

Start value	Standard Deviation (ann)	Mean	Speed of Mean Reversion	Floor	Probability of +25 bp Jump	Probability of 0 bp Jump	Probability of −25 bp Jump	Premium
					(only FOMC meeting on May 4)			
0.05%	2%	1.50%	0	0%	50%	0%	50%	8%
0.05%	2%	1.50%	0	0%	33%	34%	33%	7%
0.05%	2%	1.50%	0.002	0%	50%	0%	50%	14%
0.05%	2%	1.50%	0.002	0%	33%	34%	33%	12%
0.05%	5%	1.50%	0.002	0%	50%	0%	50%	11%
0.05%	2%	1.50%	0.002	1%	50%	0%	50%	3%
0.05%	2%	1.50%	0.002	1%	33%	34%	33%	4%

Source: Authors

"overhedge" by increasing the hedge ratio by, say, 10%. In case of a jump process, however, the premium is larger and depends on the precise dates of the FOMC meetings as well as the probability distributions of Fed action. This cannot be handled by a simple adjustment anymore. It is interesting to see the relationship of the specific problem of the daily floor to the general problem of process selection described in Chapters 2 and 5:

- If one decides to use a diffusion process, the daily floor can probably be incorporated via a rather small premium.
- If one decides to use a jump process, the daily floor needs to be modeled directly.

Bibliography

Bowman, D. (n.d.). *A User's Guide to SOFR*. Board of Governors of the Federal Reserve, https://www.newyorkfed.org/medialibrary/microsites/arrc/files/2019/Guide_to_SOFR.pdf.

Burghardt, G., Belton, T., Lane, M. et al. (1991). *Eurodollar Futures and Options*. Chicago: Probus.

Burghardt, G. (2003). *The Eurodollar Futures and Options Handbook*. New York: McGraw Hill Professional.

Burghardt, G. (2011). *Riding Yield Curve (Rides Again)*. Newedge Research Snapshot (18 January).

CME (March 2018). *What Is SOFR?* https://www.cmegroup.com/education/files/what-is-sofr.pdf

CME (April 2018). Spreading SOFR, FF, and ED Futures. https://www.cmegroup.com/education/files/spreading-sofr-ff-and-ed-futures.pdf.

CME (May 2018). Understanding SOFR Futures. https://www.cmegroup.com/education/articles-and-reports/understanding-sofr-futures.html.

CME (Q4 2018). OTC SOFR Swaps Clearing. https://www.cmegroup.com/education/files/otc-sofr-swaps-product-overview.pdf.

CME (2020). *Libor Fallback Proposal for CME Eurodollar Futures and Options*. © CME Group. https://www.cmegroup.com/education/files/webinar-fallbacks-for-eurodollars.pdf.

CME (April 2020). Initial Listing of the Options on One-Month SOFR Futures Contract. Special Executive Report 8581 (7 April). https://www.cmegroup.com/content/dam/cmegroup/notices/ser/2020/04/SER-8581.pdf.

CME (October 2021). CME Term SOFR Reference Rates Benchmark Methodology. Version 1.3. https://www.cmegroup.com/market-data/files/cme-term-sofr-reference-rates-benchmark-methodology.pdf.

CME (February 2022). SOFR Options Gaining Critical Mass, Open Interest Tops 500,000. https://www.cmegroup.com/newsletters/rates-recap/2022-02-rates-recap.html

Cox, J.C., Ingersoll Jr, J.E. and Ross, S.A., 1981. The Relation between Forward Prices and Futures Prices. *Journal of Financial Economics* 9(4): 321–346.

Dormael, A. (1997). *The Power of Money*. London: Palgrave Macmillan.

Federal Reserve Bank of New York (2018). Operating Policy: Statement Regarding the Publication of Historical Report Rate Data, March 9, 2018, https://www.newyorkfed.org/markets/opolicy/operating_policy_180309.

Federal Reserve Bank of New York (2020a). SOFR "In Arrears" Conventions for Syndicated Business Loans. https://www.newyorkfed.org/medialibrary/ Microsites/arrc/files/2020/ARRC_SOFR_Synd_Loan_Conventions.pdf.

Federal Reserve Bank of New York (2020b). Appendix 1: Simple versus Compound Interest. https://www.newyorkfed.org/medialibrary/Microsites/arrc/files/2020/ ARRC-Syndicated-Loan-Conventions-Technical-Appendices.pdf.

Federal Reserve Bank of New York (2022). Additional Information about Reference Rates Administered by the New York Fed, January 24. https://www.newyorkfed .org/markets/reference-rates/additional-information-about-reference-rates# sofr_ai_calculation_methodology.

Fusai, G., and Meucci, A. (2008). Pricing Discretely Monitored Asian Options under Levy Processes. *Journal of Banking & Finance* 32(10): 2076–2088.

Geman, H., and Yor, M. (1993). Asian Options, Bessel Processes and Perpetuities. *Mathematical Finance* 3: 349–375.

Heitfield, E., and Park, Y. (2019). Inferring Term Rates from SOFR Futures Prices. Finance and Economics Discussion Series 2019–2014. Washington: Board of Governors of the Federal Reserve System.

Horvath, A., and Medvegyev, P. (2016). Pricing Asian Options: A Comparison of Numerical and Simulation Approaches Twenty Years Later. *Journal of Mathematical Finance* 6: 810–841.

Huggins, D., and Schaller, C. (2013). *Fixed Income Relative Value Analysis*. Chichester, UK: Wiley.

Ilmanen, A. (1995). *Does Duration Extension Enhance Long-Term Expected Returns?* Salomon Brothers (July).

Keating, T., and Macchiavelli, M. (2017). *Interest on Reserves and Arbitrage in Post-Crisis Money Markets.* Finance and Economics Discussion Series 2017-124. Washington: Board of Governors of the Federal Reserve System.

Kemna, A., and Vorst, A. (1990). A Pricing Method for Options Based on Average Asset Values. *Journal of Banking and Finance*, 14: 113–129.

Kronstein, J. (December 2019). Trading SOFR Options. CME Group. https://www .cmegroup.com/education/files/trading-sofr-options-whitepaper.pdf.

Mises, L. (1924). *Theorie des Geldes und der Umlaufsmittel.* Munich: Duncker& Humblot.

Robb, R. (2012). *CFTC Ignored Warnings of LIBOR Gaming 15 Years Ago.* American Banker (4 September).

The Alternative Reference Rate Committee (ARRC) (2019). *Appendix to SOFR Floating Rate Notes Conventions Matrix.*

The Alternative Reference Rate Committee (ARRC) (2021). *An Updated User's Guide to SOFR.*

The Alternative Reference Rate Committee (ARRC) (2020). *Summer SOFR Series. SOFR Explained.*

Vyncke, D., Goovaerts, M., and Dhaene, J. (2003). *An Accurate Analytical Approximation for the Price of a European-style Arithmetic Asian Option.* Leuven: KUL Department of Applied Economic Sciences.

Index

Page numbers followed by f and t refer to figures and tables, respectively